I0010033

Hands-On High Performance Programming with Qt 5

Build cross-platform applications using concurrency, parallel programming, and memory management

Marek Krajewski

BIRMINGHAM - MUMBAI

Hands-On High Performance Programming with Qt 5

Copyright © 2019 Packt Publishing

All rights reserved. No part of this book may be reproduced, stored in a retrieval system, or transmitted in any form or by any means, without the prior written permission of the publisher, except in the case of brief quotations embedded in critical articles or reviews.

Every effort has been made in the preparation of this book to ensure the accuracy of the information presented. However, the information contained in this book is sold without warranty, either express or implied. Neither the author, nor Packt Publishing or its dealers and distributors, will be held liable for any damages caused or alleged to have been caused directly or indirectly by this book.

Packt Publishing has endeavored to provide trademark information about all of the companies and products mentioned in this book by the appropriate use of capitals. However, Packt Publishing cannot guarantee the accuracy of this information.

Commissioning Editor: Richa Tripathi
Acquisition Editor: Shriram Shekhar
Content Development Editor: Anugraha Arunagiri
Technical Editor: Abin Sebastian
Copy Editor: Safis Editing
Project Coordinator: Ulhas Kambali
Proofreader: Safis Editing
Indexer: Pratik Shirodkar
Graphics: Tom Scaria
Production Coordinator: Shraddha Falebhai

First edition: January 2019

Production reference: 1300119

Published by Packt Publishing Ltd.
Livery Place
35 Livery Street
Birmingham
B3 2PB, UK.

ISBN 978-1-78953-124-4

www.packtpub.com

To my late father, who was a living example of the Polish intelligentsia tradition for me, and to my sister (now we are even, I wrote a book too!)
To my wife, who convinced me to write this book and supported me on this long journey.

–Marek Krajewski

`mapt.io`

Mapt is an online digital library that gives you full access to over 5,000 books and videos, as well as industry leading tools to help you plan your personal development and advance your career. For more information, please visit our website.

Why subscribe?

- Spend less time learning and more time coding with practical eBooks and Videos from over 4,000 industry professionals

- Improve your learning with Skill Plans built especially for you

- Get a free eBook or video every month

- Mapt is fully searchable

- Copy and paste, print, and bookmark content

Packt.com

Did you know that Packt offers eBook versions of every book published, with PDF and ePub files available? You can upgrade to the eBook version at `www.packt.com` and as a print book customer, you are entitled to a discount on the eBook copy. Get in touch with us at `customercare@packtpub.com` for more details.

At `www.packt.com`, you can also read a collection of free technical articles, sign up for a range of free newsletters, and receive exclusive discounts and offers on Packt books and eBooks.

Contributors

About the author

Marek Krajewski has been programming in C++ since the mid 90s, and in Qt since 2008. In his career, he has been involved with Unix and Windows system programming, client-server systems, UMTS network management, Enterprise Java, satellite protocol decoding, neural networks, image processing, DVB-T testing appliances, REST APIs, and embedded Linux. He holds a Ph.D. in computer science and is currently working as an independent programmer specializing in Qt, C++, GUIs, system programming, and communication protocols. His other interests are off-piste skiing and Aikido, where he holds the rank of second dan.

About the reviewer

Nibedit Dey is a techno-entrepreneur and innovator with over 8 years of experience in building complex software-based products using Qt and C++. Before starting his entrepreneurial journey, he worked for L&T and Tektronix in different research and development roles. Additionally, he has reviewed *The Modern C++ Challenge* and *Hands-on GUI programming with C++ and Qt5* books for Packt.

> *I would like to thank the online programming communities, bloggers, and my peers from earlier organizations, from whom I have learned a lot over the years.*

Packt is searching for authors like you

If you're interested in becoming an author for Packt, please visit `authors.packtpub.com` and apply today. We have worked with thousands of developers and tech professionals, just like you, to help them share their insight with the global tech community. You can make a general application, apply for a specific hot topic that we are recruiting an author for, or submit your own idea.

Table of Contents

Preface

In today's world, programming knowledge appears to be scattered over a myriad of locations—blog posts, Wikipedia articles, conference presentations, Twitter threads, Stack Overflow questions, and the odd scientific paper to boot. Because of that, I was quite glad when the publishers approached me with an idea for a book about Qt performance—at last, a single place where program performance knowledge could be collected.

This book will try to give you an overview of program performance optimization techniques and apply them in the context of Qt programming. Qt is a cross-platform and cross-topic programming framework encompassing both GUI and system programming on desktop, mobile, and embedded platforms. Hence, while discussing Qt's performance, we will encounter a broad gamut of performance topics of every shade and color, and we will do this not in an abstract manner, but using real-life examples.

Since Qt has many different versions and releases, we will concentrate on the current (as of the time of writing) **long-term support** (**LTS**) version, namely, Qt 5.9, but will also provide information regarding later Qt versions up to Qt 5.12. Fitting the high-performance theme, we will mostly be using the epitome of high performance, that is Qt's underlying C++ language, directly.

Moreover, in order to make this book approachable, we will use open source development tools and a very widespread and relatively recent OS platform, namely, Microsoft Windows 10.

I wanted to write a book that I would enjoy reading when I first started to learn about performance years ago—we will start slowly, but then go deep, as I hope to provide you with most of the knowledge required to write performant Qt programs.

Who this book is for

This book is intended for developers who wish to build highly performant Qt applications for desktop and embedded devices using the C++ language. If you'd like to optimize the performance of a Qt application that has already been written, you could also find this book useful.

Furthermore, this book is aimed at intermediate-level Qt developers. While the *intermediate* designation is a rather broad one, we define it here as the skill level of a programmer who can implement simple Qt 5 programs using basic tooling. If you cannot do that, you should probably read an introductory Qt 5 book first.

So, let us have a look at the C++, Qt, and programming knowledge that is assumed in this book.

The Qt skills you will need include a basic knowledge of Qt Widgets, QML, and the signal-slot mechanism. You should be able to work with the Qt Creator IDE as the development environment. You should also be able to work on a Windows 10 computer.

As we will see, having a solid understanding of C++ is key to using Qt effectively. However, this book doesn't concentrate on C++ language features, so you definitively don't need to be an expert in C++ to read it.

You will, however, need to have some understanding of basic C++ features, such as object orientation, exceptions, basic templates, `auto` variables, and simple lambdas. Be aware that this book isn't about weird C++ language constructs, but rather tries to introduce you to a broader topic of performance, while using C++ as a sharp tool.

You also don't have to be that proficient in computer science or hardware architectures—we will always introduce the notions required as we go. The entry barrier isn't that high, so if you've already done some Qt programming in C++, you can embark on the journey.

What this book covers

Chapter 1, *Understanding Performant Programs*, introduces you to the world of performance, discusses modern processor architectures, and recounts some traditional performance wisdom.

Chapter 2, *Profiling to Find Bottlenecks*, looks at the tooling we use to diagnose performance problems, concentrating specifically on the tools available on Windows.

Chapter 3, *Deep Dive into C++ and Performance*, takes a closer look at the C++ 11 language, its general performance, the performance of its numerous features, and the role of compilers and linkers in the performance game.

Chapter 4, *Using Data Structures and Algorithms Efficiently*, discusses the performance impact of data structures and algorithms and then takes a closer look at the data structures used by Qt in its API and the associated performance gotchas.

Chapter 5, *An In-Depth Guide to Concurrency and Multithreading*, describes multithreading concepts, Qt multithreading classes and techniques, explains the **multithreading is hard** mantra, and offers some techniques for minimizing multithreading costs and pitfalls.

Chapter 6, *Performance Fails and How to Overcome Them*, looks back at some performance challenges I encountered during my work.

Chapter 7, *Understanding I/O Performance and Overcoming Related Problems*, turns our attention to the unglamorous theme of reading, writing, and parsing files, as well as unexpected interactions with a number of OS mechanisms.

Chapter 8, *Optimizing Graphical Performance*, looks at the main usage scenario of Qt—writing graphical UIs. We will learn about GPUs, and their performance and usage in Qt. Later, we will have a look at the main classes of Qt Widgets and Qt Quick and will discuss what their performance depends upon.

Chapter 9, *Optimizing Network Performance*, introduces basic networking concepts, the TCP and HTTP protocols, the Qt classes supporting them, and the network optimization techniques available in Qt.

Chapter 10, *Qt Performance on Embedded and Mobile Platforms*, looks at mobile and embedded usage of Qt. It builds on the knowledge we acquired in the previous chapters to examine the specific performance challenges faced by Qt on those platforms.

Chapter 11, *Testing and Deploying Qt Applications*, ends this book with a discussion of testing and deployment tools and techniques.

To get the most out of this book

As already stated, this book is aimed at intermediate Qt developers. You should be able to write small- to medium-sized Qt programs in C++ and QML using Qt Creator as an IDE on Windows 10.

You don't need to install any software before you start. Instructions will be provided at the point where specific software is needed. We will use exclusively open source programs so you won't have to purchase any licences.

Download the example code files

You can download the example code files for this book from your account at www.packt.com. If you purchased this book elsewhere, you can visit www.packt.com/support and register to have the files emailed directly to you.

You can download the code files by following these steps:

1. Log in or register at `www.packt.com`.
2. Select the **SUPPORT** tab.
3. Click on **Code Downloads & Errata**.
4. Enter the name of the book in the **Search** box and follow the onscreen instructions.

Once the file is downloaded, please make sure that you unzip or extract the folder using the latest version of:

- WinRAR/7-Zip for Windows
- Zipeg/iZip/UnRarX for Mac
- 7-Zip/PeaZip for Linux

The code bundle for the book is also hosted on GitHub at **`https://github.com/PacktPublishing/Hands-On High Performance Programming with Qt 5`**. In case there's an update to the code, it will be updated on the existing GitHub repository.

We also have other code bundles from our rich catalog of books and videos available at `https://github.com/PacktPublishing/`. Check them out!

Download the color images

We also provide a PDF file that has color images of the screenshots/diagrams used in this book. You can download it here: `https://www.packtpub.com/sites/default/files/downloads/9781789531244_ColorImages.pdf`.

Conventions used

There are a number of text conventions used throughout this book.

`CodeInText`: Indicates code words in text, database table names, folder names, filenames, file extensions, pathnames, dummy URLs, user input, and Twitter handles. Here is an example: "As could be seen in the previous example, Qt `Test` defines macros to specify pass/fail criteria for tests, namely, `QCOMPARE()` and `QVERIFY()`."

A block of code is set as follows:

```
QSignalSpy spy(tstPushBtn, SIGNAL(clicked()));
QTest::mouseClick(tstPushBtn, Qt::LeftButton);
QCOMPARE(spy.count(), 1);
```

When we wish to draw your attention to a particular part of a code block, the relevant lines or items are set in bold:

```
QSignalSpy spy(tstPushBtn, SIGNAL(clicked()));
QTest::mouseClick(tstPushBtn, Qt::LeftButton);
QCOMPARE(spy.count(), 1);
```

Any command-line input or output is written as follows:

```
$ mkdir Qt
$ cd Qt
```

Bold: Indicates a new term, an important word, or words that you see on screen. For example, words in menus or dialog boxes appear in the text like this. Here is an example: "Unfortunately, results displayed in the **Test Result** pane don't seem to work with QML tests with the Qt Creator version used in this book. We have to run a QML test project in the **Projects** view."

Warnings or important notes appear like this.

Tips and tricks appear like this.

Get in touch

Feedback from our readers is always welcome.

General feedback: If you have questions about any aspect of this book, mention the book title in the subject of your message and email us at customercare@packtpub.com.

Errata: Although we have taken every care to ensure the accuracy of our content, mistakes do happen. If you have found a mistake in this book, we would be grateful if you would report this to us. Please visit www.packt.com/submit-errata, selecting your book, clicking on the Errata Submission Form link, and entering the details.

Piracy: If you come across any illegal copies of our works in any form on the internet, we would be grateful if you would provide us with the location address or website name. Please contact us at copyright@packt.com with a link to the material.

If you are interested in becoming an author: If there is a topic that you have expertise in, and you are interested in either writing or contributing to a book, please visit authors.packtpub.com.

Reviews

Please leave a review. Once you have read and used this book, why not leave a review on the site that you purchased it from? Potential readers can then see and use your unbiased opinion to make purchase decisions, we at Packt can understand what you think about our products, and our authors can see your feedback on their book. Thank you!

For more information about Packt, please visit packt.com.

Understanding Performant Programs

In this introductory chapter, we'll start this book with some general discussions about program performance: why it's important, what are the factors that determine it, and how programmers generally go about performance themes. We'll begin with a broad discussion of performances' relevance in programming, before looking at some traditional performance-related knowledge, and we'll finish this chapter with the impact modern CPU architectures made in this field.

This chapter will therefore cover the following topics:

- **Why performance is important**: To motivate ourselves before diving into technicalities
- **Traditional wisdom and basic guidelines**: Old and proven performance knowledge
- **Modern processor architectures**: At least the performance-relevant parts of it

Why performance is important

Maybe you just started reading this book out of curiosity and you're asking yourself this question: Why is performance important? Isn't that a thing of the past, when we didn't have enough CPU power and memory, and when our networks were grinding to a halt? In today's high-tech world, we have enough resources—the computers are so insanely fast!

Well, in principle, you're right to some degree, but consider the following:

- A faster program runs more quickly, consuming less power along the way. This is good for the planet (if you're running it in a big server farm) and good for your user (if you're running it on a desktop computer).
- A faster program means that it can serve more requests in the same time than a slower one. This is good for business, as you'll need to buy or lease fewer machines to serve your customers, and, again, it's good for the planet!
- Faster software in today's business world's cut-throat competition means an advantage in respect to your competitors. This is nowhere more evident than in the world of automated trading (which is, by the way, dominated by C++), but also the fact that sluggishly-loading websites and programs needing an eternity to start won't be used that much!
- And, lastly, especially on mobile devices, we still have to cope with constrained resources—network speed is finite (light speed) and battery life is finite too—and as faster programs use less resources, they're good for users!

Our quest for performance will hence pursue a three-pronged objective: to save the planet, to strengthen your business, and to make the life of users better—not a small feat I'd say!

The price of performance optimization

So, everything is rosy? Well, not quite, as there's a dark side to performance optimization too. If we'll try to squeeze the last drops of performance from our hardware, we can end up having unreadable, inflexible, unmaintainable, and hence outright ugly, code!

So, be aware that there are caveats and that there's a price to be paid. We must decide whether we want to pay it, and at what point we'll stop the optimization to save the clarity of our code.

Traditional wisdom and basic guidelines

When I started with programming (a long time ago), the pieces of advice about performance optimization traditionally given to a newbie were the following:

- Don't do it (yet)
- Premature optimization is the root of all evil
- First make it run, then make it right, then make it fast

The first advice contained the *yet* only in its variant for the experts; the second was (and still is) normally misquoted, leaving out the "*in say 97% of the cases*" part, and the third quote gives you the impression that merely writing a program is already so difficult that fretting about performance is a luxury. It's no wonder then that the normal approach to performance was to *fix it later*!

But all of the adages nonetheless highlight an important insight—performance isn't distributed evenly through your code. The 80-20, or maybe even the 90-10 rule, applies here, because there are some hotspots where extreme care is needed, but we shouldn't try to optimize every nook and cranny in our code. So, our first guideline will be premature optimization—we should forget about it in, say, 95% of cases.

But what exactly are the 20%, 10%, or 5% of code where we shouldn't forget about it? Another old-age programming wisdom states this—programmers are notoriously bad at guessing performance bottlenecks.

So, we shouldn't try to predict the tight spot and measure the performance of a ready program instead. This does sound a lot like the *fix it later* cowboy coder's approach. Well, this book takes the stance that though premature optimization should be avoided, nonetheless, **premature pessimization** should be avoided at all costs, as it's even worse! However, avoiding premature pessimizations requires much detailed knowledge about which language constructs, which framework use cases, and which architectural decisions come with what kind of performance price tags. This book will try to provide this knowledge in the context of the Qt framework.

But, first, let's talk about quite general principles that address the question of what should be avoided, lest the performance degrades. As I see it, we can distill from the traditional performance wisdom from the following basic common-sense advice:

- Don't do the same thing twice.
- Don't do slow things often.
- Don't copy data unnecessarily.

You'll agree that all that can't be good for performance? So, let's discuss these three simple but fundamental insights in some more detail.

Avoiding repeated computation

The techniques falling under the first point are concerned with unneeded repetition of work. The basic counter measure here is **caching**, that is, saving the results of computation for later use. A more extreme example of avoiding repletion of work is to precompute results even before their first usage. This is normally achieved by hand-coded (or generated by a script) **precomputed tables** or, if your programming language allows that, with **compile-time computation**. In the latter case, we sacrifice compilation times for better run-time performance. We'll have a look at C++ compile time techniques in Chapter 3, *Deep Dive into C++ and Performance*.

Choosing the **optimal algorithm and data structure** also falls into that realm, as different algorithms and data structures are optimized for different use cases, and you have to make your choice wisely. We'll have a look at some gotchas pertaining Qt's own data structures in Chapter 4, *Using Data Structures and Algorithms Efficiently*.

The very basic techniques such as **pulling code out of a loop**, such as the repeated computations or initializations of local variables, fall into that class as well, but I'm convinced you knew about this already.

Avoiding paying the high price

The techniques falling under the second point come into play if there's something we can't avoid doing, but it has a pretty high cost tagged on to it. An example of this is interaction with the operating system or hardware, such as writing data to a file or sending a packet over the network. In this case, we resort to **batching**, also known in I/O context as **buffering**—instead of writing or sending a couple of small chunks of data right away, we first gather them and then write or send them together to avoid paying the high cost each time.

On the other hand, we can apply techniques of this type too. In I/O or memory context, this would be the **prefetching** of data, also known as **read-ahead**. When reading data from a file, we read more than the user actually requested, hoping that the next portion of data will be needed soon. In the networking context, there are examples of speculative **pre-resolving** of **Domain Name System (DNS)** addresses when a user is hovering over a link in browsers or even **pre-connecting** to such addresses. However, such measures can turn into its counterpart when the prediction fails, and such techniques require very careful tuning!

Related techniques to be mentioned in this context are also **avoidance of system calls** and **avoidance of locking** to spare the costs of system call and switching to the kernel context.

We'll see some applications of such techniques in last chapters of the book when we discuss I/O, graphics , and networking.

Another example of when this rule can be used is memory management. General-purpose memory allocators tend to incur rather high costs on single allocations, so the remedy is to **preallocate** one big buffer at first and then use it for all needs of the program by managing it by ourselves using a **custom allocation** strategy. If we additionally know how big our objects are going to be, we can just allocate several buffer pools for different object sizes, making the custom allocation strategy rather simple. Preallocating memory at the start used to be a classic measure to improve the performance of memory intensive programs. We'll discuss these technical C++ details in Chapter 3, *Deep Dive into C++ and Performance*.

Avoiding copying data around

The techniques falling under the third point tend to be somehow of a lower-level nature. The first example is avoiding copying data when passing parameters to a function call. A suitable choice of data structure will avoid copying of data as well—just think about an automatically growing vector. In many cases, we can use **preallocation** techniques to prevent this (such as the reserve() method of std::vector) or choose a different data structure that will better match the intended use case.

Another common case when the copying of data can be a problem is string processing. Just adding two strings together will, in the naive implementation, allocate a new one and copy the contents of the two strings to be joined. And as much of programming contains some string manipulations, this can be a big problem indeed! The remedy for that could be using static **string literals** or just choosing **a better library** implementation for strings.

We'll discuss these themes in Chapter 3, *Deep Dive into C++ and Performance,* and Chapter 4, *Using Data Structures and Algorithms Efficiently.*

Another example of this optimization rule is the holy grail of network programming—the zero-copy sending and receiving of data. The idea is that data isn't copied between user buffers and network stack before sending it out. Most modern network hardware supports **scatter-gather** (also known as vectored I/O), where the data to be sent doesn't have to be provided in a single contiguous buffer but can be made available as a series of separate buffers.

In that way, a user's data doesn't have to be consolidated before sending, sparing us copying of data. The same principle can be applied to software APIs as well; for example, Facebook's recent TSL 1.3 implementation (codename Fizz, open sourced) supports scatter-gather API on library level!

General performance optimization approach

Up to now, we listed the following classic optimization techniques:

- Optimal algorithms
- Optimal data structures
- Caching
- Precomputed tables
- Preallocation and custom allocators
- Buffering and batching
- Read-ahead
- Copy avoidance
- Finding a better library

With our current stand of knowledge, we can formulate the following general-performance optimization procedure:

1. Write your code, avoiding unnecessary pessimizations where it doesn't cost much, as in the following examples:
   - Pass parameters by reference.
   - Use reasonably good, widely known algorithms and data structures.
   - Avoid copying data and unnecessary allocations.

   This alone should give you a pretty decent baseline performance.

2. Measure the performance, find the tight spots, and use some of the standard techniques listed. Then, measure again and iterate. This step must be done if the performance of our program isn't satisfactory despite our sound programming practices. Unfortunately, we can't know or anticipate everything that will happen in the complex interplay of hardware and software—there can always be surprises waiting for us.

3. If you still can't achieve good performance, then your hardware is probably too slow. Even with performance optimization techniques, we still can't do magic, sorry!

The preceding advice looks quite reasonable, and you might ask: *Are we done? That wasn't that scary!* Unfortunately, it's not the whole story. Enter the leaky abstraction of modern processor architectures.

Modern processor architectures

All the classic performance advice and algorithmic foo stems from the times of simple CPU setups, where processor and memory speeds were roughly equal. But then the processor speeds exploded by increasing quite faithfully to the Moore law by 60% per year where memory access times increased by only 10% and couldn't quite hold pace with them. The problem is that the main memory (**dynamic random-access memory** (**DRAM**), contains minuscule capacitors keeping an electrical charge to indicate the 1 bit and none to indicate the 0 bit. This results in an inexpensive circuitry that doesn't have to be kept under voltage but is working basically in the analog realm and can't profit that much from advances made in the digital components.

The second change that occurred since then was the demise of Moore's law in its simple form. Up to the early 2000s, CPU manufacturers steadily increased processor frequency rates, making CPUs run faster and faster. That was achieved by increasing the number of transistors packed on chips, and Moore's law predicted that number of transistors that can be packed on a chip will double every 18 months. In simple terms, it was understood as doubling the processor speed every two years.

This trend continued until processor manufacturers hit a physical barrier, the so-called *power wall*—at some point, the densely packed transistors produced so much heat that they couldn't be effectively cooled on consumer machines (high-end, expensive water-cooling systems are, too expensive for a laptop or a mobile device), so a different approach to increasing a CPU's performance had to be found.

Caches

The attempts to overcome these problems led to a slew of architectural innovations. First, the impedance between CPU and memory speeds was fought using a classic optimization technique we already know, namely, caching, on chip level. The on-chip **static RAM** (**SRAM**) memory requires six transistors (forming a flip-flop) per bit, and all of them must be kept under voltage. This means it's expensive and it drives the power consumption up (take care not to hit that power wall!). In exchange, the memory access times are at lightning speed, as all that is needed is to apply the current to the input and read the output.

So, the idea is to add a small caching stage of expensive but fast on-chip memory in front of big, slow but inexpensive main memory. Meanwhile, modern CPUs can command up to three levels of caches, commonly denoted with **L1**, **L2**, and **L3** acronyms, decreasing in density and speed but increasing in size as the cache level goes up. The figure below shows us an overview of the memory hierarchy typically found in modern CPUs:

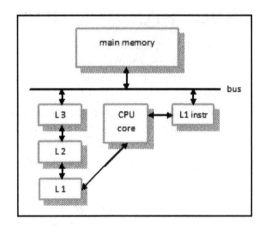

As of the time of this writing, access times for **L1** caches are in the order of **3** cycles, **L2** of **12** cycles, **L3** of **38** cycles, and main memory is around **100-300** cycles. The main memory access time is that high because the analog nature of DRAM requires, among other things, periodic charge refreshing, pre-charging of the read line before reading, analog-digital conversion, communication through **memory controller unit** (**MCU**), and so on.

Caches are organized in cache lines, which on the current Intel architectures are 64 bytes long. Each cache update will hence fetch the entire cache line from **main memory**, doing a kind of prefetching already at that level. Speaking about prefetching, Intel processors have a special prefetch instruction we can invoke in assembler code for very low-level optimizations.

In addition to data caches, there's also an instruction cache, because in the *von Neumann* architecture, both are kept in the common memory. The instruction caches were added to **Intel Pentium Pro** (**P6**) as an experiment, but they were never removed since then.

Pipelining

Another possibility to increase a processor's speed is the **instruction level parallelism** (**ILP**), also known as **superscalar computation**.

The processing of a CPU instruction can internally be split into several stages, such as instruction fetch, decode, execute, and write-back. Before the Intel 486 processor, each instruction has to be finished before the next can be started. With pipelining, when the first stage of an instruction is ready, that instruction can be forwarded to the next stage, and the next instruction's processing can begin with its first stage. In that manner, several instructions can be in flight in parallel, keeping a processor's resources optimally utilized. The next screenshot illustrates this principle, graphically, using a hypothetical four-stages pipeline:

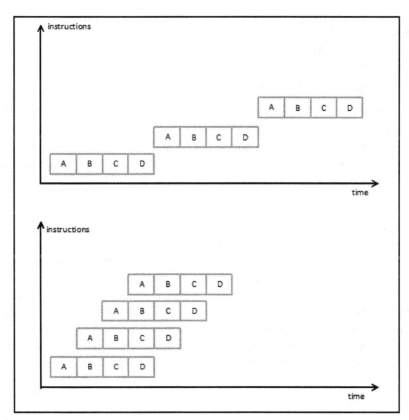

The original Intel 486 pipeline was five stages long, but on modern processors, it can be much longer. For example, the current Intel Atom processors command a pipeline of 16 stages.

That's all well and good, but, unfortunately, there are some problems lurking in the corners.

Speculative execution and branch prediction

As long as the pipeline is pumping, everything is OK. But what if we encounter a conditional branch? The pipeline has to wait till the result of the test is known, hence the next instruction can be started only when the current one has finished. Welcome to the pre-80,486 world! This is called a **pipeline stall** and defeats the whole purpose of pipelining. And because every program is literally dotted with if-then-else clauses, something must be done here.

The solution manufacturers came up with was **speculative execution**: instead of idling, we just start executing one of the branches speculatively. If we are lucky, we've just done the right thing, but, if not, we discard our speculative work, and we are on even ground with the pipeline stall case. As we decide randomly, we'll be right 50% of the time, and we just seriously increased the throughput of the pipeline!

The only problem is that the branches of the if clause are not equally probable! In most cases, they're even highly unevenly distributed: one of them is the error branch; the other is the normal case branch. But the processor doesn't know the meaning of the test, so what can we do? The solution to that is branch predicting—the processor is learning about branches in your code and can predict which branch will be taken on a given condition rather well.

This got **complicated quickly**, didn't it? If you're thinking it, you're not alone. Not so long ago, the programming world was shaken by disclosure of the Spectre and Meltdown vulnerabilities, which allowed the attacker to see contents of the memory regions where they don't have access rights. The first part of the exploit's to fool the branch predictor to take the false branch for speculative execution. After the processor sees a disallowed access, the instruction will be retired, but the protected data will be present in the cache, where they can be guessed with some complicated techniques we won't discuss here. These bugs basically put in question the processor optimizations of the last decade, as fixing them would incur meaningful performance losses.

Considering that, we are all rather curious about how CPU architectures evolve next time, aren't we?

Out-of-order execution

There's another refinement to the pipeline concept allowing an even higher utilization of a CPU's resources. Namely, as processor manufacturers started to add redundant processing units (Intel P6 already had two integer and two floating-point execution units), it became possible to execute two instructions in parallel.

Up until Pentium Pro (P6), instructions were fed into the pipeline in their order of appearance. But if there's a data dependency between two consecutive instructions, then they can't be processed in parallel, leaving the additional execution unit idle:

```
a = b + 1;   // 1
c = a + 5;   // 2
d = e + 10;  // 3
f = d + 15;  // 4
```

The solution to this problem is to take the next independent instruction and execute it before the dependent one. See the next diagram for a visual explanation:

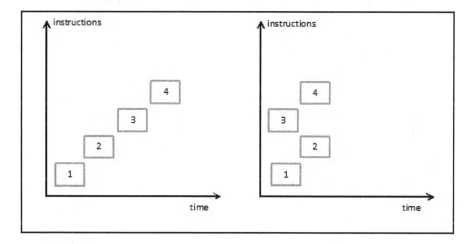

Here, on the left side, we see the traditional execution preserving the instruction order and, on the right, parallel execution with reordering, where instruction **3** will be executed before instruction **2**.

Multicore

The problem of the power wall was in the end overcome by freezing or even decreasing CPU frequencies but introducing parallelly working processor cores, adding more general registers, vector processing **single instruction multiple data** (**SIMD**) registers, and instructions. In a word, they either duplicated active processing units or added more elements that don't have to be always under voltage. In that way, the density of the transistors didn't have to be increased.

When all of the CPU cores are placed on one chip, we have a **symmetric multiprocessing** (**SMP**) CPU, because all cores can access their respective data within a local chip. The counterpart to that is a **non-uniform memory access** (**NUMA**) system, where we have several physically separate CPUs having their own internal caches. The memory access for internal CPUs will then be much cheaper than the memory access to an external CPU. Another problem is the cache coherence between the CPUs, which requires complicated cache-coherence protocols and can take down performance. In the context of Qt's application area, we normally encounter SMP machines, so we'll ignore NUMA in this book.

In a multicore chip, the processing resources can be classified in **core** and **uncore** ones—those which are duplicated for each core, and those that aren't and must be shared. For example, the top-level cache (L3 or L2, depending on the processor) is an uncore resource shared among processor cores.

One often-encountered notion is that of **hyperthreading**. This is another idea for increasing a CPU's parallelism, and hence its resource utilization. A processor with hyperthreading consists of two logical processors per core, each of which keeps its own internal state. The parts of the processor where it holds its architectural state (for example, running, interrupted, and halted) will be duplicated for each core, but the computation resources will be shared among logical cores. The intent of that is to increase the utilization of the processor's resources and prevent pipeline stalls, by borrowing resources from the stalled logical core. The operating system then uses these two logical cores as physical ones and has to be HTT-aware to optimally use such a system.

Strictly speaking, **graphical-processing units** (**GPUs**) are not a form of multicore, but we'll mention them in this context, because processors can ship with integrated GPUs on board. A GPU comprises many very simple processing units that can run massively parallel, although simple, computations. Normally, they're used to accelerate graphic processing, but they can be also used to speed up in general computations, such as the training of neural networks in deep-learning applications. In a Qt context, however, we use GPUs only for their graphical capabilities.

Additional instruction sets

As already mentioned, to increase processor performance chip, manufacturers started to add more sophisticated instructions that can either vectorize computations or execute algorithms that hitherto had to be implemented in application code.

The SIMD or vector instructions can be used to parallelize a scalar computation by executing calculations on several scalar values in parallel. For that, we have to load several float values in two sets of SIMD registers and then apply an operation to all of them at once. Intel processors introduced SIMD in a series of extensions named, namely the following:

- **Streaming SIMD Extension (SSE)**: Uses 128-bit registers and is available in several versions from SSE, over SSE2 to SSE4
- **Advanced Vector Extension (AVX)**: Uses 265-bit registers and is available in AVX2 and AVX-512 (for 512 bit) versions

As for the more specialized instructions, we mention the following Intel extensions:

- **Advanced Encryption Standard New Instructions (AES-NI)**: This implements the cryptographic AES encoding standard.
- **32-bit cyclic redundancy check (CRC32)**: This implements computation of the CRC32 correction code.
- **SSE4.2**: This SSE extension also implements basic string operations using SIMD registers.

Impact on performance

As you see, a modern CPU doesn't look like your daddy's old-fashioned *von Neuman* CPU at all. It's a very complex computer system on its own, banned on a very small chip, desperately trying out all possible tricks to squeeze out a little bit more performance from your program.

On the other hand, modern CPUs are trying to appear simple to the programmer, unfortunately leaking the implementation specifics all of the time along the way. So, what changed since the days of classic performance advice we summed up in the preceding sections?

Fortunately, not much. The basic techniques and guidelines still apply, but some additional advice must be heeded. Let's discuss these new points.

Keeping your caches hot

First of all, don't thrash your caches because main memory is very slow. This means that reading data all over the memory (also known as **pointer chasing**) isn't the best of ideas. Modern processors, such as programs that read consecutive chunks of memory in a predictable manner, allow them to leverage hardware-level prefetching. The word here is **data locality**.

A negative example for that, alas, is our old and trusty linked list! Traversing it's a real pointer-chasing feast, because all of the nodes are allocated dynamically and can be placed anywhere in memory. However, we could remedy it by using the already-mentioned techniques of preallocating and custom memory allocators. In that case, all of the nodes of a list would be located in the adjacent element of the preallocated buffer, making it again more cache friendly. Of course, we could just use an array from the start, but this is an example of how to improve data locality in similar cases.

The second classic mistake would be placing two often used integers, x and y, well apart from each other in a data structure, so that when we want to use both, we need to needlessly load two cache lines instead of one. What's used together should stay together; don't **break your data structures** on a cache line boundary!

Further optimization that's widely known is the replacement of an array of structures by a structure of arrays. This will be beneficial in the case of loading data for SIMD instructions and other techniques where we read data in parallel.

Another often-cited optimization trick is improving the performance of matrix multiplication by changing the **data-access pattern**. Instead of a straightforward triple i, j, k loop, we change it to the k, j, i loop:

```
for (size_t k = 0; k < P; ++k)
   for (size_t j = 0; j <M; ++j)
      for (size_t i = 0; i < N; ++i)
         res[i][[j] += m1[i][[k] * m2[k][[j];
```

Here, just switching the order of traversal to be more cache-friendly and reading row elements of both matrices in consecutive manner will dramatically improve performance (in some measurements, up to 94%)!

What we learn here is that the outline and structure of our data, but also its access patterns, can have a big impact on our program's performance on modern processors!

The second type of cache, that is, the instruction cache, needs some love as well. Jumping through code back and forth is equally bad, as it's in the case of your data. This **code locality** is the next important notion. One possibility to influence that is to place your normal case code before the handling error, like this:

```
if (ok) {
   do_work();
} else {
   printf("ERROR!");
   return;
}
```

This avoids a jump in normal case, hence improving code locality. We'll discuss that in more detail in Chapter 3, *Deep Dive into C++ and Performance*, when we'll look at the role of the compiler in program optimization.

Don't confuse your branch predictor

To avoid pipeline stalls, preferably, there shouldn't be any branches at all. Unfortunately, that can't be done in programming, but the next best thing we can do is to minimize branching. A classic example of branch avoidance is replacing simple conditional expressions with bit manipulations, like this:

```
const int maxValue = 16;
if (x >= maxValue) x = 0;
// is equivalent to:
x = (x + 1) & (maxValue - 1);
```

I think we can agree, these are ugly, low-level tricks, best left to the micro-optimization stage or to the compiler. Another technique of that type is loop unrolling.

A more usable technique could be helping the compiler to generate more branch predictor-friendly code such as the Linux kernel practice of macros: likely() and unlikely(), which internally use the **GNU compiler collection** (**GCC**) compiler's __builtin_expect() directive. This is supposed to support the branch-predictor, but, in reality, it allows code reordering by the compiler, which will then enable different optimizations. Older architectures with static branch predictors use special instruction prefixes indicating whether the branch is likely to be taken or not. As newer architectures are using dynamic predictors, these prefixes will be ignored and don't take any effect.

So, the received wisdom is that the branch predictors have meanwhile gotten pretty good, and that we should try to mess with them in the rarest cases only. With the exception of one thing: as a branch predictor's table has a finite (small) size, you shouldn't thrash it! And here we are again: don't use too many branches; keep good code locality!

Parallelizing your application

This is the famous *no free lunch* conundrum: if we want our program to run faster, it's not enough to buy a faster processor—we have to restructure it to be parallel and to use more processor cores! We'll have a closer look at these techniques in `Chapter 5`, *An In-Depth Guide to Concurrency and Multithreading*, when we'll discuss multithreading.

As for vector processing, we have to notice that, for SIMD instructions to be performant, the loaded data usually has to be aligned. Apart from that, as of today, any decent modern compiler will try to vectorize the code, so normally, we don't have to bother. However, the compiler will generate code for a specific architecture, but maybe you'd like to run your program on several processor and look for the more advanced extended instruction sets available? This is possible, and techniques for doing that are known as CPU dispatching.

The second theme related to parallelism to be mentioned here is the out-of-order execution. First, sometimes, we can encounter advice to break too long dependency chains so as to allow reordering, as was shown in a previous diagram. Arguably, this is a low-level technique, but sometimes every nanosecond may count.

Another theme is that there could be a time where we would like to disable instruction reordering. What could it be? Right—when synchronizing among threads, we have to know exactly in which order which variables were read or written. On the processor level, this can be forced with memory barriers, but this will prevent the possible reordering optimizations. That is the reason synchronization in a multithreaded program is already expensive on the processor level.

Summary

I hope you've enjoyed the journey so far. We acquired a basic understanding of the matter that we'll put to good use in future chapters of this book. Admittedly, in the second half, the discussion started to be a little low-level, going down into the inner workings of processors, but I hope you picked up at least a couple of buzzwords along the way.

So, we've arrived at the end of this chapter. Looking back, first we learned about benefits and caveats arising when we optimize performance and the pair, premature optimization and pessimization. Then, we discussed the basic rules for performance optimization, the well-known optimization techniques inferred from those rules, how and why memory access patterns matter, the way processors are trying to parallelize work on the instruction level, and, not to forget, what the common performance lingo's buzzwords mean.

Not bad for an introductory chapter, don't you think?

So, after we learned all of those things that we can respond to, the main question of the chapter, namely what's a performant program? The widely acknowledged response is that a performant program is a program that does the following:

- Uses the optimal algorithm for the problem
- Optimizes memory access patterns as to be cache friendly
- Fully uses the parallelization possibilities of the hardware

In the following chapter, we'll look at techniques that allow us to avoid the dreaded *premature optimization* trap. We can steer clear of this trap by measuring how our code performs and where the bottlenecks and the tight spots are located, before actually starting to optimize. In the next chapter, we'll learn tools and techniques for doing exactly that.

Questions

Here are some questions so that you can test your understanding of the topics in this chapter. You'll find the responses at the end of this book, if you'd like to look them up:

1. What is premature optimization?
2. What did Donald Knuth really say about it?
3. Why do we need performance optimization techniques?
4. Which is the worst premature pessimization?
5. Why is main memory slow?
6. What is ILP, and what has it to do with thread synchronization?
7. Is hyperthreading good or bad for performance?
8. Why do we still use the `likely/unlikely` macros in the Linux kernel?
9. Is a 64-bit program performance-wise better than a 32-bit program?

Further reading

If you would like to learn more about basic performance techniques and processor architectures, these are the resources I'd recommend:

- The short book, *The Performance of Open Source Applications*, edited by *Travish Armstrong* (available on `http://aosabook.org`, 2013) contains case studies showing mostly applications of the basic principles we discussed, for example, in the chapter about the Ninjia build system.

- Books about C++ performance, such as, this admittedly somewhat older books, *Efficient C++ Performance Programming Techniques,* by Dov Bulka and David Mayhew, Addison Wesley 1999, (by the way, this was my first computer performance book!) or a more recent *Optimized C++* by Kurt Guntheroth, O'Reiily 2013, discuss many of the traditional basic performance techniques in their first chapters.

- *Power and Performance. Software Analysis and Optimization,* by Jim Kukunas, Morgam Kaufman 2015, discusses the history and architecture of modern Intel processors, introduces tools for obtaining CPU performance data and explains some low-level performance techniques. However, this book concentrates on Linux operating systems and tools.

- An even more in-depth discussion of performance gotchas in different processor architectures can be found on Agner's Fog site (`http://www.agner.org/optimize/microarchitecture.pdf` and others, 2018) and is directed more toward compiler writers. The widely cited article by Ullrich Drepper *What every programmer needs to know about memory* (available on `http://www.akkadia.org/drepper/cpumemory.pdf`, 2007) provides many details on RAM memory, caches, virtual memory, and possible low-level memory optimization techniques.

- Lastly, *the* most famous quote about performance optimization by Donald Knuth can be looked up in his article *Structured programming with go to statements*, ACM Computing. Survey., 6(4), 1974.

2
Profiling to Find Bottlenecks

As we already described in Chapter 1, *Understanding Performant Programs*, performance bottlenecks are not distributed evenly in code. Applying the Pareto principle to performance optimization, we could say that 80% of a program's execution time is spent on 20% of the code (and, as we've seen, Donald Knuth believed this to be an even lower figure). Regardless of the exact proportions, the basic insight is the same—code optimization efforts are most effectively spent on that critical x percent of the code that is responsible for most of the program's execution time.

We saw in the previous chapter that today's hardware platforms have grown to be so complicated that the ancient adage about programmers being notoriously bad at estimating bottlenecks in their own code has now been reinforced more than ever—not only do we either understand our code, but, we don't understand the hardware on which it runs anymore either! In Chapter 1, *Understanding Performant Programs*, we introduced the notion of premature optimization as the process of blindly optimizing pieces of software without obtaining any performance data, and thus, insights relying on gut feeling only. So, this chapter will be about tooling, which enables us to measure and obtain that data. The topics discussed will include the following:

- **Types of profilers**: Some preliminary knowledge about our tools
- **Platform and tools**: Because we don't want to stick to theory alone
- **Profiling CPU usage**: Let's put our tooling to use
- **Investigating memory usage**: Putting more tooling to work
- **Going further-advanced tools**: Because there's always another tool

Let's start with what performance data is, what we are able to measure, and how can we do that.

Types of profilers

The problem is, as we mentioned, we don't know what the program, the operating system or the hardware are exactly doing, and how much time each of them needs. So, we have to obtain this information somehow. The process of doing so is called **profiling** (creating the program's execution profile), and the tools we use to do that are called **profilers**. There are the following general approaches used to obtain performance data:

- Program instrumentation
- Runtime sampling
- Reading hardware or operating system counters

Let's look at each of these approaches in more detail.

Instrumenting profilers

Code instrumentation means adding additional code to our existing code base that will measure performance and output performance data. This can be done automatically by some tools or manually, by simply writing some `printf` statements. The venerable `prof` and `gprof` GNU profilers used to work that way—the programmer had to specify a special compiler switch (`-p` or `-pg`), and the GNU compiler would add the the necessary code in each of the functions. As for a more modern example, commercial rational quantify tools use object-code insertion technology to instrument executable being tested by dynamically inserting instrumentation code. On the other hand, RAD Game Tools' telemetry provides instrumentation functions to be manually inserted into code, and Intel VTune provides such functions in its **instrumentation and tracing technology** (**ITT**) API library.

For this reason, such techniques are also called **invasive**, as they change the code they are supposed to be measuring (for your inner geek, remember the Heisenberg principle?). Thus, its advantage is high precision data and its disadvantage is changing the runtime behavior of programs (that is, diminishing accuracy).

The simpler but more time-consuming version of instrumentation, namely manually inserting the measurement and output code, also has the right to exist:

- **Profile builds**: Here, in addition to the usual release and debug build configurations, you can add a configuration where the profiling code will be enabled, to activate it when a performance problem has to be investigated or the application's performance has to be checked. For example, in Telemetry's case, you have to set `#define NTELEMETRY 1`, and recompile, and the instrumentation will be gone.

- **Custom visualizations**: Another advantage of manual instrumentation is that we can format the outputs as we wish, thus making them compatible with our preferred visualization tools. For example, Intel's ITT API functions can generate output in several visualizers' format, depending on the value of an environment variable. We will see some examples of this approach later in this chapter.

Sampling profilers

In the case of sampling profilers, the profiler will periodically examine the state of the program by taking a snapshot of its current stack and looking at the function where the program is currently at. The idea is that the most sampled functions will also be the functions that take most of the program's execution time. In the long run, these two values will converge and we will obtain an image of the most-used functions.

The first disadvantage is obvious—due to its statistical nature, sampling results for less-used functions can be imprecise; a function might be missed, but could also be sampled disproportionately, often if the profiling run is too short. The second disadvantage is more subtle—sampling records data in a non-discriminatory way providing information on every function in the system, resulting in a data deluge, when, as we already know, only a small part of the code is interesting performance-wise.

 The clear advantage of such profilers, however, is their non-invasive nature. As they are independent of build tool chains, such profilers are very easy to use and are the most commonly employed in software development today. Some examples of such profilers are the Visual Studio profiler, Very Sleepy, and Luke Stackwalker, among many others. Even the venerable gprof is a mixed-type instrumenting and sampling profiler.

In reality, you might like to use both types of profiling: manual instrumentation for your profile builds and general overview, and sampling profilers for more detailed data when investigating a specific problem.

External counters

To provide insight into low-level processor behavior, CPU manufacturers added some support for the measuring of performance directly on the chip. For example, Intel processors are equipped with dedicated hardware known as **Performance Monitoring Units** (**PMUs**). There's a dedicated PMU on each core, and optionally, an additional uncore PMU collecting data about resources shared between cores. The PMU exposes event counters that can be read by a kernel driver and exported to the user space. Specialized profilers such as Intel's VTune Amplifier XE read these counters periodically to obtain performance data while they are profiling an application. Operating systems also define performance counters and events, which can be used for the performance analysis of applications as well.

Note on Read Time-Stamp Counter

On Intel processors, there is an internally held counter, namely the **Time Stamp Counter** (**TSC**), which can be read out with a simple **Read Time-Stamp Counter** (**RDTSC**) assembler instruction. It holds a 64-bit counter of cycles since the processor was booted. I've seen legacy code that uses this instruction directly to implement performance measurements, so don't be surprised if you encounter this instruction out in the wild—it is just super-fast! However, there are some problems when we try to read that counter directly on modern pipelined and multicore CPUs, as there's simply no guarantee that a thread will start and end its execution on the same core!

Platform and tools

Now, as we already know what kinds of tools can be used for profiling, there will come a time when we will have to get our hands dirty and delve deeper into typical performance optimization work. For you to be able to reproduce it, we have to agree on the exact versions of our frameworks and tools. To make it short, we've decided on the following:

- Qt 5.9 LTE
- Windows 10
- Open source tools

This warrants some explanation, so read on. Let's start with the Qt framework.

Qt has many different versions and releases, but in this book, we have chosen to concentrate on the current (at the time of writing) **long-term support** (**LTS**) version, namely Qt 5.9—as it's the recent most stable release. Admittedly, a preview version of Qt 5.11 was present in the distribution, but we have, much to my regret, to ignore it.

Qt is a multiplatform framework; it supports Linux, as well as Mac, and Windows, all the way down to embedded operating systems. However, most of the books that teach Qt development on Linux introduce Linux development and performance toolsets.

In this book, we will take an unfamiliar path—we will choose the Windows platform in its newest incarnation: Windows 10. The reason is that most commercial Qt work is done on Windows, and, frankly, Windows is a pretty widespread platform, isn't it? For my part, I have used it in most of my projects, and I could use Qt on Linux only when working in embedded projects. Secondly, I think that Windows is treated somehow unfairly as a development platform. There's a lot of excellent tooling there that is less known than its Linux equivalents, but is well worth discovering and appreciating.

In the course of this book, we will, of course, mention Linux tools where appropriate, but for the reader to follow along, the examples and explanations will be Windows-specific.

Moreover, to make this book approachable to everyone, we will try to use open source tools where appropriate. Commercial alternatives will be mentioned as well, which hopefully will lead to some thrilling comparisons.

Development environment

As Qt comes with batteries included in the form of its own IDE, our choice here is simple—we will use Qt Creator because it is a complete development environment and has one unbeatable advantage, namely its built-in support for QML debugging and profiling.

To install Qt platform and Qt Creator go to `https://www.qt.io/download`, choose the Qt open source version, and start the download of the Windows installer for the latest Qt version. In the installer, choose Qt version 5.9.6 (the latest one at the time of writing), and under **Tools**, select Qt Creator 4.7.0 (or later, if there has been an upgrade) with its debugger support. Additionally, select MinGW 5.3.0 compiler, which we will be using in Qt Creator. You will have to sign in to your Qt account before the real installation starts. Then, just wait till everything is installed. If you'd like to shorten the installation time, you can deselect some components for several platforms that Qt supports.

So, our final setup will be as follows:

- Qt 5.9.6
- Qt Creator 4.7.0 or later
- MinGW compiler 5.3.0

As the MinGW compiler contained in the distribution is 32 bits only, we could try another possibility; for example, using some of Microsoft's Visual Studio's free editions. This has one clear disadvantage: namely, the QML support is lost; but when installed, you can work with the Qt plugin quite comfortably with applications using only Qt Widgets. You can also use Qt Creator as your IDE and configure it to use the Visual Studio compiler. In this way, we could have 64-bit builds, but for the sake of simplicity, in this book, we will constrain ourselves to a simpler setup, using the preinstalled MinGW compiler.

Profiling tools

As for tooling, there seems to be no problem, Qt Creator integrates them already under the **Analyze** menu—the QML profiler, the CPU, the function profiler, and the memory analyzer. Unfortunately, this integration only works on Linux, as the tool used by Qt Creator is Valgrind, which is not available on Windows. The QML profiler is Qt native, but the other profilers won't work on Windows, so we have to look for some alternatives.

Now, the often-heard advice is to whip up a VM instance with Linux installed, and do your profiling there using Qt Creator's built-in Valgrind integration. In this book, we do not endorse such techniques because we aren't developing on Windows just to switch to Linux at the first opportunity. Though Qt draws an abstraction layer over different operating systems, underneath these are different platforms, with different implementations, and different behavior. We do not want to go profiling on another platform running the application in a VM to boot. However, for memory leaks detection, that could be a viable but labor-intensive option, so if there are any alternatives, we'd prefer to avoid it.

So, let's have a quick look at what tools we have at our disposal on our chosen platform.

Just use gprof?

One piece of advice you'll often encounter is to use the venerable `gprof`, the precursor of all sampling profilers, because it will already be there in your MinGW installation. It's easy to integrate `gprof` with Qt Creator, but really, it's only useful for the simplest of cases, because it doesn't support multithreaded programs and dynamically loaded libraries. So, for any serious performance work, its standard version is simply not usable.

Windows system tools

Additionally, we can use an excellent suite of general-purpose Windows tools, namely the Windows Sysinternals tools, available on the `https://docs.microsoft.com/en-us/sysinternals/downloads/sysinternals-suite` page. As we will see later, some of them can be used for performance evaluation and troubleshooting. The Sysinternals suite contains many tools, so we'll present only a selection of tools that are most useful for our purposes, namely the following:

- **Process Explorer**: This is a **Task Manager** on steroids. It can query and visualize several system and performance counters for each process, and I regularly use it for preliminary investigations. We will see some usage examples later in this chapter.
- **System Explorer**: This shows all system calls issued by any running processes in a long list and supports filters to select processes we'd like to observe. Admittedly, it is more of a debugging tool, but it provides a very simple way to find out what our application has done recently, which can be sometimes also be helpful in performance analysis.
- **RAMMap**: Let's examine the system's global memory usage, which requires quite a bit of Windows internal knowledge.
- **VMMap**: Shows detailed info on a single application's memory usage.
- **Coreinfo**: The Windows equivalent to Linux's `cpuinfo` gives detailed information about the processor, information you might need when doing low-level optimization work.

The following two screenshots show a sample of **Coreinfo**'s output, and you will see and recognize many topics that were discussed in Chapter 1, *Understanding Performant Programs*, in the *Modern processor architectures* section. Try to make sense of them!

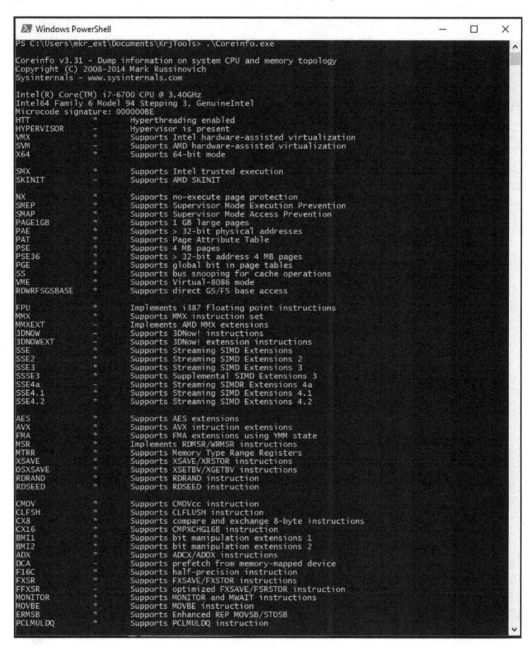

```
Windows PowerShell                                              —    □    ×

LAHF-SAHF         *      Supports LAHF/SAHF instructions in 64-bit mode
HLE               *      Supports Hardware Lock Elision instructions
RTM               *      Supports Restricted Transactional Memory instructions

DE                *      Supports I/O breakpoints including CR4.DE
DTES64            *      Can write history of 64-bit branch addresses
DS                *      Implements memory-resident debug buffer
DS-CPL            *      Supports Debug Store feature with CPL
PCID              *      Supports PCIDs and settable CR4.PCIDE
INVPCID           *      Supports INVPCID instruction
PDCM              *      Supports Performance Capabilities MSR
RDTSCP            *      Supports RDTSCP instruction
TSC               *      Supports RDTSC instruction
TSC-DEADLINE      *      Local APIC supports one-shot deadline timer
TSC-INVARIANT     *      TSC runs at constant rate
xTPR              *      Supports disabling task priority messages

EIST              *      Supports Enhanced Intel Speedstep
ACPI              *      Implements MSR for power management
TM                *      Implements thermal monitor circuitry
TM2               *      Implements Thermal Monitor 2 control
APIC              *      Implements software-accessible local APIC
x2APIC            *      Supports x2APIC

CNXT-ID           -      L1 data cache mode adaptive or BIOS

MCE               *      Supports Machine Check, INT18 and CR4.MCE
MCA               *      Implements Machine Check Architecture
PBE               *      Supports use of FERR#/PBE# pin

PSN               -      Implements 96-bit processor serial number

PREFETCHW         *      Supports PREFETCHW instruction

Maximum implemented CPUID leaves: 00000016 (Basic), 80000008 (Extended).

Logical to Physical Processor Map:
**------    Physical Processor 0 (Hyperthreaded)
--**----    Physical Processor 1 (Hyperthreaded)
----**--    Physical Processor 2 (Hyperthreaded)
------**    Physical Processor 3 (Hyperthreaded)

Logical Processor to Socket Map:
********    Socket 0

Logical Processor to NUMA Node Map:
********    NUMA Node 0

No NUMA nodes.

Logical Processor to Cache Map:
**------    Data Cache         0, Level 1,    32 KB, Assoc   8, LineSize  64
**------    Instruction Cache  0, Level 1,    32 KB, Assoc   8, LineSize  64
**------    Unified Cache      0, Level 2,   256 KB, Assoc   4, LineSize  64
********    Unified Cache      1, Level 3,     8 MB, Assoc  16, LineSize  64
--**----    Data Cache         1, Level 1,    32 KB, Assoc   8, LineSize  64
--**----    Instruction Cache  1, Level 1,    32 KB, Assoc   8, LineSize  64
--**----    Unified Cache      2, Level 2,   256 KB, Assoc   4, LineSize  64
----**--    Data Cache         2, Level 1,    32 KB, Assoc   8, LineSize  64
----**--    Instruction Cache  2, Level 1,    32 KB, Assoc   8, LineSize  64
----**--    Unified Cache      3, Level 2,   256 KB, Assoc   4, LineSize  64
------**    Data Cache         3, Level 1,    32 KB, Assoc   8, LineSize  64
------**    Instruction Cache  3, Level 1,    32 KB, Assoc   8, LineSize  64
------**    Unified Cache      4, Level 2,   256 KB, Assoc   4, LineSize  64

Logical Processor to Group Map:
********    Group 0
PS C:\Users\mkr_ext\Documents\KrjTools>
```

Program profiling tools

There are no CPU profilers supported and integrated in Qt Creator on Windows. We will thus have to fall back on a profiler started in a standalone manner.

Very Sleepy (http://www.codersnotes.com/sleepy/) is a simple and popular open source profiler. Admittedly, its UI is rather spartan but is probably sufficient for many non-graphic applications. In the following screenshot, we can see the results of a CPU profiling run with one of Qt's demo programs:

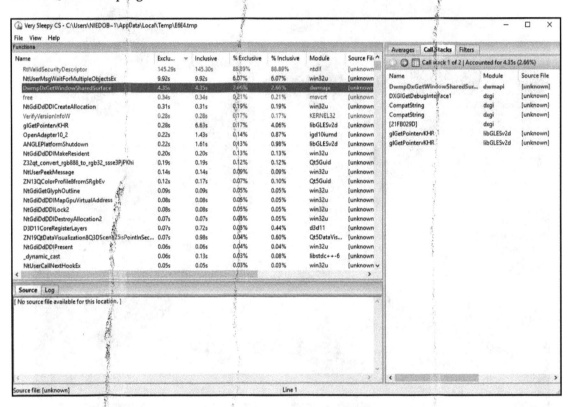

There is another open source profiler that could be used: MD's **CodeXL** profiler. It has a much richer UI than Very Sleepy, and is in fact much more than a CPU profiler. It supports GPU debugging, frame analysis, GPU profiling, shader analysis, and power profiling. In the following screenshot, you can see the results of a CPU profiling run with one of the contained demo programs displayed in its UI:

The screenshot shows the **call graph visualization**, where clicking on the functions with most samples will take us down along the hot path, but there is also a list of most-sampled functions and modules in separate tabs.

Microsoft's Visual Studio contains its own integrated profiler even in the Community Edition, but we decided on Qt Creator as the IDE, so we won't discuss that. Luke Stackwalker (http://lukestackwalker.sourceforge.net/) has a much better UI than Very Sleepy and is available for Windows, but unfortunately it only supports Microsoft compiler's debug information format. Because we are using MinGW's GNU compiler, we must dispense with it. The same pertains to the open source Orbit Profiler. Google's **perftools** suite supports Windows, and it contains its own sampling profiler, but the profiler is not available on Windows.

Visualizing performance data

When it comes to the visualization of performance data, we are presented with two alternatives: either use the visualizer that shipped with the used profiler, or a standalone one.

Sampling profilers usually come with their own visualizations integrated in their GUI, as already explained. To instrument profilers, there is, as a rule, a visualization tool available; for example, look at Telemetry. Intel's ITT instrumentation API data is normally viewed in VTune Amplifier, but we can transform the data format to view it with different viewers. This is done with Intel's open source **Single Event API** (**SEAPI**) project, which supports formats such as these: Windows ETW, Android's Systrace, Google JSON trace, Qt Creator's QML profiler, open source Trace Compass, and the old and trusty GraphViz. How cool is that!

So, there are many viewers we could use, and we are somehow spoilt for choice. But lately, the Google JSON trace format has stirred quite a bit of attention, because of the built-in support for it in the ubiquitous Chrome browser! You have to open a new browser tab and type `about:tracing` in the omnibox, and the profiling page opens. Here, you can profile the Chrome browser itself, but also load recorder traces. Now we only need to find (or write) a set of instrumentations generating data in the prescribed JSON format and we have a custom visualizer for our data for free.

Now we have gained an overview of the available performance tools, let's do a little practical exercise to try out these tools!

Memory tools

Here, I must admit, we don't have a nice open source memory profiling tool comparable to Valgrind's Massif on Linux, which can show a memory usage trace and attribute parts of the used memory to a C++ class, which consumes it. We can obtain a general overview of used memory through Sysinternal tools, but to see what consumes the memory we'd have to use a program introspection tool such as a GammaRay or a debugger.

As for Valgrind's memcheck, a comparable tool for Windows would be **heap observer** (**heob**), which is even integrated with Qt Creator, or Dr. Memory. These tools can detect memory leaks and buffer overflows.

Profiling CPU usage

On Linux Qt, Creator integrates with Valgrind's callgrind, which, alas, isn't available on Windows, so we have to look for other tools. Before we jump to the dedicated tools, let's discuss a very basic, little-known (as far as I can judge), but surprisingly effective, technique.

Poor man's sampling technique

I call that technique the **poor man's sampling** technique. It is really simple. In its most basic form, you run a program in a debugger, stop it several times, and examine the call stack of the randomly chosen breaks. The idea is (as with sampling profilers) that the most-used function will show most often in the stack trace. Simple as it is, this quick technique will sometimes will give us enough information to diagnose the problem.

Unexpectedly, this can be done most elegantly with the **Process Explorer**. We just need to get to the **Threads** tab, double-click on a selected row, and the stack trace of this thread will be shown, as in the following screenshot:

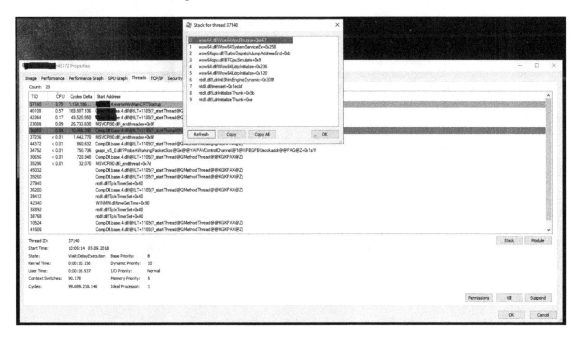

Besides that, the **Threads** tab gives us an overview of the single thread's memory usage, thread's creation and deletion (the color red signifies deletion, green creation), and the changing workload.

In the following sections, we will at last show how to use some more specialized tools, and how to quickly locate the problematic spots in an application that's not working very well.

Using Qt Creator's QML profiler

For this purpose, we will use a small program inspired by one of the technical videos from Qt's site about integrating Python and QML. It uses QML for UI definition, but defines a C++ model; thus, it is a mixed application. After starting, it will fetch data from the web to answer a question we posed, as can be seen in the following figure:

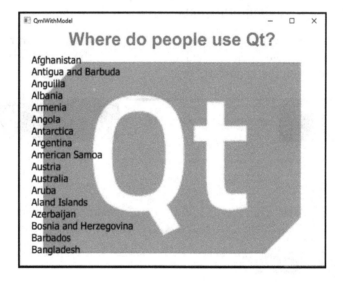

The source code of the program is contained in this book resources (`https://github.com/ PacktPublishing/Hands-On-High-performance-with-QT/tree/master/Chapter%202`). We will use this application in the following examples. First, we will have a look at the performance profile of the QML part.

The **QML Profiler** is integrated with Qt Creator, so we only need to open the example project and select **Analyze | QML Profiler** to show the profiling view and then select the Start button to start the application with profiling enabled. QML debug support has to be enabled for the application for doing that, but in debug mode Qt Creator enables it by default. We can also attach the **QML Profiler** to a running application if we wish.

I started the **QML Profiler** for the example project previously mentioned, waited till it fetched the HTTP data with country names, and then scrolled the list up and down a little. Then, I stopped the profiling session and the following screen appeared:

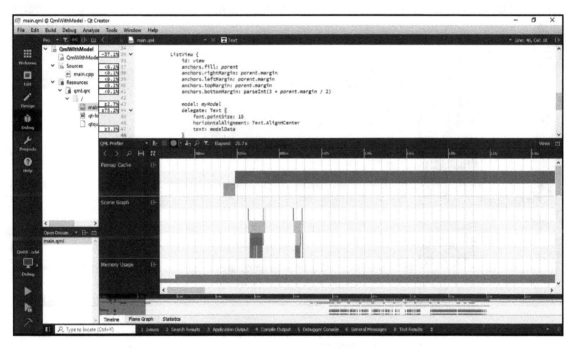

We can see that, on the upper panel, the percentage of samples for each code line is shown, indicating that most of the work was done in the **Text** delegate, namely more than 75%. This is understandable, as I scrolled and flicked through the country names list. You'll also notice that not all the HTTP work appear in the profile, as **QML Profiler** does not look into C++ code.

On the lower end of the window, you'll notice a small **Timeline** panel, where the entire course of our performance data is shown in a minified manner, and which can be scrolled along the time coordinate using an opaque scene rectangle.

In the middle of the profiling screen, there is a list of different performance indicators. We can see some **Scene Graph** activity at the beginning, amounting to initialization. If we scroll the graphs using the opaque scene rectangle in the **Timeline** panes, we arrive at the following visualization:

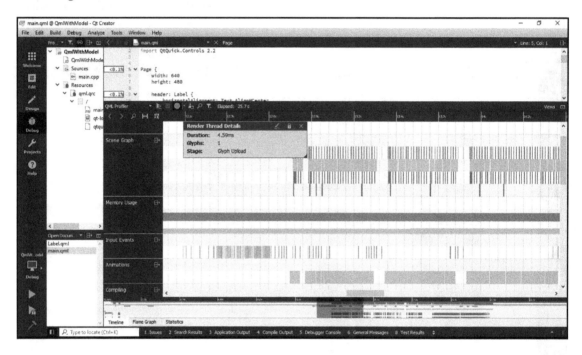

We see that there was much activity in the **Binding** and **JavaScript** categories, and when we click on some of the bars in the **Binding** sections, the corresponding QML line will be selected, in our case, the `text:modelData` line, where the binding of C++ model data takes place. When we scroll up back to the **Scene Graph** category, we can see that here, too, a lot of fork was done when we were scrolling:

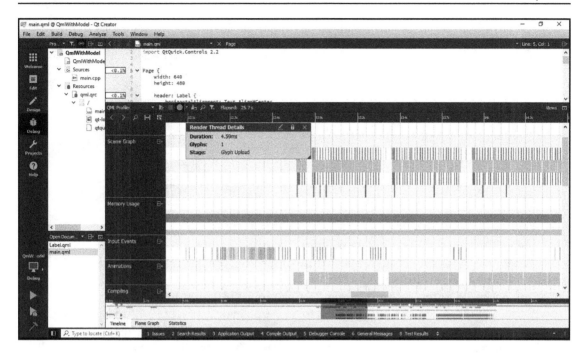

When we click on the smallest purple bar, down in the **Scene Graph** area, a popup with a description of that activity (here, **Glyph Upload**) and performance data shows up. If you want to learn more about data collection and analysis with the **QML Profiler,** please refer to the excellent Qt documentation.

We have seen that, when using the integrated **QML Profiler,** we can look rather deeply into the inner workings of QML code, and can obtain both a lot of detailed information and a good general overview of the behavior of our code. However, one thing immediately catches the eye—the absence of performance data between initialization and the scrolling of the list, that is, the HTTP communication. This is because **QML Profiler** is blind to C++ code, and that is why we need one additional tool: a general C++ CPU profiler.

Using standalone CPU profilers

To simulate excess CPU usage, we will add the following two lines to the `main.cc` file of the preceding example project before the `return` statement:

```
// waste time
wasteCpuCycles();
return app.exec();
```

The `wasteCpuCycles()` function will waste time with floating-point divisions in the following manner:

```
void wasteCpuCycles()
{
  size_t count = 10000000;
  double result = 0;
  for(size_t i = 0; i < count; ++i)
  {
    result += i / 2.33;
  }
  qDebug() << QString("Wasted %1 divisions, result=%2")
              .arg(count).arg(result);
}
```

First, we will try out the Very Sleepy profiler. To install it, go to `https://github.com/ VerySleepy/verysleepy`. Because, at the time of writing, the last released version, v0.90, cannot read the debug information of newer MinGW compilers, you will need the latest development build of the yet-unreleased 0.91 version. You can find it under the **Download** section of `Readme.md` as a link to an AppVeyor artifact (v0.90-154-g3220232 in my case). It contains an installer, so just start it and accept all defaults. After you start the profiler, you can either attach it to a running program from the list on the left-hand or click **File | Launch** and select a program to start, as shown in the following screenshot:

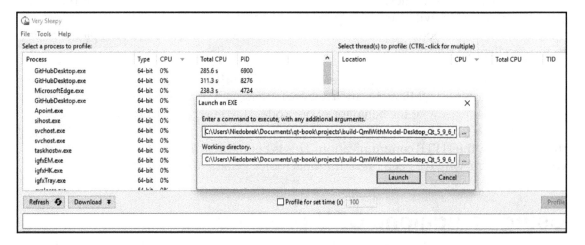

You'll see that we have to specify the executable and its working directory; for the latter, just use the directory where the application is located. After clicking **Launch,** the application will be started under the control of the profiler, as seen in the following screenshot:

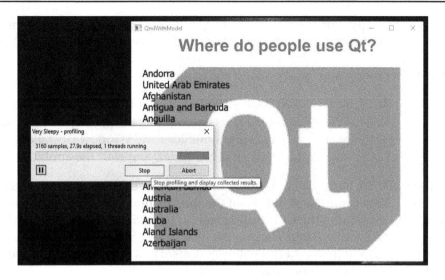

When you have all the required profiling data, click on the **Stop** button in the **Very Sleepy** dialog. The profiler will then collect the data and display it in a new window, as can be seen in the following diagram:

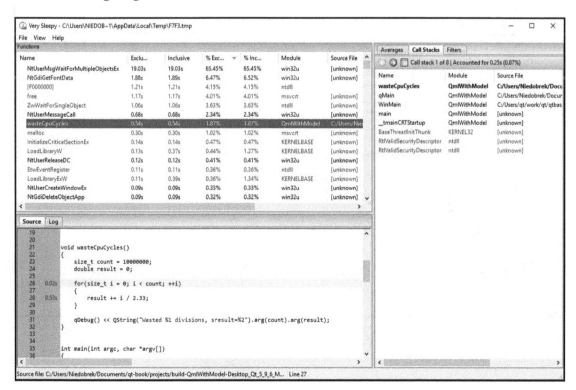

We see that **Very Sleepy** found our CPU wasting function, and shows it as the most CPU-intensive non-system function. In the lower panel, the source code is shown with lines annotated with sampled time durations. We can see that the most time was wasted in floating-point operations, and some on loop mechanics.

Next, let's try out the current CodeXL's CPU profiling support. To install it, go to `https://github.com/GPUOpen-Tools/CodeXL/releases/tag/v2.5` or the product site (`https://gpuopen.com/compute-product/codexl/`) and download the Windows installer (`CodeXL_Win_2.5.67.exe`). Install it on your computer, and start the application.

To be able to profile the example application, you will have to create a new project by clicking on **File | New Project** and filling out the the executable location. After that, you can start profiling by clicking the **CPU Profile** icon in the toolbar. When you think that you have all the required profiling data, click on the rectangular Stop icon next to the **CPU Profile** icon. CodeXL will then collect the data and display it in a new profiling session, which can be seen in the following screenshot:

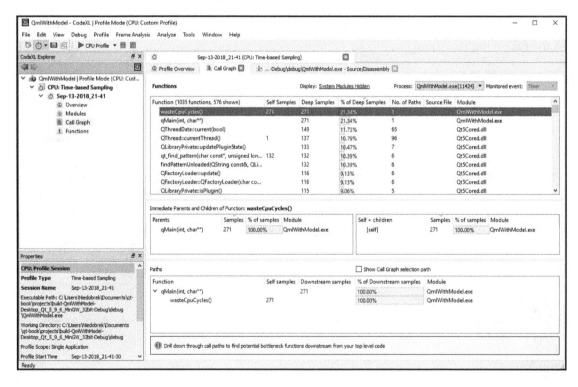

We see that the CPU wasting function is shown on the first row this time. This is because CodeXL will, by default, filter out system functions. We have several other views in which the data is organized in a different manner. However, CodeXL seemed to have a problem displaying the source code of the function and only displayed the disassembly in the **Source/Disassembly** tab. Nonetheless, the instructions were all annotated with sample rates, which gives us a nice insight into the workings of the generated assembler code.

Reiterating sampling profiling's limitations

As already stated at the beginning of this chapter (which you may have forgotten or just plain refused to read), there are some limitations as a consequence of statistic nature of the sampling data. Let's illustrate this with an example now, as it will then become more plausible than in a theoretic discussion. Let's have a look at the **Call Graph** tab of the CodeXL profiling results shown in the previous screenshot:

- You could be tempted to say that the qMain() function called only the wasteCpuCycles() function, as shown in the **Call Graph**, but we just don't know that for certain. What we can say is that the stacks collected in the sampling process have never seen that function calling something different than wasteCpuCycles().
- We cannot say how often function wasteCpuCycles() was called either. Was it called once, spending 21.34% of the time overall, or 10 times, taking 2.134% each time?

As we said already, if you want super-precise information, you will have to resort to instrumentation.

Investigating memory usage

On Linux Qt, Creator integrates with Valgrind's memcheck, which, alas, isn't available on Windows, so we have to look for other tools. Before we jump into dedicated tools, however, let's first have a look at Windows system tools.

Poor man's memory profiling

Unexpectedly, sometimes, much can be done just by using the old and trusty **Process Explorer** tool we introduced in the *Widows system tools* section earlier in this chapter. Let's discuss this with a real-life example.

In a project for one of my customers, there was a Qt application that suffered from timeouts when fetching frames from a camera. This is arguably a performance problem, so I started an investigation. As a first measure, I started a long-frame acquisition run, and **Performance Graph** view of **Process Manager** for the problematic application to monitor its behavior. You can see the measurement time series in the following screenshot:

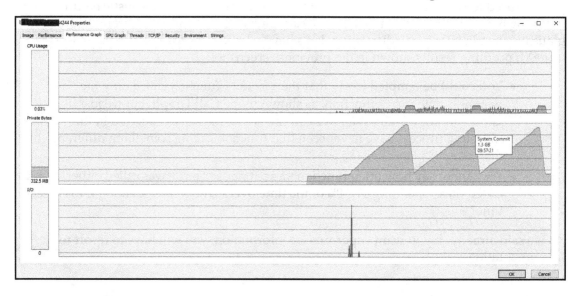

What stands out is that the memory usage spikes and then falls rapidly. It can be observed that the timeouts occur on the falling flank of the memory usage curve. Thus, the suspicion arose that, somehow, the process of releasing memory prevents frame grabbing. A quick look into debug traces confirmed this:

```
AppMainWindow::outOfMemoryHandler() -> leaving out of memory handler
ImageCollector::waitForImage(): timed out !!!!
```

It turned out that the main window would free excess memory, blocking Qt's main message loop, so that when the ImageCollector got activated, its internal timer was already stale. Of course, this was a bug, not a real performance problem, because a grabber ran in another thread.

Using Qt Creator's heob integration

Sometimes, the previous analysis isn't enough, as it will only show that our program accumulates memory, but cannot say if it is doing that by design (building up a great cache?), or because we have a memory leak. In such cases, we will have to check whether memory is leaking—a very arduous task that is best left to specialized tools.

For that reason Qt Creator supports Valgrind's Memecheck application on Linux, which unfortunately isn't available on Windows. Admittedly, in the case of memory profiling, the situation isn't quite as dim as with CPU profiling, because Qt Creator has built-in integration for the heob memory-checking tool.

However, heob isn't contained in Qt Creator's installation and has to be installed manually. Go to https://github.com/ssbssa/heob/releases and download the latest compressed archive (heob-2.1.7z in my case). It contains heob's two binaries, for 32-bits and 64-bits, decompress it and save it in your tools folder. As we are using MinGW, we will additionally need the dwarfstack DLLs to be able to read program symbols information. Go to https://github.com/ssbssa/dwarfstack/releases, download the latest compressed archive (dwarfstack-2.0-dlls.7z in my case), and decompress it in the same directory you saved the heob executables in.

To test leak detection, we will add the following two lines to the main.cc file of the example project, exactly as we did in the CPU case:

```
// induce memory leak
makeLeak();
return app.exec();
```

The `makeLeak()` function will allocate 10,000 bytes and simply leak it. Now click **Analyze | Heob,** and the following dialog will appear:

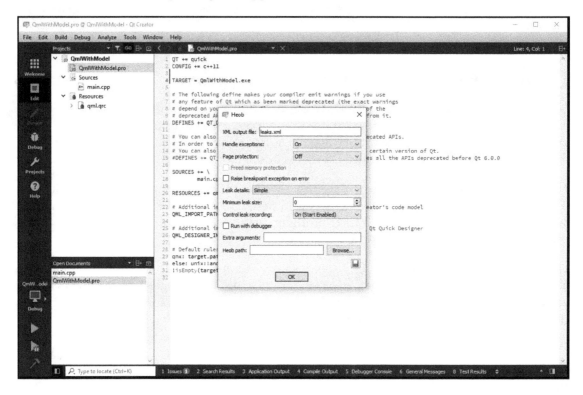

Caution: Due to a bug in the Qt Creator version we are using, this dialog won't be shown; instead, an error message that a path couldn't be found will appear. The bug has been reported but probably won't be fixed because workarounds for it exist. First, as shown in the previous screenshot, add a `TARGET=` line to the `.pro` file of your project, containing the name of your executable before you start **Heob**. Don't forget to remove it when you want to build your project again. The second workaround is to add an empty file along with your executable with the same name as the executable, only without the `.exe` extension (`QmlWithModel` in the example project's case).

After you have fixed the problem with a workaround, open the **Heob** dialog, and enter the path where you stored the heob executables in the **Heob path** field, accept all the default settings, and click on **OK**. As seen in the next screenshot, heob will start the tested executable and inject its instrumented memory management functions:

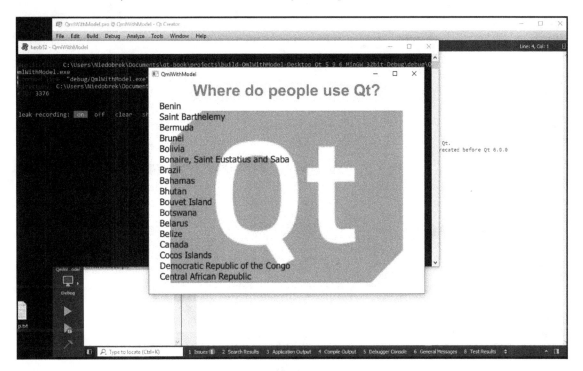

After we stop the tested application, the detected memory problems will be reported in the **Memcheck** output panel, as seen in the following screenshot:

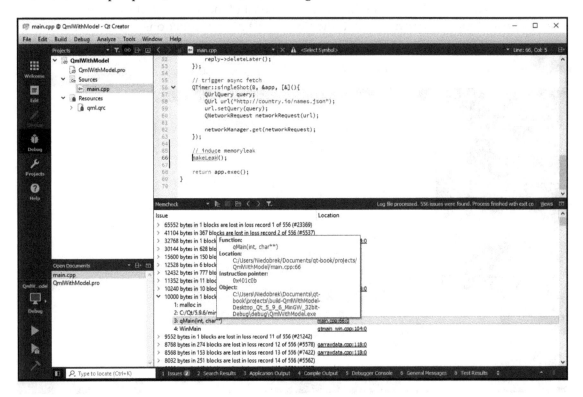

We see that our self-inflicted memory leak got detected. When we click on the link with the source location, the referenced line will be shown in the editor. Additionally, a tooltip containing information about the detected leak will be displayed when we hover the mouse above a given line.

Heob can do more than that, though; for example, it can check buffer overflows and invoke an exception or start a debugger when they occur. **Qt Creator Manual** provides documentation for the options shown in the dialog (see `https://doc.qt.io/qtcreator/creator-heob.html`), but there are more options than that. You can get a quick overview of the supported options when you invoke heob with the `-H` option, either from the dialog or directly.

Manual instrumentation and benchmarks

Is there too much complicated tooling for your taste? Don't panic; it doesn't always have to be a profiler; there is a set of simpler techniques, which oftentimes can prove to be quite sufficient.

Debug outputs

Sometimes, the simplest thing we can do is just to add some `printf`s reporting times spend in critical parts of the code as debug outputs (that is, they will disappear in your Release build). This is the simplest form of manual instrumentation we can have—no sophisticated output formats; just simple human-readable log lines.

We can use it in two ways: first, when investigating some incumbent performance problem, and, second, for an overview of the general timing of our application when it is evolving.

Qt can support us in that endeavor because it provides a C++ class that can be used to measure short-time intervals—the `QElapsedTimer` class. We can use it like this:

```
QElapsedTimer timer;
timer.start();
// work, work ...
qDebug() << QString("work-work took %1 msecs").arg(timer.elapsed());
```

When working with QML, we can use the console's support for time measurements in our JavaScript code, for example:

```
console.timeStart("moreWork");
// more JS work ...
console.timeEnd("moreWork");
```

This would print the following line to the JavaScript console:

```
moreWork: XXX ms
```

XXX stands for the measured time. You can also **nest** time measurements, as in the following example:

```
console.timeStart("totalWork");
console.timeStart("firstPart");
// JS work ...
console.timeEnd("firstPart");
// even more JS work ...
console.timeEnd("totalWork");
```

Benchmarks

Another tool we can use is **benchmarking**; this is a technique for measuring the performance of certain isolated features or some synthetic workloads. Benchmarking is best known as a technique for comparing programming languages' or SQL databases' performance, but we can also use it in Qt programming to measure the performance of some aspects of our code.

The Qt Test module contains a QBENCHMARK macro to support such measurements, which is used to denote these lines in a test case that has to be benchmarked, for example:

```
void BenchmarkTest::test1 {
  QBENCHMARK {
    // code to be measured ...
  }
}
```

The code inside the macro will be rerun as often, as it is needed to get a stable and accurate measurement. There is a whole lot of logic needed to ensure that benchmark measurements are not biased, but this all is hidden from us by the Qt Test module. However, if we want, the -iterations option can set a fixed number of iterations for the benchmark test. There are more benchmarking macros and options, so please consult the Qt documentation if needed.

Benchmarks in regression testing

If you are using continuous integration for your project, you could set up a suite of performance tests that must pass before the newest code change can be accepted, thus introducing a bit of **performance culture** to your project. I have seen such tests in real-world projects, and I must say that they can sometimes be a mixed blessing. The reason is that they can fail when the build server is overloaded, so an extra bit of caution is needed here. Admittedly, it is border territory between testing and profiling, but as it's an important technique, it doesn't do any harm to mention it twice.

Manual instrumentation

As already stated, using the Chrome tracing tab (`chrome://tracing/`) as a performance visualizer is a popular technique. We could either whip up a set of instrumentation functions by ourselves or, preferably, find an existing, already-implemented library. And, indeed, there are such libraries in the wild, and one of them is SPDR (`https://github.com/uucidl/uu.spdr`); another example is Minitrace (`https://github.com/hrydgard/minitrace`). In the following screenshot, you'll see an example showing Chrome's own performance trace:

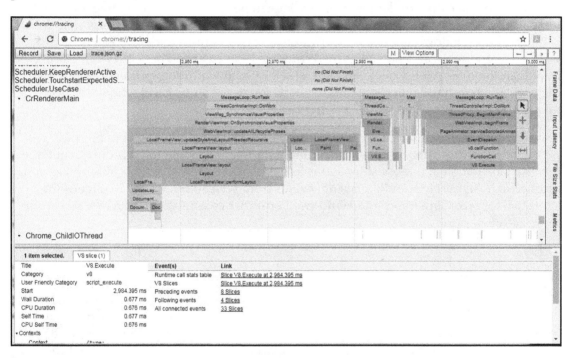

As you can see, Chrome displays performance data in the form of flame graphs. This is a relatively recent visualization introduced by Linux perftools author, Brendan Gregg. A flame graph shows nested function calls in the vertical direction and the time flow in the horizontal direction. It is very suitable for visualizing deep function-call hierarchies. Upon clicking each rectangle in the graph, its performance data will be shown. We can use the previously mentioned projects to generate our custom call hierarchy and performance graphs in that format and view them with Chrome. That would look very professional!

Further advanced tools

Besides the basic performance tools introduced so far, there are many more specialized tools we can use. We will introduce some of them in detail and only briefly mention some others.

Event Tracing for Windows (ETW) and xperf

On Linux, we have the excellent and widely known perftools suite for reading any imaginable kernel counters that might be relevant for performance. A little less well-known is the fact that Windows sports an equally excellent free performance toolset, namely the **ETW** and **xperf** tools, also known as the **Windows Performance Toolkit** (**WPT**). ETW traces can show the total system behavior, and that is how different processes influence themselves. We can use it in more difficult performance analysis cases where we need information from Windows kernel and hardware.

The acronyms that are used in connection with ETW can be a little perplexing, so we will explain them in more detail. **ETW**, the acronym for **Event-Tracing** for **Windows**, contains the instrumentation of the key subsystems in the Windows kernel, a high-quality sampling profiler, and support for sending custom events from your software. WPT contains the xperf tool for recording traces and **Windows Performance Analyzer** (**WPA**)—a visualizer for collected performance data.

Installation

ETW and xperf were famous for their very cumbersome usage, and that is maybe the reason why ETW is not more widely known. It has improved a lot since then, but we will nonetheless use a GUI tool, aptly named **UI for ETW**, written by Bruce Dawson, who was so kind as to make the barely usable tools approachable by everyone. To install **UI for ETW,** go to `https://github.com/google/UIforETW/releases`, download the current distribution (`etwpackage1.49.zip`), unpack it, and start the installer. The installer will automatically fetch a matching version of WPT for your machine, if there isn't one already. When **UI for ETW** is started, it shows the following window:

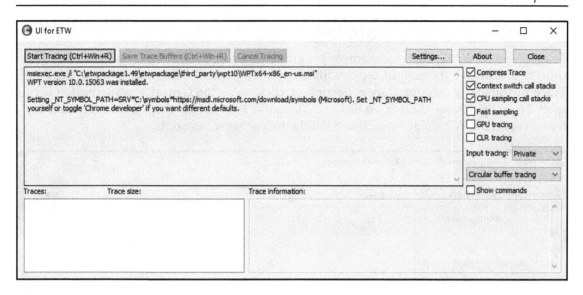

When the **Start Tracing** button is clicked, **UI for ETW** will start to continuously collect ETW traces and write them into a circular memory buffer. When we want to save the current contents of the trace buffer, we have to click on the **Save Trace Buffers** button, or just use the **Ctrl+Win+R** shortcut from anywhere. We will then see the last-recorded trace in a list, as we can see from the following screenshot:

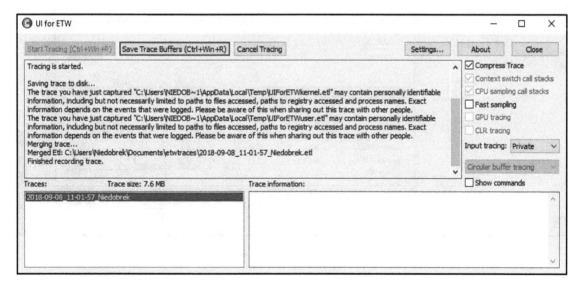

Recording and visualizing traces

To create an ETW trace for our example program, we open **UI for ETW**, start trace collecting, launch our example, work with it, close it eventually, and then click on **Save Trace Buffers**. You can stop trace collection by clicking on the **Cancel Tracing** button if you wish. Now, by double-clicking on the trace filename, as visible in the previous screenshot, we can open the WPA viewer, as shown in the following screenshot:

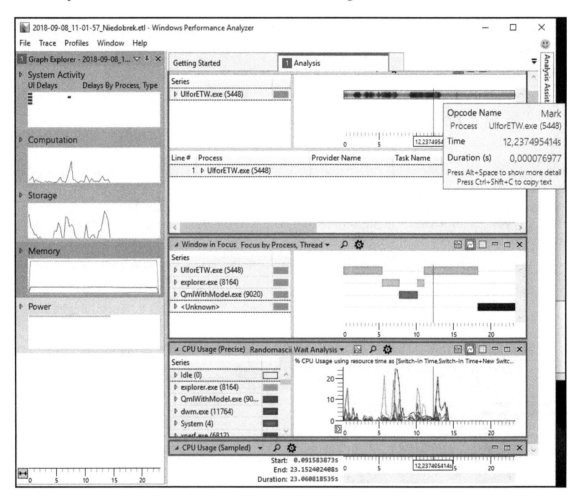

We can see that **UI for ETW** is not only a better GUI for the xperf tool, it also adds its own providers, recording power consumption, heat, keyboard input, flame graphs, and so on. Moreover, it provides its own preset analysis tab. In the previous screenshot, we can see the **System Activity**, **Window in Focus**, **CPU Usage (Precise)**, **CPU Usage (Sampled),** and other analysis windows on the right-hand side. As there is very little documentation for the wealth of counters displayed in the UI, you will have to go to Bruce Dawson's blog, where he provides some descriptions of them.

On the left-hand side, several performance categories are shown. When we click and expand the **System Activity** category, the available counters will be displayed, as shown in the following screenshot:

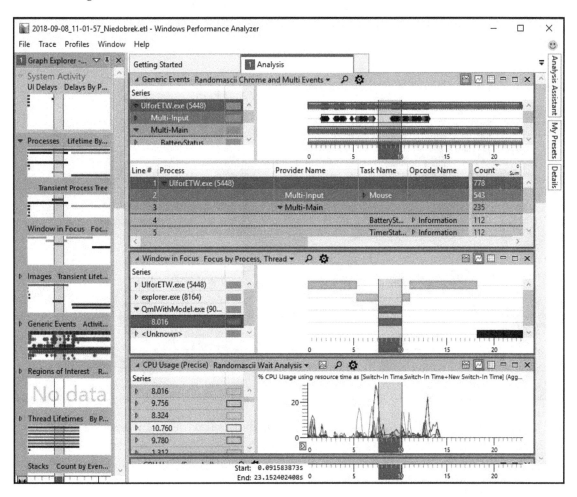

Then, we can go to the **Windows in Focus** window and select our `QmlWithModel.exe` process. We see, in all the other windows, the relevant trace portions are highlighted as well! If you'd like to display some of the counters visible in the left **Graph Explorer** panel on the right-hand side, you can click it and choose **Add Graph to New Analysis Window** from its context menu. For example, when we do that for the CPU counter form, the *Computation* category, we will be presented with the view shown in the following screenshot:

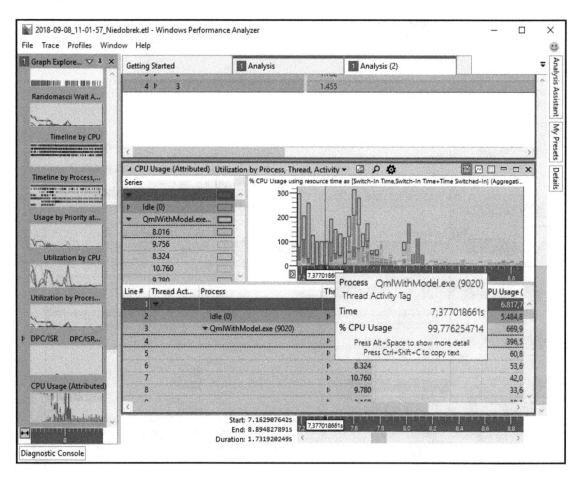

We then select a portion of the **Utilization by CPU** diagram with the mouse and select the Zoom option to zoom into the section we are most interested in. You will see the light-green bars corresponding to our example program scheduled in in parallel with other programs. Beneath the diagram, the counter values for threads we have are displayed and can be examined.

As GPU events are also enabled by **UI for ETW**, there is another visualization available for collected traces. In **UI for ETW,** click on the trace filename in the trace list window, open its context menu, and select **Open** in **GPUView**. This tool (included in the WPT distribution) lets us investigate interactions between the CPU, the graphics driver, and the GPU, and is shown in the following screenshot. We won't discuss it here, though, as we only want to hint at a further possibility for ETW data visualization:

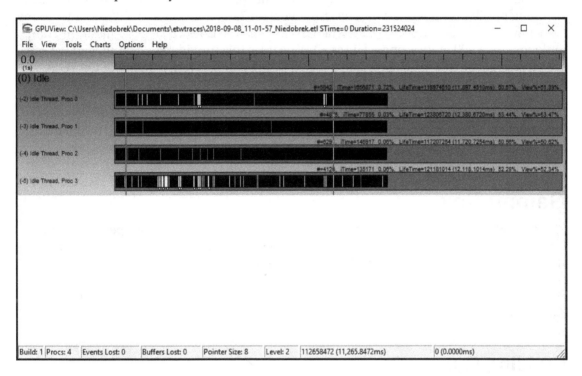

Conclusion

We only looked at very little of ETF's and WPA's functionality—only enough to get you started. This tool is so powerful! An example ETW trace is included with this book's resources for you to browse through; maybe you will detect that a little problem occurred when starting the example program I didn't tell you about!

ETW enables programs to emit custom events, which can be very convenient when we want to mark some boundaries in the program to make finding the relevant information easier. Example implementation for user event is provided with **UI for ETW**, so consult it for further information.

But where ETW really shines is the analysis of UI hangs. This is something that your typical sampling profiler cannot do. Windows, from version 7 up, includes an ETW provider in the kernel, which will generate an event when the application doesn't check its message pump for longer than 200 milliseconds. **UI for ETW** enables this provider by default, and we can see those events in the **UI Delays** graph from the **System Activity** window of the WPA. This can prove very useful when analyzing hangs in your GUI.

If you want to learn more about ETW, and maybe read a series of non-trivial performance investigation cases solved using ETW, have a look at his Random ASCII blog (available at `https://randomascii.wordpress.com`, beginning with the ETW Central blogpost).

GammaRay

This is another specialized tool coming from KDAB, a German company specializing in Qt. It is not so much a profiler, as an application inspector, allowing a peek into the object structure of a running application. But because performance optimization sometimes amounts to finding excess resources, such a tool also has a place in your quiver! Qt Creator even has built-in integration for GammaRay; unfortunately, it's only available in Qt Automotive Suite.

Building GammaRay

Unfortunately, there are no prebuilt binaries for Windows, and MinGW and must be built from sources. For that purpose, we have to go to `https://github.com/KDAB/GammaRay`, fetch the latest code, and set out to compile it with Qt Creator.

The build project is configured as a CMake project, so we have to install the current CMake version from `https://cmake.org/download/` (3.12.2 in this case). Qt Creator has CMake integration built in, so we will just have to enable it. For that, we open **Projects | ManageKits** dialog, then select the **CMake** tab, and add your installed version by specifying the CMake's executable path.

Next, we open GammaRay's `CMakeLists.txt` project file and start the build. It will report some errors, but after we disable the multibuild option by setting the `-DGAMMARAY_MULTI_BUILD=FALSE` property for CMake, the errors will disappear. After some time, we will be able to start the compiled GammaRay application and attach it to the running instance of our example program, as can be seen in the following screenshot:

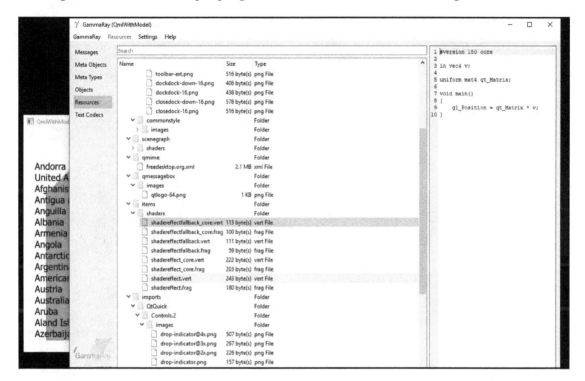

You can see the resources used by the QML in its scene graph, complete with used shaders and their code. You can also browse Qt object hierarchies (in the **Objects** tab) and look at properties of single object instances, for example, the elements of **QQuickListView** showing the list of countries, as can be seen in the next screenshot:

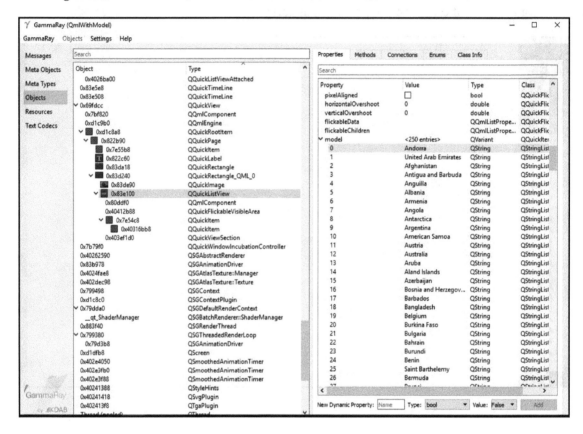

When can we use it?

As an example of this tool's usability for performance work, KDAB mentions debugging high video memory usage by accumulating textures. In its latest versions, GammaRay can show textures relating to single Qt Quick items, allowing you to locate culprits. Another example is the debugging of 100% of the CPU load caused by a constantly firing, zero-millisecond timer, which, erroneously, isn't set to `singleShot`. A quick glance through the list shown in the **Timer**'s view during runtime reveals the problematic guy in an instant.

Additionally, we can also use the tool's capabilities in the visualization of graphic scenes, state machines, and Qt models to examine complex hierarchies at runtime, which can indirectly benefit our performance work.

Other tools

There are a number of other interesting tools we'd like to mention, just to see how many possibilities are out there.

Graphic profilers

Let's start with AMD CodeXL. I know, we had that one already, but as already stated, CodeXL is much more than a simple sampling CPU profiler. On AMD processors, it can additionally use hardware support for event profiling, instruction-based sampling, and sophisticated power analysis. It can debug C++ code, OpenCL, and OpenGL API calls, as well as OpenCL kernels. It supports frame and shader analysis, and it can profile GPU usage. It is a comprehensive graphic profiler tool oriented toward AMD hardware.

Intel Graphics Performance Analyzers (Intel GPA) is a game and graphic performance analyzer, and it is oriented toward Intel hardware, and is free as well. It shows CPU, GPU, Graphics API, and power metrics in real time, supports frame and trace capturing and analysis, and lets you override graphics pipeline state and parameters without recompilation. Wow! These graphic analysis tools are really sophisticated!

While the previous analyzers relied on sampling or hardware support, RAD's Telemetry Performance Visualization System is a tool using instrumentation. It is also oriented toward games, and, as the name suggests, it is a visualizer for the information created by the instrumentation code. It has a rich UI and is designed to keep up with real-time outputs. It displays classic CPU profiling information, visualizes locks and lock contentions, and shows context switches and thread affinities. It is quite good for an instrumenting profiler!

Apitrace is a tool for tracing the OpenGL calls your application is making. It works by preloading an instrumented implementation of OpenGL and recording its trace outputs. Apitrace comes with a GUI program for trace visualization and is widely used for graphic performance optimization work.

Commercial Intel tools

The commercial Intel performance suite comprises of VTune Amplifier, Intel Advisor, and Intel Inspector. VTune Amplifier is an advanced sampling profiler using hardware and OS counters, providing information on CPU, threading, memory, cache, and storage. Intel Inspector is a memory and threading debugger, which can detect races, deadlocks, and memory leaks. Intel Advisor is a prototyping tool that can estimate how your design will perform on real hardware pertaining to threading and vectorization, and propose-necessary adjustments. Some cool tool suite, huh?

Visual Studio tools

As mentioned, newer versions of Microsoft's Visual Studio contain their own integrated profiler, thread, and memory analyzers. Some commercial Visual Studio versions also contain support for automated code instrumentation. The integrated profiler shows a very nice CPU performance diagram, where you can zoom in on a suspiciously-looking diagram section and show the usual function hierarchy and other views for this section only. You can see an example CPU profiling overview in the next screenshot:

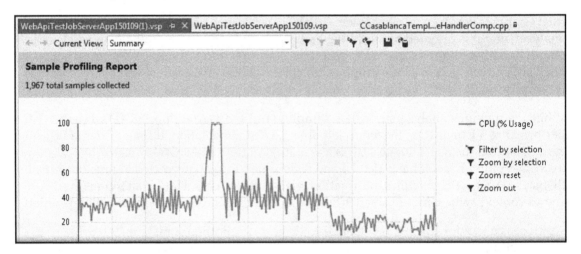

There's also the commercial **GlowCode** profiler, which integrates neatly with Visual Studio, uses just-in-time instrumentation, has a very small runtime overhead, and, additionally, contains a leak detector.

Summary

So, there was an awful lot of tools in this chapter, and then some more. What did we really learn from this chapter, besides a litany of tool names? Although it doesn't look like this at first glance, we indeed learned several important things, namely the following:

- What kinds of tools are programmers using for performance analysis?
- What platform, Qt version, and development environment will we be relying on in this book?
- What open source and free tools can we use on Windows in addition to Qt Creator?
- Much insight can be gained by relatively simple means.
- How to profile a QML application's CPU usage.
- How to profile a C++ (and mixed QML/C++) application's CPU usage.
- How to investigate memory usage and find memory leaks.

There are even more specialized performance tools you could use, so there's virtually no limit to the amount of data you can collect. In the next chapter, we will let the tools rest for a little while and return to programming questions. As Qt is written in C++, and C++ will be used for any high-performance work in Qt (as we will see in the following chapters), we will turn our attention to that language. As you are at least a middle-level developer, you will already know a lot about C++, but we want to look at it from a different angle. Let's ignore the discussion of the most recent hot language feature or the newest annoying quirk and instead have a look at it from the vantage point of a performance engineer.

Questions

Here are some questions so that you can test your understanding of the topics in this chapter:

1. What does this mean: Apitrace preloads an instrumented implementation of OpenGL? Explain.
2. Isn't there a way to use the `gprof` after all?
3. How would you look for a lock convoy or a waiting chain causing your UI to stutter or, even worse, to freeze?
4. What is the difference between **CPU Usage (Precise)** and **CPU Usage (Sampled)** in ETW traces?

5. How would you find timers running amok or QML items accumulating video memory?

6. What can you do when your favorite open source performance is not supported by Qt Creator?

7. What is that thread and lock analysis feature some of the tools seem to have?

8. If you try to launch the example program directly or from an external CPU profiler, this won't work. Why not? How do you fix it?

9. If we don't use any custom ETW events in our program, will we be able see any information about the program in ETW traces?

10. Which one is better—sampling or instrumentation?

3
Deep Dive into C++ and Performance

In this chapter, we will take a closer look at Qt's underlying language and its standing in the matter of performance. We will look at the design philosophy of C++, some problematic and some good features, and the impact the recent C++ standard updates have had on program optimization. We will also discuss what compilers and other tools can do for program performance.

The topics that will be covered are as follows:

- C++ philosophy—what were Bjarne's guidelines when designing C++
- Traditional C++ optimizations—the basics we have always done
- C++11/14/17 and performance—what performance nuggets are hidden there
- What your compiler can do for you—a lot, you'd be surprised
- Optimization tools beyond compiler—because the story doesn't end there

Admittedly, an entire book could be written on these topics and, indeed, there are some of them out there (see the *Further reading* section later), so you cannot expect to learn all of it from a single chapter. What we strive for is to give the reader an overview of the important themes, so that we will have a strong basis when discussing Qt's performance.

C++ philosophy and design

C++ started as a humble preprocessor for C, so it's only natural that it inherited C's low-level character with its direct map to hardware, memory allocation control (stack and heap), pointer arithmetic, casts between types, dangerous lack of boundary checks, and also that of implicit initialization. Much of the early success of C++ has its roots in the decision to maintain backward compatibility with C in order to be able firstly to compile old C sources, and secondly to maintain the high performance of the resulting code.

Hence, one of the first and most important design guidelines for C++ was, and still is, the *zero-overhead abstractions* principle, or rephrased, *you don't pay for what you don't use*. The meaning of it is that each new language feature should incur no overhead if it is not used. For example, if we don't explicitly use virtual functions there's nothing added to the class definition, whereas in Java every method is virtual, and we have to mark it as final if we don't want to pay the price. Another example could be garbage collection support, which is optional in C++.

Other cornerstones of the C++ philosophy were the use of constructors and destructors for automatic resource management (the famous **resource acquisition is initialization (RAII)**), support of polymorphism and multiple inheritance and sometimes unbridled usage of template wizardry and operator overloading. You might feel that this is a lot of additional features crammed in on the old C language's base and might ask yourself whether C++ still pursues the high-performance goal. So, let me cite from a recent document of the standard committee titled, *Directions for C++* (available on `https://wg21.link/P0939`):

> **Technically, C++ rests on two pillars**: *A direct map to hardware (initially from C) and zero-overhead abstraction in production code (initially from Simula, where it wasn't zero overhead). Depart from those and the language is no longer C++.*

This sums up the C++ philosophy nicely—while maintaining a link to low-level functionality as low-level languages do, it offers advanced high-level abstractions like the most sophisticated languages out there. And that's with zero overhead! That's why we love C++—not many languages are able to pull off this trick!

From the point of view of our performance assessment of C++, the most important principle is the *zero-overhead* principle. By and large, this principle was adhered to when designing the classic C++ features with two notable exceptions—exceptions and **run-time type identification (RTTI)**. Another basic feature that stirred up much controversy in its time was the cost of the virtual functions. We, hence, will shortly discuss these two features and their corresponding performance impacts.

Problems with exceptions

Exceptions are, 20 years after their inception in C++, still such a controversial topic that some major C++ guidelines (Google's being the most notable example) prohibit their usage. While they are often banned due to difficulties in writing exception-safe code, in some projects, such as in real-time or safety-critical environments, they runtime space and time because they violate the *zero-overhead* principle with respect to binary image size.

By the way, the Qt API doesn't have exceptions, but not for any of the preceding reasons! In the past, compilers on some target platforms, which Qt wanted to support, simply didn't implement exceptions at that juncture!

Run-time overheads

Performance-wise, we have two problems with the existing exception model:

- **Binary code bloat**: Just turning on exception support for a program that previously didn't use exceptions at all (that is, isn't throwing or catching anything) will considerably increase the size of the binary. Numbers such as 15% or even 38% were reported.
- **Runtime costs**: With today's prevalent table-based exception implementations, there's practically no cost when an exception is not thrown, but there can be a really big runtime overhead when an exception *is* thrown.

This runtime cost stems from the creation of the exception object, either on heap or, under Windows, on stack, and then the matching of the dynamic exception type using RTTI, which has its own set of performance problems. That does not even mention the stack unwinding!

Non-determinism

The second runtime problem is the non-determinism of exceptions—we just cannot say how long it will take to handle a thrown exception! And as new exceptions can be generated in the handler of the current exception, there can be multiple exceptions in flight, which cannot be folded using normal optimizations, so they will require an arbitrary amount of memory too.

When allocating memory for an exception, we either use dynamic allocation, which requires unpredictable amounts of time in general, or the current stack, which must however be partially preserved, leading to dead-stack-pinning techniques for potentially several exceptions in flight, multiplying the stack usage.

RTTI

Today's dynamic exceptions require RTTI to match the exception handlers and RTTI is the second C++ feature violating the zero-overhead principle. It does it in two ways:

- First, it requires support for `typeid::name()`, which in turn requires storage of metadata, increasing memory usage. This is the only place in C++ where metadata is used!
- Second, the performance of RTTI lookup is unpredictable, because linking in an unknown, third-party, shared library can increase the time needed to resolve it dramatically!

Because of that, RTTI was also banned in many project's coding guidelines (for example, Firefox), hence effectively prohibiting the use of exceptions in one sweep.

Conclusion

We see that exceptions, as they are defined today in C++, are problematic performance-wise, mainly due to their unpredictable runtime costs. Recently, there was even a C++ standard proposal (P0709) for adding zero-overhead, static, exception-handling mechanisms to C++, so the future developments here will definitely be interesting to watch.

Having said that, in Qt programming, the trade-off the modern table-based exception implementations make, that is, zero overhead when no exception is thrown and big overhead (reported to be in the order of 1000-2000 CPU cycles in one study) when it is, is acceptable given that the exceptions occur very infrequently. Hence, the usual advice given to beginners is: don't use exceptions to break out of the loop!

As for RTTI, we have to be wary of its unpredictable costs. So, be forewarned. The best thing you could do is to replace `dynamic_cast<>` usage with a virtual function, if you can.

Virtual functions

The first and foremost accusation raised against C++ in the early days was the allegedly high cost of virtual functions. Nowadays, this criticism seems to have come back in vogue in some programming communities, for example, among games developers. So, what about its performance costs?

As we know, virtual functions are implemented by means of *vtables*, that is, tables containing function pointers for all the virtual functions of a class. An instance of a class will contain a pointer to the global instance of this class's vtable. Hence, a call of virtual functions goes through two indirections; first, it follows the pointer to the vtable and then the pointer to the function. This cannot be good for performance, right? It's a classic example of pointer chasing, isn't it?

The direct cost of a virtual function call is taking the pointer to the vtable and following it. This could cause a cache miss but probably won't, if the vtable is accessed anywhere close to often. Then the pointed-to method will be called, which may again cause an instruction cache miss, but in tight loops, it probably won't.

The other cost of virtual function calls is indirect, as they could refuse to be inlined (but bear in mind that that's not always the case), disabling further compiler optimizations, as we will discuss in one of the following sections.

An even more indirect cost of virtual function calls is the manner in which polymorphism is traditionally used, that is, by creating polymorphic objects dynamically using `new`. Dynamic memory allocations incur high costs regarding CPU time data locality, as we will see in one of following subsections, so overusing them would have a negative impact on performance. So, watch your program design!

So we can see, there is a cost to virtual functions but it's not so big that it would justify always avoiding them. Here, as always, the measure-first strategy is to be applied.

Traditional C++ optimizations

We will first discuss the performance problems encountered when using the *classic* C++, that is, its pre-C++11 version. This is the very basic knowledge that we, in fact, expect the intermediate programmer to master, but we will nonetheless provide a quick refresher about it.

Low-hanging fruit

As we already said in `Chapter 1`, *Understanding Performant Programs*, there are some techniques that are so simple that they cost you nothing and buy you small but consistent performance gains.

They are more like habits than real techniques, to be frank. In C++ such absolute basics are, for example, as follows:

- Using ++i instead of i++—a compiler should optimize that away, but why rely on that?
- Passing function arguments by const reference—note that, in C++11, we may choose to pass by a value in cases when we will copy it inside the function. For details, look at the discussion about move constructors later.
- Using initialization over assignment—for example, when initializing class members in a constructor, look at the discussion of temporaries later.

Be aware: not heeding this basic advice would amount to premature pessimization!

Temporaries

The *old* C++ was haunted by temporaries—intermediate objects that were created by a compiler only to serve as sources of data and were immediately discarded, eating away at performance. Temporaries can emerge in two places:

- When returning data by value from a function
- When converting from one class into another while passing a parameter to a function

Return values and RVO

When we are returning an object from a function by value, actually the compiler should construct a temporary object, fill inside of the function, return it to the caller, and then use assignment to copy the contents of the temporary object into the result object. Pretty inefficient, huh?

Because of that, very early on compilers implemented a simple optimization allowing the called function to fill the result object directly, skipping the unneeded creation of a temporary. There are two cases of that optimization, simple **return value optimization (RVO)**, when we return an unnamed object, and **named return value optimization (NRVO)**, when, true to its name, we return a named object:

```
T func1()
{
    ...
    return T(); // RVO
}
```

```
T func2()
{
  T t;
  ...
  return t; // NRVO
}
```

C++89 compilers normally used to implement NRVO, but could sometimes become confused whether a function could return an object from two or more different control paths. The standard itself stated that these optimizations were optional, so you couldn't bet on that.

Another place where RVO couldn't be applied was in cases of the chaining of operators, as shown in the following example:

```
std::string s1, s2, s3, s4;
...
s1 = s2 + s3 + s4;
```

The addition on the left side would create two temporary objects (each for one addition) and then assign it to the destination object. The usual workaround was the following ugly one:

```
s1 += s2;
s1 += s3;
si += s4;
```

Conversions

Another context where temporaries could arise was in the case of constant reference parameters in function calls. As such, references would be allowed to bind to a temporary object and implicit conversion could be triggered, creating a temporary only used inside of the function:

```
struct T
{
  T(int i) { ... }
};

void func(const T& o);

main()
{
  func(1); // creates temporary object T!
}
```

For that reason, the `explicit` annotation for constructors was introduced, which blocks such unwanted implicit conversions.

Memory management

C++ allows a pretty fine-grained memory control by allowing us to choose explicitly between stack and heap memory, and it goes even further, by providing customization points for the used memory allocation strategies. We can do it by doing the following:

- Replacing the global memory allocator for the program
- Using own allocation strategies for a single class
- Using custom `std::Allocator` for **Standard Template Library** (**STL**) container classes

Basic truths

The most basic truth we need to learn is that `new`, that is, the dynamic allocation, is bad because it is expensive! And that is because of two reasons—first, the allocation operation in itself is quite expensive, and second, it results in bad data locality. As we learned in `Chapter 1`, *Understanding Performant Programs*, bad data locality results in pipeline stalls and cache misses, ruining the smooth instruction flow in the processor.

Obtaining a fresh memory form the memory allocator is a costly operation because the system allocator must fulfill many different requirements at once and, to achieve that, it has to observe several trade-offs. First of all, it has to do the following:

- It has to support multithreading, so it has to have some form of synchronization. In the older days, that was a major problem, as the allocator had simply a global lock and hence a single point of contention, but modern allocators use some form of per-thread memory pools. Nonetheless, there is a cost to pay for the remaining synchronization when these pools become exhausted.
- It has to support efficient allocations of many same-size objects, many variable-size objects, some very big objects, and some very small objects, and do all of that fast!
- It shouldn't deteriorate over time, waste memory, or fragment the memory.
- Sometimes, it has to call the kernel to give us additional memory. (This one can take quite a long time!)

We see that memory managers have their work cut out for them, so it's not a surprise that the overhead of a memory allocation is rather heavy!

Technically, in C++, we can replace the default memory manager (which is the `malloc()` function) both globally (that is, for the entire program) or only for a single class. We are doing that either by overriding the global `new()` operator or the `new` operator for a specific class as shown in the following:

```
// override global memory handling
void* operator new(size_t size) { ... }
void operator delete(void* p) { ... }
void* operator new[](size_t size) { ... }
void operator delete[](void* p) { ... }

// or only for a class
class Person
{
public:
  void* operator new(size_t size) { ... }
  void operator delete(void* p) { .. }
  // etc...
```

Technical note: The preceding example shows C++11 code. C++17 adds overloads to specify alignment. C++98 used the now deprecated `throw()` specifier.

So, we can do that, but do we want to do it? Let's have a look at that.

Replacing the global memory manager

Admittedly, modern memory managers became very good at satisfying these conflicting requirements, so has any change been made to beat them at their game? I'd say, probably not. But there are alternative general memory managers that are touting their performance advantages over the standard `malloc` function. Should we use them instead?

There are some alternative, high-performance memory managers that have to be taken seriously, such as Google's **tcmalloc**, **ptmalloc2** used in the GCC compiler, and jemalloc from FreeBSD. However, as one study has shown, they are all on a par, and more importantly, each of them can outperform the other ones under certain conditions. So, changing the memory manager isn't a silver bullet. You will have to test their impact in your specific setting.

For example, one study that has tested replacing the default GCC allocator in an embedded device, reports 300 ms faster startup times of a QML application when using *tcmalloc*. However, the overall startup times decreased from 5,325 ms to 5,045 ms, hence the overall improvement amounts to less than 6%. In this case, it seems that the startup is rather dominated by reading and parsing the QML files.

One counter-example widely used in games is the *VMem* memory allocator, which is specifically optimized for the constrained environments of game consoles.

Custom memory allocators

A custom memory allocator will allocate a large segment of memory once, and then allocate pointers within that block of memory in response to allocation requests. So, how can we use this basic scheme to improve memory allocation performance?

We could indeed do it if we could relieve some of the requirements that the general-purpose memory manager has to observe, as in the following:

- Only create objects of fixed size or/and instances of specific classes.
- Do not support multithreading.
- Do not support the releasing of objects.
- LIFO allocation/deallocation order.

Because such an allocator would be very specialized, it could have an edge over general-purpose global allocators. Additionally, as their implementation can be really simple, such allocators offer a potential for inlining that won't ever be the case with a generic allocator. Second, we can control and avoid the memory fragmentation, optimize the memory locality, and even control the alignment for SIMD operations. And at last, as we preallocated our memory at the start, we will avoid the kernel calls that could be made by a general allocator to get fresh memory! So, summing up, the advantages are as follows:

- Fast and simple implementation
- Good memory locality and no memory segmentation
- No unexpected trips to kernels

This looks like a clear win! So, should we always use custom memory allocators for our classes? Sorry to disappoint you, but probably not if your program isn't allocating thousands and thousands of objects on the fly! Having said that, there are cases where we can use it to a good measure.

Where they do make sense

In game programming, custom allocators are widely used because of very specific requirements, as they are constantly creating objects at runtime, such as meshes, sprites, textures, and so on. In this regard, the following allocator types are used:

- **Single-frame memory**: This contains memory for operations that occur within one frame cycle. After the frame is rendered, we don't have to deallocate all memory, but we just reset the pointer in the memory buffer of our allocator (ideally without running destructors of any contained object!). This is also called an arena in standard contexts.
- **Object pools**: Also called fixed size allocators, they contain many same-sized objects (particles, projectiles, spaceships), and hence they simplify the allocation logic extremely. Additionally, they cater for good memory locality. You would like to have all of your particles in a nice array, wouldn't you?

Another example where a custom memory manager could make sense is for the serialization and deserialization of objects for network transmission. If we have complex objects containing dynamic sub-objects (remember a string object will be dynamic!), the dynamic allocation costs can be heavy. We could optimize network communication by using a custom allocator for message serialization on a per-message basis. As an example, Google's Protocol Buffers offer a `protobuf::Arena` class, which can be used as a custom allocator for serialization.

Yet another possible scenario would be using an allocator to assure that all objects of a given type are stored in a contiguous sequence, thus improving the memory locality of some inefficient data structure (think of a list and its nodes) in a refactoring step.

Stack allocators

We can allocate that memory buffer regularly on the heap, but there's another rather ingenious alternative—if you are careful with your objects' lifetimes, you can also allocate the memory buffer directly on the stack, shaving off the dynamic allocation costs completely! Unsurprisingly, such allocators are called **stack allocators**.

Conclusion

With that, we've finished our overview of custom allocator types. We won't present any example implementations here, because there are enough of them already. If you are using *Boost* in your project, then you'll be glad to hear that it has a fixed-memory manager library called *Pool* (`https://www.boost.org/doc/libs/1_68_0/libs/pool/doc/html/index.html`).

Howard Hinnant implemented an on-stack allocator
called `short_alloc` (https://howardhinnant.github.io/stack_alloc.html). These are
high-quality implementations; use them if you need a custom allocator.

Custom STL allocators

If we are using an STL container, we cannot simply replace its allocator in the manner that
has been discussed previously, because their elements often have an implementation-
defined type we cannot access. For that reason, we had the `std::Allocator` class, which
could be passed to the collection and used to allocate its single elements. However, owing
to the language limitations of C++ at that time, these allocators were extremely clunky to
use and generally were little loved (not to say hated) in the C++ community. This is a pity,
as allocators were designed as a way to customize the behavior of STL containers.

However, C++11 simplified the allocator API to such an extent that they can now
indeed be used without that much pain. To prove that, here is a standard example of a
simple, stateless C++11 allocator:

```
template <class T>
struct TestAlloc
{
  typedef T value_type;
  TestAlloc() = default;
  template <class U> constexpr TestAlloc(const TestAlloc<U>&) noexcept {}

  T* allocate(std::size_t n)
  {
    if(auto p = static_cast<T*>(std::malloc(n*sizeof(T)))) return p;
    throw std::bad_alloc();
  }
  void deallocate(T* p, std::size_t) noexcept { std::free(p); }
};

template <class T, class U> bool operator==(const TestAlloc<T>&, const
TestAlloc<U>&)
{ return true; }
template <class T, class U> bool operator!=(const TestAlloc<T>&, const
TestAlloc<U>&)
{ return false; }
```

We see there is still some amount of plumbing needed, but not too much. If you'd like to
learn more about implementing allocators, please refer to the C++ books in the *Further
reading* section.

Template trickery

Template wizardry was a landmark of C++ for a long time. After it was accidentally discovered that templates constitute a Turing complete language of their own, their usage exploded. Unfortunately, it was a very verbose and ugly language that was close to being incomprehensible. Today, the tricks of olden days have been largely replaced by more sane constructs from the newer C++ standards, but the templates still have their place in C++.

We will look now at some classic template techniques which were used to improve performance. As this book is neither an introductory C++ text nor a template metaprogramming primer, we assume that the reader can read basic template syntax.

Template computations

As templates are instantiated at compile times, they were used to optimize code by removing the computational burden from runtime and transferring it to the compile time. It is hence a classic example of the precomputation optimization technique. As templates are allowed to take an integer argument and may contain static class members, the following recursive technique can be applied:

```
// recursion step
template <unsigned int Base, unsigned int Exp>
struct Power
{
  static const
    unsigned long long result = Base * Power<Base, Exp - 1>::result;
};

// base case
template <unsigned int Base>
struct Power<Base, 0>
{
  static const unsigned long long result = 1;
};

std::cout << " --> 2**5 = " << Power<2, 5>::result << std::endl;
```

Today, we wouldn't use recursion anymore, but that's how it was done. The preceding example is a simple exponentiation, but we could do more complicated stuff using that technique. For example, using our `Power` template, we could compute the *N* first digits of PI using the Bailey-Borwein-Plouffe formula (see `https://en.wikipedia.org/wiki/Bailey-Borwein-Plouffe_formula`). Try to do it, if you feel like it!

Expression templates

Expression templates were an optimization technique introduced by Ted Veldhuisen in his implementation of the Blitz++ numerics library. It may be too complicated to explain them in an intermediate-level book, but the general idea is to build up a nested type definition containing all of the information about an expression, and then, after all of the information has been gathered, to create the final code.

One example could be concatenating strings: instead of naively creating temporary strings after each concatenation (as shown in the previous section on temporaries), we could first collect all of the string information, then allocate a buffer big enough to store all of the strings to be concatenated and fill it in the last phase.

It sounds like magic—can we do that all at compile time? Yes, with enough ugly template code we can. The idea is to use operator overloading and somehow *poison* the expression so that the expression template overload will be chosen. Look at the following code to get the general idea:

```cpp
template <typename L, typename R>
StrgSumExpr { ... };

template <typename L, typename R>
StrgSumExpr<L, R> operator+(const L& lhs, const R& rhs)
{
  return StrgSumExpr<L, R>(lhs, rhs);
}

class String
{
  ...
  template <typename L, typename R>
  String& operator=(const StrgSumExpr<L, R>& expression)
  {
    reserve(expr.size());
    auto count = expression.count();
    // concatenate in reverse order
    for(size_t i = 0; i < count; ++i)
    {
      append(expression[count - 1 - i]);
    }
    return *this;
  }
};
```

Does it help? Well, it is a technique that avoids the creation of temporary objects while still supporting clear code, hence it is a workaround for a C++ limitation. So, the answer is: yes, it can help in some cases.

CRTP for static polymorphism

But, what if you still don't want to pay the price for polymorphism? One possibility is to switch to static polymorphism. The **curiously recurring template pattern** (**CRTP**) is one of the older template techniques popularized by Jim Coplien in the 90s. CRTP defines a kind of mix-in, which adds some functionality to a given class but doesn't use virtual functions for that, as in the following example:

```
template<class T>
class OracleBase
{
  // within base we can use members of derived class T!
  int whatsTheAnswer() const
  {
    return static_cast<T>(this)->getAnswer() * 2;
  }
};

class Oracle1: public OracleBase<Oracle1>
{
  int getAnswer() const { return 22; }
} o1;
class Oracle2: public OracleBase<Oracle2>
{
  int getAnswer() const { return 21; }
} o2;

// now use the base class
template<typename T>
void answerFrom(const OracleBase<T>& base)
{
  std::cout << "answer: " << base.whatsTheAnswer() << '\n';
}
answerFrom(o1);
answerFrom(o2);
```

We see that, instead of overriding a virtual function, we call the method of a derived class directly by casting to the subclass and using its interface. So, we spared one pointer indirection, but was it worth it? Well, on the positive side, it could enable the inlining of that function by the compiler, hence enabling further optimizations.

As always, we should use this technique only when calls over the vtable were identified as the bottleneck. And it isn't a real replacement of dynamic polymorphism as we cannot store such objects in a single container!

Allow me to make a digression here that is not performance-related: a really cool use case for CRTP is the grafting of new functionality onto existing classes, as is illustrated in the following example, which adds an equality operator to `struct X`, assuming the less-than operator is defined:

```cpp
template <class Derived>
class Eq {};

template <class Derived>
bool operator == (const Eq<Derived>& lhs, const Eq<Derived>& rhs)
{
  Derived const& d1 = static_cast<Derived const&>(lhs);
  Derived const& d2 = static_cast<Derived const&>(rhs);
  return !(d1 < d2) && !(d2 < d1);
}

struct X: public Eq<X> { int size; };
bool operator < (const X& lhs, const X& rhs)
{
 return lhs.size < rhs.size;
}
```

A concrete example of CRTP used in that way in C++11 standard is the `std::enable_shared_form_this<T>` class—look it up!

Removing branches

With this technique, we can avoid branches by generating a matching template specialization instead of executing a runtime test, as in the following example taken from the financial industry:

```cpp
float calculatePrice(Party party, float value, float credit)
{
  return party == Party::Buying ? value - credit : value + credit;
}

// replacement:
template<>
float Pricing<Party::Buying>::calculatePrice(float value, float credit)
{
  return value - credit;
```

```
}
// the same for Party::Selling ...
```

We can use this technique every time when we can resolve the context (in our case, the involved party) already at compile time. So, akin to the *static polymorphism* technique we discussed before, this one could be called **static branching**.

C++11/14/17 and performance

After a long standstill of nearly 10 years and after the bug-fixing C++ standard of 2003, the new C++11 brought so many innovations that we might sometimes think it were a completely new language. There are many features which dramatically improve its usability, the definition of the memory model for modern processors, support for multithreading, and much more, but we will only provide a short overview of features that are directly connected to performance. The first and foremost of these was the introduction of move semantics.

Move semantics

As we've already discussed in this chapter, the creation of temporary objects was a real performance problem in classic (or should I say old?) C++, so one of the first innovations that was introduced in "modern" C++ was the possibility to mark some objects as throwaway objects. For example, the temporary objects created in the earlier example of operator chaining are only throwaway objects which just pass their data to the next operation.

This is suggestive of the notion of a *movable* object, that is an object that can give away (that is, move) its congaing data when it finds itself in a specific context. Such an object will define a move constructor and a move assignment operator and will bind to a new type of reference in function calls—a movable reference (called *rvalue* reference) denoted with &&:

```
struct X
{
  std::string s;
  // move constructor, it eats away the contents of x argument!
  X(X &&x) : s(std::move(x.s)) {}
};

// function using move semantics
void func(X &&x);
```

In that manner, the problem with temporaries, which get created only to copy out their contents and then perish, was solved, or at least amended, by replacing it with movable objects that just pass their data further on. This alone can provide substantial performance gains.

There are much more technical details concerning move semantics, so if you want to learn more, please consult one of the books from the *Further reading* section.

Passing by value fashionable again

The introduction of move semantics slightly changed the long-standing advice about passing function arguments by reference. Namely, if we are using a const reference only to copy the object for local usage, as discussed previously in this chapter, then we create a temporary and then copy out its contents. If we have a movable object, this is a waste of time, and we might want to define an overload taking a movable reference. A small optimization in code size is to pass the object by value, hence sparing one of the overloads:

```
// two overloads
func(const T& t);
func(T&& t);

// replaced with one:
func(T t);
```

The replacement function will, in the case of a const reference, perform one copy and one move and, in the case of an rvalue reference, it performs two moves, hence only paying the price of one extra move compared to the case of two separate overloads (check it!). So, it is OK if the moves are cheap, which they are supposed to be.

Compile time computations

We have seen how compile time computations were conducted using templates before C++11. One disadvantage of all template techniques is the bloated syntax. Another is the impossibly long and unhelpful error messages typically produced by compilers. This made templates somehow inaccessible for non-expert C++ programmers. In C++11, an entirely new concept was introduced to make compile time computation accessible for everyone—the constexpr functions, as shown in the following example:

```
constexpr long long factorial(int n)
{
  // C++11 constexpr funct use recursion instead of iteration
  // return n <= 1 ? 1 : (n * factorial(n - 1));
```

```
// C++14 constexpr funct can use variables and loops
if (n <=1 )
  return 1;

long long result = 1;
for (int i = 1; i <= n; ++i)
{
  result *= i;
}
return result;
}
```

As may be seen, we can achieve the same effect as with template metaprogramming, but don't have to agonize about convoluted, unreadable, and verbose syntax. In the C++11 standard, there were quite a few restrictions to constexpr functions, but they were lifted by and by in the later editions of the standard.

Additionally, we can use constexpr functions in conjunction with another new C++11 feature, namely user-defined literals, and let the compiler parse them in compile time, as shown in this example:

```
constexpr std::uint64_t
  constexprHash(char const* str, std::uint64_t lastValue = hashBasis)
{
  return *str
    ? constexprHash(str + 1, (*str ^ lastValue) * hashPrime)
    : lastValue;
}

constexpr unsigned long long operator "" _hash(char const* p, size_t)
{
  return constexprHash(p);
}

// test:
auto hash = "fiuma di fiumi"_hash;
```

This example defines a user literal operator _hash() computing a simple hash for a given string. Check out in Compiler Explorer (which will be introduced in the next section) whether the computations for both the previous examples are really performed in compile time!

Other improvements

We will mention some more new features of *modern* C++, which can be used to improve performance, but for a detailed discussion, please refer to your favorite C++11/17 book:

- **Guaranteed copy elision**: As we said, RVO/NRVO was only an optional compiler optimization in C++89. C++11 renamed it to copy elision and extended its function to catching exceptions. C++17 introduced guaranteed copy elision for the case of unnamed RVO as a mandatory optimization technique.
- **Better allocators**: We already highlighted the fact that, in *old* C++, the STL allocator classes were little loved and little used. C++11 simplified the creation of custom allocators, with the intention that they should be more widely used to customize the memory management of STL container classes. Additionally, a new type of allocators was introduced, namely polymorphic allocators, which are non-templated and can be used to change allocators for collections without changing collections' effective types, hence plugging in an allocator that's better suitable in a specific context. Admittedly, it is an advanced and relatively new technique.
- **In-place construction**: The STL containers got new method overloads using move semantics, but in order to spare the move, a kind of new type of reference passing was introduced—that is, passing only the object's constructor parameters and creating the object in-place inside of the SLT container. This was made possible using new language features such as perfect forwarding and variadic templates. An example of such a method is `std::vector<T>::emplace_back()`.
- `noexcept` **modifier**: This is also an optimization that's performed for STL containers. When you define the constructors of your data type as `noexcept`, STL can optimize certain operations, that is, use move semantics for the copying of data.
- `std::string_view`: This class was introduced in C++17 and it allows you to pass "slices" of a string, hence alleviating the need to construct substring objects in some contexts.

What your compiler can do for you

C++ is a high-level programming language and offers many abstract programming constructs that make programmers amazingly productive. But, the higher the abstraction level is, the greater is the threat of obscuring the low-level performance details. Optimally, we want to write clear, understandable and maintainable code but without compromising performance in the process. For this reason, compilers will try to optimize the code automatically and improve the performance so that we can have the better of two worlds—readable code and good machine-level performance.

One must say that compilers have become quite sophisticated in doing so over the years. They have many amazing tricks up their sleeves as we will see, so we should be better focusing on clear, understandable code rather than trying to optimize code manually that then ends up being cryptic, fragile, and hard to maintain. This is a classic case of premature optimization—doing something we don't need to do as the compiler will do that anyway. It can even have a detrimental influence on performance, as our attempts to micro-optimize may prevent the compiler from applying its standard tricks.

We will now have a look at what exactly compilers are trying to do. And don't worry, there's enough work left for us! Compilers cannot replace a bad algorithm with a more efficient one or change the layout of a data structure to improve its locality—we have to do this.

Examples of compiler tricks

Let's start with something fun, to show you that compilers are really clever. Unfortunately, you can often hear that compilers are dumb, but you shouldn't believe that. In ancient times, compilers were dumb and there was a difference in writing ++x instead of x = x +1 as they resulted in different PDP-11 instructions. But not anymore. Let me convince you with some examples of compiler cleverness.

We will start with simple summation. But, in order to check what the compiler really makes out of our code, we need yet another performance tool which we didn't mention in Chapter 2, *Profiling to Find Bottlenecks*— the **Compiler Explorer** by Matt Godbold. In order to use it, you just go to https://godbolt.org and paste your code in the left pane as seen in the following screenshot.

The assembler output for a selected compiler will then immediately appear in the right pane:

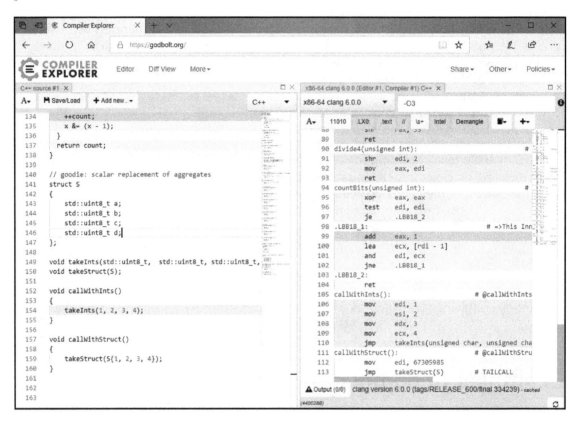

In the following examples, I used *clang 6.0.0* and *gcc 8.2* 64-bit compilers with **-O3** optimization level. In this book's resources (https://github.com/PacktPublishing/Hands-On-High-performance-with-QT/tree/master/Chapter%203), there's a file with all of the examples. Take it to *Compiler Explorer* and play with it!

Let's go back to our summation. We can write a simple function adding elements of an array like this:

```cpp
int sum()
{
   int a[] = { 1, 2, 3, 4, 5, 6 };
   int sum = 0;
   for(auto x : a)
   {
      sum += x;
```

```
    }
    return sum;
}
```

Then, both compilers are able to replace the whole grand logic with a simple code:

```
mov   eax, 21    # set return register to 21
ret
```

Isn't that amazing? The compiler just provided compile time computation on its own, because it understood what is going on in the code. Clever! Now, we try something more difficult—we will sum up an unknown number series as in the next example:

```
unsigned int sumSeriesTo(unsigned int x)
{
  unsigned int sum = 0;
  for(size_t i = 0; i < x; ++i)
  {
    sum += i;
  }
  return sum;
}
```

Now, when we call this function with a constant value, `return sumSeriesTo(20)`, the compiler is again able to look through it and replace it with the result straight away: `mov eax, 190`! If we then use a variable function parameter, `return sumSeriesTo(arg)`, it simply inlines the whole `sumSeriesTo()` function on the spot. And now it gets interesting—GCC automatically vectorizes the summation in the inlined function using SSE2 instructions, but *clang* pulls off an even better trick; it replaces the whole code by a closed summation formula, that is, `sum = x*(x+1)/2`. Clever!

The usual optimizations of replacing multiplication and division by shifts are automatically applied too, but with a little twist. For smaller arguments, the shift is replaced by an even more efficient `lea` (that is, calculate address) instruction as shown here:

```
lea   eax, [0 + rdi*8]   # multiply arg 1 by 8, save in return register
ret
```

You see, you don't have to sweat over small optimizations! The very costly modulo division should equally be replaced by a bitwise and operation for operands that are powers of two, such as the following:

```
x % y  =>  x & (y - 1)  // if y is a power of 2
```

And indeed, both compilers spotted the opportunity:

```
mov    eax, edi    # copy param into return register
and    eax, 31     # x & (32 - 1)
ret
```

Another simple optimization we already mentioned in Chapter 1, *Understanding Performant Programs,* namely the replacement of ternary expressions with bit manipulations for integer values, got applied for a simpler expression such as int x=a<0?1111:2222;, but in case of other common transformations removing the need for branching, that is, a+=(b?0:c)=>a+=(b-1)&c, this possibility couldn't be detected by any of the compilers. We can see that compilers cannot do everything they theoretically should. If your code is *really* performance-critical, you can do such optimizations yourself. Here, the usual caveats apply:

- Measure for bottleneck and measure after the change was made. Reverse the change if the trick didn't help.

But let's look at another quite marvelous trick that compilers are proficient in—the heap elision. Let's say I write a very dumb code like this:

```
int dumb()
{
  auto val = new int(44);
  return *val;
}
```

Then, both compilers are able to reduce it to a simple mov eax, 44! No dumb allocation, no memory leak! Here is a more complicated code using smart pointers:

```
int smartDumb()
{
  auto val1 = std::make_unique<int>(22);
  auto val2 = std::make_unique<int>(22);
  return *val1 + *val2;
}
```

It can be simplified as before and it results in the same mov eax, 44! If we return to our first summation example and replace the a[] array with std::vector<int>, *clang* is still able just to return the value without calculations. The vector will however still be allocated, probably because of its internal dynamic memory, but it won't be used. With the last experimental version of *clang* (as of the time of this writing) even that allocation is gone. Doubly clever! Good boy!

The last example is the classic popcount, that is, count of bits set in an integer value. We are using the classic C implementation shown as follows:

```
unsigned int countBits(unsigned int x)
{
  unsigned int count = 0;
  while (x)
  {
    ++count;
    x &= (x - 1);
  }
  return count;
}
```

The x &= (x - 1) line resets the last nonzero bit. Here, both compilers were first unable to optimize the code, but after adding the option, `march=haswell`, to hint at the additional instruction sets, interesting things should be seen. The GCC compiler used the special `blsr` (that is, **reset lowest set bit**) instruction for the x &= (x - 1) line, which is admittedly clever. But *clang* was able to up the ante: it replaced the whole mess by one single `popcnt` instruction! Nice one! We should probably do the same, using a compiler intrinsics, but more on that later.

You have seen that compilers can be pretty smart—and they are improving every day! This should teach you something, namely, that you shouldn't try to optimize small stuff. Of course, compilers aren't perfect; they can get confused and omit some optimizations, but we should optimize by hand only after we already identified the bottleneck. Chances are that we end up with convoluted and unreadable code that, in turn, will inhibit other compiler optimizations. I know, I said it before, but this one is really important!

More on compiler optimizations

After having had a look at some show-off examples of compilers replacing the whole logic of a function by a single instruction and substituting costly instructions with cheaper alternatives, let's have a look at the unspectacular work compilers do that's nonetheless very important.

Inlining of functions

The first of the unspectacular optimizations is function inlining, which amounts to the copying of the function code into the call site instead of calling it. We basically save the function invocation overhead, increasing the code size as a price. So, how big can the performance gain be, really? You might think that calling a function surely cannot be the big showstopper! With respect, you would be wrong. Inlining a function not only shaves off the function call overhead, it also enables many other optimizations as a result. The gains achieved by inlining can lie in the double-digit percentage range and it has also been reported to be as high as 150%.

However, inlining is a double-edged sword—make too much of it and you can actually slow down your program due to the code bloat! For that reason, compilers provide a fine-grained control for it, with annotations to disable it, such as GCC's `__attribute__((noinline))` and Microsoft's `__declspec(noinline)` , and to force it, that is, `__attribute__((always_inline))` for GCC and `__forceinline` for Microsoft. We also have the `inline` hint directly in C++, but it's only that—a hint.

These annotations allow us to correct a compiler's work in both directions—both when it gets overzealous and when it gets too parsimonious.

Loop unrolling and vectorization

Loop unrolling is a technique for replacing loop control code with a repetition of the loop body, as shown in the following example:

```
// not unrolled
for (i = 0 ; i < 100 ; ++i)
    dest[i] = src[i];

// unrolled
for (i = 0 ; i < 100 ; i += 4)
{
    dest[i] = src[i];
    dest[i + 1] = src[i + 1];
    dest[i + 1] = src[i + 1];
    dest[i + 1] = src[i + 1];
}
```

As with inlining, the gains achieved by loop unrolling can lie in the double-digit percentage range and be much higher for a well-placed, very hot, unrolled loop. And as with inlining, overdoing it results in code bloat, hurting performance instead of improving it.

For loop unrolling, we do not have as much control as for inlining. You can enable or disable it at compiler level using compiler options, but you cannot control single loops. So, we either trust the compiler and enable loop unrolling (-funroll-loops for GCC) or disable it and unroll the loops manually. One technique that you might want to look up in that context is Duff's device.

One could argue that vectorization too is a form of loop unrolling—the compiler replaces several calculations with one vector (that is, SIMD) instruction. A SIMD instruction can address several elements of an array and use them as input for a vector operation. Assuming that v1 and v2 are floating point arrays, the following SSE assembler code will take the first four elements of v1 and add to them the first four elements of v2:

```
movaps   xmm0, [v1]    # load v1[0 .. 3] to xmm0 register
addps    xmm0, [v2]    # add v4[0 .. 3] to xmm0 register
movaps   [v1], xmm0    # copy results back to v1
```

Admittedly, a compiler may sometimes miss an opportunity for vectorization and we could speed up the program by including it manually (do not write assembler code though, use compiler instrinsics instead!). But, as this is an intermediate-level book, we won't discuss that further. However, looking up your compiler's documentation for hints about writing code that will get vectorized easily is always worthwhile.

What compilers do not like

As we've seen in the subsection about compiler tricks, compilers are at their best when they know exactly what data is being used in their computations. We've seen that, in such a case, they can even optimize entire algorithms away, replacing them with a simple mov   eax, NNN. However, when a compiler isn't sure about the data, it has to generate extra-defensive code! There are two such sources of uncertainty, as is discussed next.

Aliasing

Let's assume we wrote the following simple function:

```
void addThroughPointers(int* ptr1, int* ptr2, int* ptrValue)
{
  *ptr1 += *ptrValue;
  *ptr2 += *ptrValue;
}
```

What could be difficult here? Well, in C and C++ there is no guarantee that all three pointers do not point to the same place in memory and hence that changing one pointer won't affect the other pointers. So, the compiler cannot use cached values but it has to reread the pointed-to values every time.

The C99 standard introduced the `restrict` modifier for the pointers exactly for this reason and it hints to the compiler that the pointers do not alias each other, allowing it to skip the rereading of values to assure consistency. Unfortunately, C++ still doesn't support it, and the best that we can do is to use compiler-specific extensions, that is, `__restrict` in GCC and `__restrict__` in Microsoft compiler. In the case of the MinGW compiler, we are using the following:

```
void addThroughPointers2(int* __restrict ptr1, int* __restrict ptr2,
                         int* __restrict ptrValue)
```

An interesting fact is that the `memcpy` function is defined in the C99 standard with restricted source and destination pointers, hence making its behavior in cases of overlapping pointers undefined. C++ doesn't have the restrict qualifier, but it defines the same undefined behavior, hence implicitly treating those pointers as restricted!

External functions

A similar problem poses itself to the compiler when we are calling a function that isn't in the current compilation unit and is hence somewhere the compiler cannot peep into. In such a case, a compiler has to assume the worst. Let's discuss it using another summation example:

```
int mutatingFunc(int value);
int sum(const vector<int>& v)
{
  int sum = 0;
  for(std::size_t i = 0; i < v.size(); ++i)
  {
    sum += mutatingFunc(v[i]);
  }
  return sum;
}
```

So, where's the problem? The compiler cannot assume that the `mutatingFunc()` didn't change the input vector. How come? Well, if the vector is somehow globally visible to the function, it can be theoretically mutated as well! Maybe you have heard about the concept of the pure functions used in functional languages such as Haskell. These are functions that only use their input parameter to calculate the result and don't touch anything else. C++ doesn't have a pure keyword for now, so we have to fall back on compiler extensions, such as GCC attributes, to denote a function's purity:

```
int mutatingFunc2(int value) __attribute__((pure));
```

So, as I think that we have gained enough knowledge on compilers' inner workings by now, we are in a position to answer the following question: since the compiler helps us so much, what can we do, in turn, to help the compiler?

How can you help the compiler?

How can we help the compiler, after it has done so much for us? We already mentioned the first and perhaps most important thing to do—write understandable, maintainable code.

We have seen in the examples in this chapter that we can trust the compiler to transform a readable but suboptimal code into a more performant one. So *primum non nocere* (first don't harm), so to speak.

But there are more specific measures we can take, like the following:

- **Use compiler options**: First, we will want to use the -O option to set the optimization level (typically 2 or 3, note that 3 can sometimes perform worse than 2!). Giving a compiler more context by specifying the target architecture may also help. We might also try to enable loop unrolling, speeding function calls by omitting frame pointers, enabling noncompliant but fast floating-point mathematics and more. Get to know your (compiler's) options!
- **Use compiler directives**: You might want to use compiler-specific function attributes, examples of which we have already seen in the section on inlining. We could also, for example, change the default call convention to the faster *fastcall* in that way.
- **Use intrinsic functions**: Intrinsics are functions for which implementations are provided directly by the compiler. On the one hand, they allow us to use some low-level functionality (for example, _mm_prefetch() for doing manual memory prefetching); on the other hand, the compiler knows everything about their implementation which facilitates many optimizations!

The two last techniques are not very portable and not very pretty, so pay the price only if you desperately need to optimize that single spot! However, there is another, less intrusive technique which will give a compiler more knowledge about the code, as discussed in the next section.

Profile Guided Optimization

Profile-guided optimization (**PGO**), sometimes also called **feedback-driven optimization** (**FDO**), uses additional knowledge about the real-world behavior of the program to help compilers to optimize code for the most common use cases.

This is done by providing execution profile information to the compiler. For this purpose, the program will be complied and linked using special compiler options, which will enable instrumenting the resulting binary with code, which will measure and store the profile data in a format which the compiler can understand. After the application has been run under typical load, we will gather the generated execution profile and then feed that profile back into the compiler, which recompiles the application. In that manner the application will be optimally adapted for the typical environment.

In the course of PGO recompilation, a compiler can change inlining, replace calls to a frequently called virtual function with direct calls, optimize register allocations and the location of functions in sections, and reorder code blocks to optimize branch performance. The two last optimizations are aiming at improving code locality or, in other words, at keeping the instruction cache warm.

This method has its downsides too, namely, the high run-time overhead of profile collection (due to instrumentation) and an awkward two-stage compile model (again due to instrumentation). Besides that, it can be difficult to decide what the previously mentioned *typical load* is under real conditions.

When compilers get overzealous

We have seen the compilers are crazy smart. But smart is a neighbor of too smart and that is a neighbor of dangerous! So, with the crazy improvements in compiler optimizations some dangerous edge cases have found their way in, which can show us the dark side of compilers.

The first (and maybe biggest) of these problems is the treatment of C++'s **undefined behavior (UB)** by compilers. The C and C++ standards define some program errors as UB and do not require compilers to diagnose or report it. The behavior stays *undefined*, which means it can be anything whatsoever. Hence, the old joke that on UB your program might format your hard drive and send you an email. Examples of some common undefined behaviors are as follows:

- Null pointer dereference
- Out of bound read
- Signed integer overflow
- Modification of a scalar more than once in a single exception

Now, what has that to do with dangerous optimizations? These are simple runtime errors, aren't they? Yes, in the old days UB amounted to HW-specific behavior, that is, normally to a crash during runtime. But recently, compilers started to exploit their *license to optimize* to the fullest and to treat malformed programs as impossible programs, thus assuming that programs cannot ever display UB. So, consequently, compilers started silently to remove the offending code.

Now, think about irony of that—a compiler doesn't have to diagnose UB, which was intended to simplify the compilers' jobs, but they do that anyway, but keep the knowledge to themselves. But compilers don't do that because they are mischievous; the impossibility assumption is used to simplify the optimization logic.

One well-known example of UB in action, recently seen on the Stack Overflow website, is this loop:

```
std::complex<int> delta;
std::complex<int> mc[4]= {0};
for (int di=0; di < 4; di++, delta = mc[di])
{
   printf("%i\n", di);
}
```

This loop should run four times, but runs endlessly instead. Here, the `mc[i]` access after `i` was incremented is UB, so the whole loop test was removed by the GCC 8.2 compiler! However, other compilers didn't spot it and compiled the loop normally. Another well-known story is GCC removing a check for a null pointer in Linux kernel code (check it out!).

But, UB isn't the only surprise optimizers have got up their sleeves. A second problem is that a compiler is entitled to remove all code which doesn't have any visible effect. A very famous example of that is the case of the disappearing `memset()` function, as shown in the following code:

```
void GetData(const char* RemoteAddr)
{
  char passwd[64];
  if(AskForUserPassd(passwd, sizeof(passwd)))
  {
     // get data from remote ..
  }
  // erase the passwd form cache!
  memset(passwd, 0, sizeof(passwd));
}
```

Here, we were trying to zero out the password buffer to remove it from memory to guard off against side-attacks and the reading of memory crash dumps. Unfortunately, for the optimizer, this is nothing but a *dead store write*, that is, writing to a memory location that won't be read by anyone, and it can be optimized away! This is an open problem and there are even special functions such as `SecureZeroMemory()` on Windows, `explicit_bzero()` in FreeBSD, and `memset_s` in the C11 standard library to be used in such cases. Their specifications directly disallow dead store optimization for those functions.

Optimization tools beyond compiler

Now, we have learned about various compiler optimization techniques, and they are really great, so we don't need anything else, do we? Unfortunately, there are limits to the optimization the compilers can do, and these limits stem from the fundamental compiler limitation, which is that the compiler can see only one file at a time! This restricts all of the optimizations to the contents of that file only, and everything that happens in other parts of the program is like black magic to the compiler. We have already seen the pessimizations the compiler is forced to do when it sees an external function, haven't we? So, there are many optimization opportunities which have to be omitted because of the narrowed view the compilers are forced to take. What we need is **whole program optimization** (WPO), but how can we achieve that? One possibility is to use linkers to take over that job.

Link time optimization and link time code generation

This technique is unsurprisingly called **link-time optimization** (**LTO**) and exploits the fact that the linker will see the whole of the program when it's finished linking. But linkers are not optimizers, so what could be done here? The trick is to call back the compiler to do the optimizations! For that, the object files emitted by the compiler do not contain machine code, but the **intermediate representation** (**IR**) of the code. The linker puts all of the parts of the program together and then calls back the compiler to optimize the whole program. For that reason, this technique is also called **link-time code generation** (**LTCG**), as the compiler will generate the final machine code only in the link phase.

Sounds complicated? Yes, and it has a couple of problems too: it is very slow, and it requires large amounts of memory, which can be prohibitive for large programs and smaller machines. Additionally, it kills incremental linking. There are attempts to fight these problems. For example, ThinLTO keeps all of the compilation units separate, but imports information about external functions in each unit, this is able to parallelize the optimizations. The GCC compiler contained in MinGW supports base LTO.

Another optimization linkers can do is removing duplicate function definitions, which decreases the size of the executable and improves the code locality. This is known in the Windows world as **identical COMDAT folding** (**ICF**) and is supported by GCC linker.

Workaround – unity builds

A unity build (also known as a **Single Compilation Unit** or **jumbo**) is actually a means to speed up the compilation of C++ projects, because it cuts down on times needed for the processing of single files. A unity build looks as simple as the following:

```
// UnityBuildFile.cpp
#include "Widgets.cpp"
#include "Gui.cpp"
#include "Main.cpp"
```

As we can see, one has only to include all the implementation files in a single main build file. The time savings, reported to be as high as 90%, come from parsing the common includes only once, less instantiation of templates, less invocations of compiler, and less work for the linker.

But apart from that, we get our WPO free of charge as everything is in one place and totally visible to the compiler!

There are some caveats though, starting with its tremendous memory usage and ending with miscompilations as some overloads can be suddenly better than in a non-unity build or some macros are applied out of their scopes. An incremental build is also out of the question. Despite those problems, this technique is used in the industry, for example, for *WebKit* and the *Unreal* game engine. There are plugins for *CMake* supporting unity builds, and Visual Studio 2017 even contains experimental native support for that.

Beyond linkers

There are optimization tools even beyond linkers, although it might sound incredible. However, they aren't widely used and are rather more at the advanced end of what's available, so read this section only if you are interested in cool technologies.

We already introduced profile-guided optimization as a possibility to guide the compiler in its optimizations by providing a real-world execution profile. This is a great technique; however, it has its limitations. When parts of the code are coming from assembly or third-party libraries, compiler lacks the code and cannot apply the profile accurately. Other limitations are the previously mentioned problems of deciding what the *typical load* is to conduct the measurements and the high cost of obtaining performance data, especially for big applications.

Because of these problems, a different class of optimization tools was tried out, that is, post-link optimizers, which will take an already linked binary and optimize it without knowledge of its source code. One of the recent examples of post-link optimizers is Facebook's BOLT. It turned out that it's possible in this way to achieve improvements even for applications already optimized with PGO and LTO. The idea is simple—instead of obtaining profile data by instrumentation we obtain it by sampling, making the whole process a lot cheaper! The other problem, namely, the lack of source code can be solved by a code decompilation, which can only concentrate on interesting aspects of code, like the control flow. The Facebook tool mentioned uses the reconstructed control flow to reorganize the binary layout of code to improve the cache utilizations and take away pressure from the branch predictor. The reported improvements lay in the range from 2% up to 8%-15% and the tool is able to group the often-used code in a quite compact region of memory.

As we can see, the quest for improving performance goes onward!

Summary

We've seen in this chapter a whole slew of optimization techniques applied either by compilers or left for programmers to use. After such exposure to cool tricks like these, you can forget the big picture, hence it is expedient at this point to restate the basic truths.

Herewith, we (again) state that for performance, only three things really matter: the first is the correct choice of algorithm; the second is correct parallelization and the avoidance of blocking calls; and the third is attention to data locality. The remainder of the tricks, and hence all of the little helpers discussed in this chapter, are potentially useful, but only on a case-by-case basis when a bottleneck has already been identified. Otherwise, we would be sailing in the dangerous waters of premature optimization!

After that periodic reminder, let's recall what we learned in this chapter. We discussed the following topics:

- The zero-overhead principle and its violations
- Temporary objects in C++
- Custom memory managers
- Some template tricks
- C++11 features, such as move semantics and `constexpr` functions
- Compiler tricks and optimizations
- Whole program optimization

The next chapter will cover the greatest cause of poor performance—the choice of correct data structures and algorithms. We will have a look at the data structures that Qt provides, discuss their peculiarities, and provide guidelines for their efficient usage. We will also restate the basic advice for choosing the right algorithm and we will review the use of C++ standard containers from the point of view of performance.

Questions

As in previous chapters, here are some questions so that you can test your understanding of the discussed topics:

1. What did Linus say about C++ performance?
2. What is an arena?
3. What are PGO, FDO, LTO, LTCG, and WPO and what do they have in common?

4. Have you looked into the compiler optimization example code from this book? Do you know what **scalar replacement of aggregates** is now?

5. What do you think? How big is the overhead of a function call?

6. What is **dead stack pinning**? Wasn't it a movie? Or was that dead stack walking?

7. What is RTTI and is it expensive or not?

8. What would change in the `mutatingFunc()` example discussed in the section about compiler optimization tricks, if it were defined in the same compilation unit?

9. What is register pressure? Hint—it has to do with one of a compiler's main tasks, that is, register allocation.

Further reading

There are several books about specific C++ performance techniques. We already mentioned two: the slightly older *Efficient C++ Performance Programming Techniques* by Dov Bulka and David Mayhew (Addison Wesley, 1999) and *Optimized C++* by Kurt Guntheroth (O'Reilly, 2013). Both books discuss basic C++ optimizations in more detail than we are doing here and contain a fair number of general performance techniques. There are also example implementations of custom memory management techniques and, in the second book, there are also STL allocators.

There is also a newer book focused more on the recent C++17 language version: *C++ High Performance* by Viktor Sehr and Björn Andrist (Packt Publishing, 2018). These books focus more on C+ usage in a standard setting, that is, without using Qt.

The two-part article *What Every Programmer Should Know About Compiler Optimizations* (2015) by Hadi Brais, available on `https://msdn.microsoft.com/en-us/magazine/dn904673.aspx` and `https://msdn.microsoft.com/en-us/magazine/dn973015.aspx`, discusses some compiler optimization techniques used by Microsoft C++ compiler in more depth.

"Optimizing software in C++: An optimization guide for Windows, Linux and Mac platforms by Agner Fog (2018), available on `http://www.agner.org/optimize/optimizing_cpp.pdf`, contains an in-depth discussion of general performance, compiler optimizations, and the efficiency of different C++ language constructs.

4
Using Data Structures and Algorithms Efficiently

It has repeatedly been stated that algorithmic choice is the biggest single factor concerning performance, before asynchronous and concurrent programming issues, and memory allocation and memory access overheads.

Bad programmers worry about the code. Good programmers worry about data structures and their relationships.

– Linus Torvalds

As we all want to be good programmers, we have to know about data structures and, consequently, their associated algorithms. In this chapter, we will first have a look at data structures and algorithms in general, then we will discuss the specifics of Qt-provided data structures, and at the end we will deliberate about ways to improve performance using algorithms and data structures.

This chapter will thus cover the following topics:

- **Algorithms, data structures, and performance**: General overview
- **Using Qt containers**: Because there are some peculiarities
- **Qt algorithms, iterators, and gotchas**: Because there will be gotchas
- **Working with strings**: How to optimize it
- **Optimizing with algorithms and data structures**: General algorithmic advice

Algorithms, data structures, and performance

This is an intermediate-level book, so you will probably know a lot about algorithms and data structures already, but we will nonetheless first provide some high-level overview for these topics before we discuss the Qt-specific use cases and gotchas. Let's start with algorithms.

Algorithm classes

Algorithms are recipes for calculating something. As you are an intermediate programmer, you might surely have heard about the $O(n)$ (that is, the big O) notation which ranks the algorithms performance-wise. This notation describes the relative theoretical performance of algorithms by measuring how the runtime of an algorithm increases with increasing input size. The variable n stands for the input size, and for us the big O notation expresses the independence of any constant factors. Its other meaning will be ignored in this explanation.

The algorithm classes you will encounter in real life are $O(n)$, $O(n \log n)$, $O(\log n)$, $O(n^2)$, $O(n^3)$, ..., $O(n^x)$, $O(x^n)$. These are, in order of appearance, logarithmic, linear, linear-logarithmic, quadratic, cubic, polynomial, and exponential.

The speed of logarithmic algorithms decreases slower than the increase of input size, while the speed of linear ones decreases proportionally to that. The speed of linear-logarithmic algorithms decreases a little slower than pure linear ones. These are the good guys we'd like to use all the time. The other ones are bad and dangerous dudes, which you should omit if you can. The most innocent-looking is the quadratic (that is $O(n^2)$) algorithm—it can be written so easily and doesn't look very dangerous:

```
for(int i = 0; i < count1; ++i)
{
  for(j = 0; j < count2; ++j)
  {
    ...
  }
}
```

But then, look at the graphical illustration of their relative running time in the next figure:

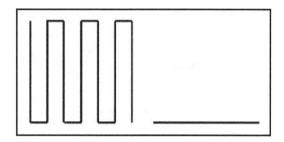

On the left side, we see the amount of work the quadratic algorithm is doing; to the right is the work of a linear one. When it is shown in this way, the difference is quite pronounced! So, stay with the good guys: *O(n)*, *O(n log n)*, and *O(log n)*.

So, what's the difference between a performant algorithm and a bad one?

- A performant algorithm will use additional knowledge of the structure of the data; the simple and inferior algorithm will not.

Using the knowledge about the structure of the data is an example of the basic **don't do unnecessary work** optimization principle. And if we do less work, then we improve the overall performance!

The simplest example is the search for some value in an array of data. The simplest solution would just go over the array and check its elements. The binary search would use the knowledge that the data in the array are sorted and achieve logarithmic performance. For that, the data has to be sorted, but this will only pay out if we are looking at the elements very often. We can discern two things from this: the design of an algorithm is a trade-off and, secondly, it is intimately bound to the data structures we are using.

Now, we see the reasoning behind Linus's warning, so be a good programmer and think about organizing your data structures so that they match the hidden structure of your problem! Then, use the standard algorithms defined for that data structure. Thus, for the next topic, we will take a short look at data structures that we can use in a program, but before that, let me formulate a short warning.

Algorithmic complexity warning

Complexity analysis is a thriving academic discipline, but we have to know that its results are true only at the limits. This means the theoretically faster algorithm could scale better and outperform the slower one only for big enough inputs, as it might have a big constant overhead. So, to restate it more succinctly, we'd like to cite Bob Pike's third rule of programming:

> *Fancy algorithms are slow when n is small, and n is usually small.*

> *-Bob Pike*

As has already been said—measure first, optimize later. Don't use complicated algorithms when there isn't any need for them. Judge wisely about if and when they are really needed.

Types of data structures

There aren't that many types of data structures we use in day-to-day programming. What we said about fancy algorithms before does apply in the same measure to fancy data structures—they will be needed very seldom! We can achieve good performance using some well-known data structures.

Arrays

This is the old, vanilla, simple data structure—just a chunk of memory with consecutive objects stored in it. But this simplicity is also its biggest strength, because it guarantees a superior memory locality. When we iterate over an array, the processor hardware is at its happiest—automatic prefetching works, caches stay hot, and branch predictors are 100% correct.

So, no problems at all? Alas not. Arrays are not very malleable. If they are too small, a bigger chunk of memory has to be allocated (first performance sin) and the the old data has to be copied over (second performance sin). Even if we have enough space to insert an element, if we have to insert it in the middle of the array, all the consecutive elements have to be moved one position to the right (by copying, a performance sin as we know) to make a place for a new element. So, we'd like a better data structure please!

`std::vector` and `QVector` are examples of containers which use arrays internally and take care of their automatic resizing. `std::array` doesn't do that and is only a thin wrapper over the naked C++ array.

Strings could also be said to be disguised arrays, as internally they just hold an array of characters, as the `std::string` and `QString` classes do. As the strings are oftentimes very heavily used, extra care has to be applied here to avoid unnecessary copying and reallocating of their buffers. One generic technique which can be applied in that context is **small string optimization (SSO)**.

SSO always preallocates some storage to be used directly to accommodate small strings. Only when a string is too big will dynamic memory be allocated. This strategy has proved to provide consistent performance benefits and is now widely supported. The GCC compiler also switched to this implementation and replaced the previously used copy-on-write technique. Unfortunately, in some Linux distributions, the old implementation is still used due to backward compatibility reasons.

The same optimization can be applied to vectors, but GCC doesn't support it yet. However, Facebook's `Folly` library and `Boost` library's `small_vector` implement it already.

We can search for an item in an array in *O(n)* time, but if the array is sorted, we can speed it up with binary search to *O(log n)*. However, sorting an array will take *O(n log n)* time, so we do not want to do it often.

Lists

The favorite from the days of yore: you can insert and remove elements without any copying, and traversing it requires only one pointer dereference. What sounded like a good idea back then is rather unappealing today—inserting new elements requires dynamic memory allocations each time and traversing the list amounts to a classic pointer chase. That's why lists have fallen quite out of favor with the performance folks of today.

We can search for an item in a list in *O(n)* time, so there's no improvement over arrays. However, inserting elements in the middle doesn't have to pay the price of moving the elements as the array does.

Trees

Trees organize their elements in a hierarchical branched structure (hence the name) and are very good when we are searching for items. Due to their hierarchical organization, the search has the *O(log n)* complexity (assuming a well-balanced, nondegenerate tree). However, the same caveats as with lists apply—there are bad memory locality and dynamic allocations.

But the search times are very nice indeed. Could we keep them, somehow? Well, if we wanted to maintain this search speed, we could replace a tree structure with a sorted array, assuming we won't be changing it often. For a more general case, there is a `Boost` implementation of `flat_map` which projects the tree structure onto an array, preserving the hierarchies but improving the data locality of the container.

Hash tables

When looking up elements, this data structure gives us an unparalleled *O(1)* performance! It uses a key, which is then encoded by a hashing function into an integer, which is in turn used to access a position in an array. It's instant access. We have only to translate our key into an index and remember which key denotes which data.

But, as always, there are also problems. The hashing function can from time to time produce the same index for different keys (this is called a collision). We can resolve that problem in two ways - either we form a list of elements for a given index (chaining), or we just look for another free place in the array, in the simplest case for the next one (open addressing). The first method results in bad data locality; the second is more complicated to implement and requires users to define a special value denoting a deleted element. However, because of such a good lookup performance, there is much research ongoing to optimize both those strategies, with open addressing generally held to be more performant.

The **Standard Template Library** (STL) uses the chaining implementation because the C++ standard requires pointer stability for an `unordered_map`. If you want to use the open addressing scheme Google's `dense_hash_map` is a well-known implementation and there is a recent `F14` hash table from Facebook's `Folly` library.

The second problem with hash tables is the handling of the internal array growth - when the hash table is automatically resized, all its elements have to be rehashed! Thus, we say that the *O(1)* search complexity is only an amortized complexity—with a choice of the right growth strategy, the reallocation costs counted together with the regular access times still give us the asymptotic *O(1)* complexity.

Another problem with hash tables is that for bad hashing functions the hash table will have too many collisions and will degenerate! For example, a chaining implementation could degenerate into a single list with search times back to the array's *O(n)*!

Using Qt containers

Let's start with the statement that there's a raging debate when it comes to Qt data structures. There are proponents of Qt data structures and in the opposite camp the champions of standard STL algorithms and data structures.

What can we say about that? Qt containers were designed long ago when some platforms didn't support STL. The design objectives were for them to be good enough for GUI programming, easy to use, and discoverable, whereas STL containers were designed to be general-purpose, efficient, and correct. Thus, Qt containers lack many features of their STL counterparts and they also were neither modernized nor have they acquired many new features since the times of Qt 4. They are just good enough to build GUIs. As they are used pervasively in all Qt APIs, it would be a performance sin to copy their data to STL containers only to be able to use a better implementation.

So, we have to cope with them and be wary of their limitations and performance profiles. For that reason, we will discuss the things to watch out for when using Qt data structures.

General design

The first step on the road to understanding a data structure's performance is to acquire knowledge about its internal workings. So, let's have a look at how Qt containers are implemented, because it may come as a surprise to some programmers.

Implicit sharing

The first thing that catches the eye is that Qt containers support implicit sharing, which is a fancy name for a combination of reference counting and **copy-on-write** (COW). Let's have a look at the inner structure of a typical Qt container, as depicted in the next figure:

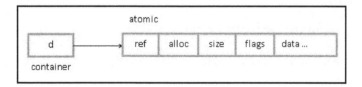

The container itself is a thin wrapper around the pointer d, which points to its real data. The payload data is preceded by a header containing a reference count, the allocated size, and sometimes further optional data, such as the used size and flags. Now, when a container gets copied only a shallow copy will take place, so that the two containers will share the data, as shown in the next figure:

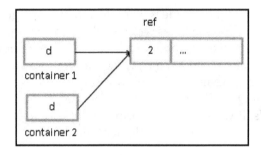

When **Container 2** will try to change some of its data now, the detach() operation will be executed, performing a deep copy of the container's data, before changing the value in the copied data buffer, as demonstrated in the following diagram:

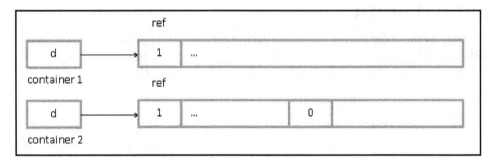

In cases when the data is not changed after copying, it will be freed when the reference count falls back to zero. To be frank, the deep copy will be done not just if the container's data has actually been changed, but also on every invocation of a non-const member function. So, watch out for those accidental copies! We will discuss that in more detail in the forthcoming *Iterators and iterations* section, which discusses iterating over containers.

This implementation technique was used when there wasn't yet the support for move semantics in the language, to optimize out the creation of temporaries, which we discussed in Chapter 3, *Deep Dive into C++ and Performance*. For example, the GCC implementation of std::string used it before C++11.

By the way, if you'd like to implement your custom implicit-sharing data structures, you can use the two Qt helper classes QSharedData and QSharedDataPointer<T>.

Relocatability

The second optimization used in Qt containers is the tagging of data types with type info to perform some optimizations, just as STL would use memcpy for data structures which are trivially copyable (see the std::is_trivially_copyable<> trait).

Qt has three type traits that can be used: Q_PRIMITIVE_TYPE for types without a constructor and destructor, Q_MOVABLE_TYPE for types which need constructors but can be relocated by bitwise copy, and Q_COMPLEX_TYPE for all the rest. By default, your custom types are complex and if you want the relocation optimization to be enabled, you have to tag the type using the following macro:

```
Q_DECLARE_TYPEINFO(MyType, Q_MOVABLE_TYPE);
```

What is the benefit of a relocatable type? For example, if we had an array of relocatable objects we would need to call copy constructors for each of them in case of array resizing, but we would just call memmove a single time. In standard C++, there is a similar trait proposed for C++20, namely, is_trivially_relocatable_v<T> and a corresponding [[trivially_relocatable]] attribute.

Now, having learned the most important things about the general design of Qt containers, let's have a look at the most used ones.

Container classes overview

The Qt containers can be divided into two sets. The first is made up of the ones following the well-known data structures we discussed at the beginning of this chapter and then there is some other, which can come across as rather unusual. Let's start with the former.

Basic Qt containers

Most of the Qt containers are roughly equivalent to some STL containers, as shown in the next table:

Qt	STL	Qt	STL
QVector	std::vector	QLinkedList	std::list
QMap	std::map	QMultimap	std::multimap
QHash	std::unordered_map	QMultiHash	std::unordered_multimap
QSet	std::unordered_set	QVariant	std::any

The implementation of the basic containers is similar to that of the standard library: QLinkedList is a doubly linked list, QMap is a red-black tree (although in Qt 4 it used a skip-list implementation), QHash uses bucket chaining, and QVector uses a double-the-space reallocation strategy.

The difference is that they are all implicitly shared. Another difference is their comparatively limited functionality, having among other things a lack of exception guarantees and a lack of support for custom allocators. So, you cannot use the stack or pool allocators we discussed previously in Chapter 3, *Deep Dive into C++ and Performance*, with them. Also the new STL APIs from C++11 up to C++17, such as all the emplace() methods, aren't available. Even some C++98 APIs are missing, for example those for range construction and insertion.

The containers shown in the previous table can all be paired with a correspondent STL container. However, there are two containers without direct equivalents in STL and we will discuss them in the following in a little more detail.

QList

This container is used very often in the Qt API and, before the advent of Qt 5, was taught to Qt programmers to be the default Qt container. However, today it has fallen into disrepute and its usage is discouraged because it can be problematic for performance.

First and foremost, QtList isn't anything like std::list. Internally, it holds an array of void* pointers. And now the complications begin. There are two modes for using those pointers—the first one is when they are just pointing to object instances; the second one is when they are reused as direct storage for small objects. The small objects optimization will be triggered when the object size is smaller or equal to the size of void* and if Q_MOVABLE_TYPE was specified for this object's type.

There is a second optimization which somehow warrants usage if **list** is in the class name. QList leaves a free place at the start of its internal data buffer, thus accelerating front insertions and deletions as well as middle-of-the-list insertions.

The third optimization was the attempt to reduce the amount of code generated for templated containers because QList uses common, type-independent code for the management of the void* array. That was indeed important in former days when compilers and linkers still couldn't really cope with the **template bloat** but the issue is not that acute today.

So, what do we think about this class and why is usage of QList discouraged? The problem with it is that the small object optimization doesn't work for all small Qt classes, because not all of them are tagged as relocatable. This was probably an oversight, but because of the **abstract binary interface** (**ABI**) compatibility, it probably won't be fixed. So, if a class isn't suitably tagged, QList will internally use an array of pointers to objects with all the performance penalties of the linked list—allocator calls and pointer chasing. Some often-used Qt classes will trigger small object optimization though, for example QString, QByteArray, QFileInfo, QIcon, QBrush, and QPen among others, but many others do not.

So, what is the conclusion? If you fully understand the performance implications, use it, otherwise the safer alternative is to use QVector or std::vector.

QVarLengthArray

This is another container with attitude—it is not implicitly shared. It preallocates memory for a certain number of elements specified in its template argument, by default 256. If then more space is needed, the container allocates a new buffer dynamically and uses it thereafter.

Keen readers will notice that QVarLengthArray implements the small vector optimization we already discussed. This optimization can be extremely useful when we know in advance that in common cases, the size of a container will not exceed a certain number of objects.

QCache

This lesser known Qt container is implemented as a hash table for quick lookup times, but it additionally implements a **least recently used (LRU)** caching strategy, purging the least used elements automatically to make room for new ones.

When inserting an object into QCache, you can specify the cost parameter which should be some approximate estimation of that object's size. When a sum of all objects' costs exceeds the cache limit (maxCost(), by default 100), the cache starts deleting the less recently accessed objects to make room for new ones.

The second Qt class providing cache implementation is QContiguousCache. It adds a requirement that the elements within the cache are stored in a contiguous manner. It was developed to provide efficient caching of items for display in user interface views. Differently from the general QCache class, it doesn't implement the LRU strategy, but rather purges items from the opposite side of the cache relative to the position where the current item was appended or prepended.

C++11 features

One will often hear that Qt containers haven't changed since the Qt 4 days, but that is not entirely true. Not much work has been done, but there hasn't been a standstill either. First, the move constructors and assignment operators were added in Qt 5.2 for the container classes, as can be seen in the definition of QMap:

```
QMap(QMap<Key, T> &&other)
QMap<Key, T> & operator=(QMap<Key, T> &&other)
```

As the Qt containers all support COW copies, they are cheap but they are not completely free. So, the move semantics were added for additional optimization.

Another change which was done in Qt 5.4 was adding the support for C++11 reference qualifiers, a move-semantics-related feature we haven't yet discussed. The idea for that feature is to optimize away a copy in a situation like the following one:

```
auto lowerCaseStrg = QString::fromUtf8(data).toLower();
```

Here, `fromUtf8()` returns a temporary, which then will be used by `toLower()` only as a throwaway input. It would be nice if `toLower()` could reuse the memory allocated by the string constructor and perform the transformation in place. To be able to detect such situations in your code, C++11 added the **reference qualifier** syntax as shown in the next example:

```
class QString
{
  ...
  QString toLower() const &; // normal, returns a copy
  QString toLower() &&;      // rvalue, can convert in place!
  ...
};
```

The `&` and `&&` at the end of `toLower()` denote the context from which the method is called and define overloads depending on the reference type of the `this` pointer. When a method is called on a temporary (an rvalue reference), the overload with `&&` will be chosen and the in-place optimization will be applied.

In Qt 5.4, many methods of `QString` (for example `toUpper`, `toLower`, `toLatin1`, and so on), `QByteArray` (`toUpper`, `toLower`), `QImage` (for example, `convertToFormat`, `mirrored`, `normalized`, and so on), and `QVersionNumber` had this optimization added.

Memory management

As we already stated, Qt containers lack a feature equivalent to the `std::Allocator`, which can be used to customize memory allocations in containers. Thus, if we'd like to manage memory differently, we have to write custom data structure or just start using STL right away.

However, we have some control over the memory usage of the Qt containers, as many of them implement the `capacity()`, `reserve()`, and `squeeze()` methods, which can be used to query, preallocate, and decrease the memory held by containers.

At this point, this seems to be a good place to look at the growth strategies specific to Qt containers, as they are different from the standard library ones. As the Qt documentation states:

- `QString`: It will increase by four Unicode characters up to the size of 20, then up to 4,084 it will allocate a buffer of double the size, and higher than that, it will always allocate blocks of 2,048 characters (that is, 4,096 bytes).

We didn't discuss the QString class yet, but its allocation strategy is used in other container classes, such as in QByteArray and QList.

- QVector: If its elements are relocatable, that is, they were tagged with Q_MOVABLE_TYPE, then the same growth strategy as with QString will be applied, otherwise the double-space strategy will be chosen.
- QHash: The internal size of the hash table will grow by powers of 2, and the same applies to QSet and QCache.

Should we use Qt containers?

The standard advice you will hear a lot these days is not to use Qt containers, as they are old and ugly. We tend to be told to use STL classes instead.

First, as we already stated, we receive the data from Qt APIs packaged in the Qt containers, so, from a performance point of view, repackaging them into standard containers is seen as wasting resources. Anyway, Qt containers are here to stay, as Qt does not want the standard library in its API, because of backward compatibility concerns and the fear of changed standard container definitions, as in the case of GCC string implementation.

From an alternative viewpoint, standard containers offer better functionality and reportedly even Qt 5 is using them internally. So, there's no single unambiguous guideline, as you have to trade off the ease of use versus the performance losses when copying data to and fro. If your decision is to use the Qt containers, don't forget to apply the Q_DECLARE_TYPEINFO tag for the contained types, and be very suspicious of QList.

But there's another big problem when using Qt containers, which we already hinted at before. It can really come quite unexpectedly and will cost you performance. So, keep reading on to the next section to discover what it is.

Qt algorithms, iterators, and gotchas

There's isn't that much to say about Qt algorithms, as they were deprecated in Qt 5 and it is now recommended to use the algorithms from the STL—also with Qt containers. The Qt algorithms included basic ones like qFind, qCount, qBinaryFind, and so on. However, some of the algorithms are not deprecated, namely the bit algorithms such as qCountLeadingZeroBits, qCountTrailingZeroBits, and qPopulationCount. Additionally, the qDeleteAll algorithm is still supported because there's no direct counterpart for it in the standard library.

Iterators and iterations

The simplest algorithm you can imagine, though, is iterating over a collection. For that purpose, you should use iterators instead of directly accessing the index operator. The Qt containers offer two types of iterators. First, there are the standard STL-type iterators, which point at the elements and which can be used with STL algorithms instead of the deprecated Qt counterparts, and additionally there are the Java-style iterators, which point between elements.

The Java-style iterators can come in handy when we want to delete some elements of a collection. The following example shows the usage of a Java-style iterator when deleting all elements of a collection:

```
while (iter.hasNext())
{
  iter.next();
  if (iter.key() == ...)
  {
    iter.remove();
  }
}
```

In STL, the iterator becomes invalidated after you remove items from its container, so code such as that preceding would not work.

Qt also has `Q_FOREACH()` and `foreach()` macros that were introduced before C++11 added this feature directly to the language. You shouldn't use them anymore, but if you do so, at least take care and don't use them with STL containers, as this will result in a deep copy of the whole container at the beginning of the loop. These macros were designed for usage with Qt containers.

Gotcha - accidental deep copies

We have just noticed that iterating over containers in Qt can become quite dangerous performance-wise. So, what would you say about this innocent-looking code:

```
QVector<int> vector;
for(const auto& v: vector)
{
  if (v == 1)
    std::cout << v;
}
```

Well, the bad news is that there will be a deep copy of the container's data in this loop. We will trigger a dynamic memory allocation and copy only for the time of this loop's duration. A performance nightmare!

Why is that? We aren't doing anything to the container and are accessing it by a constant reference! However, the compiler will generate a code using `QVector::begin()` and `QVector::end()` function members, which are not constant and thus will trigger a detach of the container! The following often-seen code would trigger an unneeded copy of the container as well:

```
for (auto iter = vector.begin(); iter != vector.end(); ++iter)
{ ... }
```

If we aren't mutating the container, the correct code is of course:

```
for (auto const iter = vector.cbegin(); iter != vector.cend(); ++iter)
{ ... }
```

With STL classes, we will get through with it when we use COW containers. To convince the compiler of using the `const` iterators in the `for` loop we have to use one of the following tricks:

```
QVector<int> vector;
// Qt utility:
for(const auto& v: qAsConst(vector)) ...
// C++17 utility
for(const auto& v: std::as_const(vector)) ...
// manually
auto const& cvector = vector;
for(const auto& v: scvector) ...
```

The same applies to direct access to single elements of container-held data:

```
QStringList list = getList();
if (list[0] == "casimir") ... // triggers deep copy!
if (list.at(0) == "svatopluk") ... // no deep copy

const QStringList& clist = getList();
if (clist[0] == "misiko") ... // no deep copy
```

But wait, even such an innocent code, as in the following example, can trigger a deep copy:

```
QMap<int, int> map;
auto iter = map.find(key);
```

Surprisingly, the detach was triggered because the `find()` method is not a `const`. We should have been using the `constFind()` method instead. The `find()` method is not a `const` because it returns a non-`const` iterator ready for working with.

This gets rather complicated and ugly rather quickly. Fortunately, there is an open source tool for diagnosing such problems called **clazy** (`https://github.com/KDE/clazy`). Unfortunately, it is a compiler plugin for **clang**, so not available for other compilers.

Now you've learned all this, maybe you'd like to think twice before iterating over Qt containers. STL alternatives, which do not use implicit sharing, are much safer performance-wise.

Working with strings

Working with strings is a big part of every programmer's job. Qt provides its own string implementation, but in this case the problems we had with Qt containers should not deter you from using `QString`—it is so much better than the `std::string` class. It has built-in support for Unicode and many convenient functions lacking in `std::string`. So, we will first have a look at how `QString` and its supporting classes can be used in an efficient manner.

Qt string classes

The problem with string classes in general is that they will copy the content of the `char*` string literal when they are created. Avoiding this cost, will be one recurring theme in our discussion. Another problem is avoiding the unnecessary creation of temporary strings. Let's see what Qt classes have to offer in this respect.

QByteArray

`QByteArray` represents a sequence of bytes without any encoding, thus it can be seen as an equivalent of `std::string`. Use it to store byte arrays. It is implicitly shared, so the usual COW caveats apply. Its constructors will allocate an internal buffer and copy the string data into it.

If we'd like to avoid that copy, we can use the `fromRawData()` member function, which will only store a pointer to the data but won't take over its ownership. The caller has to ensure that the pointed-to data remains valid for all of the lifetime of the `QByteArray`.

Another possibility is to use the `QByteArrayLiteral()` macro. This macro will generate a `QByteArray` out of the `char*` literal at compile time and place it in the read-only memory segment. Since Qt 5.9, it is guaranteed that it will never result in an allocation on all supported platforms.

QString

`QString` represents a UTF-16 encoded Unicode string and supports Unicode-aware manipulations. It is implicitly shared and its constructors will allocate memory. Needless to say, it doesn't support SSO. Analogously to `QByteArray`, if we want to spare these allocations we can use either the `fromRawData()` member function or the `QStringLiteral()` macro.

There is an additional string class called `QLatin1String` which provides a thin wrapper around ASCII-/latin1-encoded `char*` literals. It is meant as an optimization to avoid the construction of any `QString` object from string literals, and it defines some basic string-processing methods. However, if a non-`const` method is called, a copy of string data will be made. Moreover, as it is not a Unicode string, it will use half of the memory of the equivalent `QString`.

Alternatively, this class can be used to mark function overloads, which can offer a faster implementation avoiding Unicode string logic.

QStringBuilder

We already discussed the usage of expression templates for the optimization of string construction. Qt provides an internal template class called `QStringBuilder`, which provides the expression template base optimization for concatenations of `QString` instances. This class isn't meant to be instantiated directly, but will be automatically invoked when its overloaded `%` operator is used, instead of the normal + concatenation operator, as in the following example:

```
QString s1("Hello ");
QLatin1String s2("you'all ");
QString msg = s1 % s2 % "how are you doing?";
```

By setting the global option `QT_USE_STRING_BUILDER`, the + concatenation operator will always be automatically replaced by the `QStringBuilder` template class's `%` overload, and you don't have to change your code by hand to profit from that optimization.

Substring classes

In Qt 4, there was already a class encapsulating substrings of a given string, named `QStringRef`. It doesn't store any data besides pointers to a portion of the original `QString` instance. In that way, substrings can be passed cheaply to functions without allocating any new memory. An example of this class's usage is string tokenization—instead of generating an array of `QString` and copying the data out of the original string, we can just return an array of string references, as in this example:

```
QString s("alfa, beta, gamma, zeta");
QVector<QStringRef> alfaBet = s.splitRef(", "); // instead of split()!
```

However, in Qt 5.10, a new class for representing substrings was introduced, namely the `QStringView` class, modeled after the C++17 `std::string_view`. The difference between these two classes is that `QStringRef` requires a `QString` instance as a source, whereas `QStringView` provides a view on an arbitrary UTF-16 string or string literal. Because of this, it is probable that `QStringRef` will be deprecated in the future.

However, in the Qt version used for this book (that is, 5.9), we can only use `QStringRef`.

More string advice

We have seen that we can use special constructors to avoid allocations: the `%` operators for concatenation and substring classes to provide views on string instances. Is there more we can do to optimize the string usage besides clever use of the Qt API?

Interning

Ever heard of Java's string interning? Basically, doing `String.intern()` on a series of strings in Java will ensure that all strings that have the same content share the same memory. This is cool, because it saves space but also allows for fast string comparison for equality by comparing just the pointers. Using a standard proposal **N3599**, which is already supported as an extension in GCC and clang, we could implement compile time interning in pure C++ in the following manner:

```
template <char... String> struct Interned
{
   static constexpr char const value[sizeof...(String) + 1]{String...};
};
template <char... String> constexpr char const
Interned<String...>::value[];
```

```
// using N3599
template<typename CharT, CharT ...String>
  constexpr const char* operator""_intern()
{
    return (Interned<String...>::value);
}

// test: only one copy?
static_assert("foo"_intern == "foo"_intern, "");
```

The `char*` literal gets wrapped into a type and becomes represented by a pointer to the wrapper type's (one and only) static member. Note that GCC will compile this code only in C++14 mode—in the book's resources (`https://github.com/PacktPublishing/Hands-On-High-performance-with-QT/tree/master/Chapter%204`), there's an (ugly) workaround for C++11 to be found.

There are some open source libraries implementing interning for C++ and C, but as the astute reader would notice, interning is just one variant of the classic flyweight **Gang of Four (GoF)** design pattern. This pattern defines flyweight proxies, which avoid duplication of frequently used objects, and that is what we want to achieve with interning. `Boost.Flyweight` library implements this pattern and we could use it for interning like so: `boost::flyweight<std::string>`.

Hashing

We have already seen that we can represent strings with their integer-valued hashes at compile time using a `constexpr` technique we discussed in *Chapter 3, Deep Dive into C++ and Performance*. This could speed up things when strings are used as keys in lookup tables.

However, as always with hashing, there's a danger of collisions. Thus, even if the strings compare as being equal, we still cannot be sure if they are really equal. However, when using a good hash function, this danger can be minimized. The **FNV-1a** 64-bit hash was tested with 219,606 lowercase English words mixed with some numbers and didn't create any collisions. So, using hashes for a limited set of strings can be a viable optimization.

Some open source C++ libraries implement a combination of the two previous approaches: that is, interning and hashing.

Searching substrings

When your performance is dominated by searching for substrings, then the good news is that C++17 adds an implementation of the **Boyer-More-Horspool** string-searching algorithm, which is often faster than the standard STL search. This algorithm doesn't check every character of a string, but rather tries to skip over some of them using a table generated from the string searched for (that is, the needle). Look at the following example for its usage:

```
QString text = "Lorem ipsum dolor sit amet, consectetur adipiscing ...";
QString needle ="amet";

auto iter = std::search(text.constBegin(), text.constEnd(),
                        std::boyer_moore_searcher(
                            needle.constBegin(), needle.constEnd()));
```

In C++11, we can use `Boost` implementation of the Boyer-More-Horspool string-searching algorithm. As always with fancy algorithms, there is a price to pay in the form of string table creation, so this algorithm will bring performance improvements only for bigger inputs. This would then be a classic case of the use of a better algorithm optimization technique.

Fixing the size

If we want to avoid allocations, we could just use the `const char*`, old-school C-style strings. However, that's not very comfortable. Fortunately, the **Electronic Arts Standard Template Library** (**EASTL**), a custom implementation of the standard library created for games, contains a fixed size of strings, which won't allocate any additional memory, namely `eastl::fixed_string`. You can set the maximum size of memory which will be used and, for pathological cases, dynamic allocations can also be enabled.

As long as we don't want to change it, we could also use `QStringLiteral` for a fixed size string.

Optimizing with algorithms and data structures

We have learned much about Qt classes and their pitfalls and a couple of techniques for working with strings. But it is always said that the choice of algorithms is the most important part for influencing performance. We will try to give some more high-level advice on that to wrap up for this chapter.

Optimizing with algorithms

The basic rule for optimizing your algorithm could be stated as, "Don't repeat yourself," or rather, "Don't repeat computations." You can do it in several ways, for example by:

- Omitting work using knowledge about the structure of the problem: For example, divide a task into subtasks and combine the results.

When you are doing that, you are trying to write your own algorithm. As we have already said, we are aiming at linear algorithms. So, if you have a double loop (and thus $O(n^2)$ complexity) somewhere, it had better not crop up in the critical path! With big inputs, even an $O(n)$ algorithm can get rather slow, so sometimes logarithmic complexity is the safest one. Recursively dividing up work into smaller chunks will get you there.

You could of course go extreme and refuse to do any computation work altogether, thus:

- Compute the results offline and provide the results as program data. For example, do not compute the factorials, find them in a table.

Or, maybe choose the middle way and:

- Save the results computed for later use (such as caching or memorizing): When we combine that with dividing into subtasks, we arrive at the **dynamic programming** technique.

One cool example of saving the results to save time is the **Schwartzian transform** known from Perl. The original problem, which triggered its invention, was to sort text lines by their last words. The sort algorithm had thus to extract the last word from the line, again and again. The original transform thus extracted the last word, enhanced the corresponding line with it, ran the sort using the extracted data, and discarded that data at the end. All this was done with three lines of Perl code—a thing of beauty.

The technique is however more general, so we can apply it when we can process some proxy data faster than the original. And there is, of course, still the basic technique of saving the computed data in a lookup hash table. In this vein, we can, for example, use a vector of pointers to big data structures as a proxy and sort the pointers to avoid costly copying and moving of data.

There's another interesting technique we could use, namely:

- Optimize for the hot path; use a slower path as fallback. If the hot path is hit in the majority of cases, we will have solved our problem.

One interesting example of this approach is the use of a **Bloom filter** data structure. A Bloom filter is a space-efficient, probabilistic data structure, which saves information about set membership. Since it's probabilistic, though it means that we could get a false response. The good thing is, Bloom filters can only lie to us when it says that an element is in the set. If it says the element isn't contained, that is guaranteed to be true.

So, why would we like to use a data structure that loses information? The reason is, that the test is very fast, and that a very large number of elements can be recorded. So, we first test if an element is in the filter, and if it's not, we are done—there is the fast path. If the filter says that the element is contained, we have to check it using a slow algorithm. However, if most of the elements have to be discarded, our normal case is very fast! This explains the name **filter**.

Sometimes, we have no idea how to design an optimal algorithm, but we can save ourselves some trouble and:

- **Invent a heuristic**: A heuristic is a practical method, not guaranteed to be optimal, or even logical, but sufficient for reaching a given goal.

For example, let's suppose we noticed that for some parameters our algorithm is performing well with one set of inputs and with other parameters for another. We do not understand why, but if that is sufficient to speed up our program significantly, we will just hardcode that and move on.

Maybe you have heard about NP-complete problems. They are algorithms with insanely high running costs, for which no good solutions are known as yet today. Such problems can be nonetheless solved in practice by using a heuristic.

And lastly:

- **Be cache-friendly**: Let yourself be inspired by the **cache-oblivious** algorithm and do as much work as possible after you have touched a specific piece of your data.

Because of the prominent importance of memory accesses in modern processor architectures, there is a lot of research going on about optimization of the classic algorithms with respect to memory caches. Cache-oblivious algorithms try to achieve this by recursively dividing a problem's dataset into smaller parts and then doing as many computations of each part as possible. Once data fits into a cache, it will do as much work as possible without touching any other memory.

Reusing other people's work

You can invent an algorithm by yourself, but you can try to reuse other's work. For example:

- **Use a better algorithm**: Algorithms are a heavily studied topic and probably your problem has already been solved. So, look for an existing algorithm.

However, fancy algorithms can have a high constant cost (for example initialization overhead) as we have seen before in the case of the Boyer-More-Horspool string-searching algorithm. So, sometimes a middle way could be a good idea:

- **Use a hybrid algorithm**: Fancy algorithms are often only effective for big inputs, so use trivial implementation for small inputs and switch to optimized ones later.

Hybrid (or adaptive) algorithms are very often used when combined with heuristics.

C++17 just added execution policies such as `std::execution::par` that can be passed to STL algorithms, which will then try to run a parallel version of the algorithm, so why not:

- **Use a parallel algorithm**: Because C++17 has support for that to the standard library, or use another parallelization framework like **OpenMP**, which is supported by the GCC compiler.

Good candidates for parallelization are algorithms running in $O(n)$ or larger and having large inputs, say $n > 2000$. However, execution policy is not a magic wand. If you don't understand the problem at hand, you can easily end up slowing down the algorithm. Qt also offers some parallel algorithm implementation in the `QtConcurrent` module, which we will discuss in a subsequent chapter on concurrency.

Optimizing with data structures

When it comes to data structures there is one basic piece of advice:

- Choose a matching data structure for your problem.

You will do that by looking at your usage pattern and choosing a data structure with the best speed for the operations you need. We already learned about basic data structures at the beginning of this chapter and saw that the two most performance-friendly data structures are arrays for simple object storage and iteration and hash tables for a keyed lookup. Tree structures also have their place, but are rather for more specialized use, like quad trees, interval trees, or tries. Lists can be used too of course, but not in performance-critical code.

Let me quickly illustrate the importance of data structure choice on a small example from the trenches. I know about a game engine which replaced `std::list` with `std::vector` and `std::map` with `std::unordered_map` (that is hash map) and it started to run four times faster. Then, they replaced `std::string` with a custom string class implementing interning and hashing and it started to run seven times faster. All this occurred thanks to a better choice of data structures.

As the proverbial astute reader would certainly notice, the previous performance gains stem mainly from the better memory access locality of the chosen data structures. Unsurprisingly, the biggest gains can be achieved from the improved locality of your data, as well as from better access patterns. Let's look at some techniques to achieve that.

Be cache-friendly

When designing your structures and classes, there are the following simple methods to make your cache happy:

- Don't mix frequently and rarely used fields; group them together.
- Don't mix frequently and read-only and read-write fields.
- Sort fields according to their alignment requirements so as not to waste space for padding.
- Place often-used fields at the beginning.

You might also sometimes want to duplicate some of your fields to improve lookup performance. In the field of database design this is called denormalization and denotes a holding of the same data in different tables instead of creating a new table and referencing its contents.

Flatten your data structures

We have already seen that we can improve the performance of a list or tree data structure by using a custom allocator improving the locality of the data. We also briefly mentioned specially crafted implementations flattening trees in an array, that is `Boost` library's `flat_map`.

Another possibility is simply to rewrite your complicated, possibly tree-like data structure manually, by placing all of its data in a single buffer—the POD data at the beginning, then string data, then any vector data at the end. Pointers to strings and vector data may stay as pointers or be replaced by offsets. I know of one old and very complicated program where such a manual flattening of a complicated data structure caused the program to run five times faster. However, it was a really complicated beast, so you cannot expect such speed-ups every time.

One interesting trick with flattening I have heard of is to use Google's Flat Buffers network serialization library for that. As it can represent hierarchical data in a flat binary buffer, the idea is to serialize a complicated data structure and then use its serialized version in future work. The problem, however, could be that not every mutating operation is supported for the serialized data structure.

Improve access patterns

Ideally, we'd like to have our data stored neatly in contiguous arrays and access them in a linear manner. There are a couple of techniques trying to achieve that. We have already seen one such technique, namely pool allocators. Let's look at some other examples.

Structure of arrays

The full name of this technique is **structure of arrays instead of array of structures**. The idea is to make the following replacement:

```cpp
// before
struct Data { ObjA a; ObjB b; int x };
std::vector<Data> myData;

// after
struct Data
{
  std::vector<ObjA> a;
  std::vector<ObjB> b;
  std::vector<int> x;
} myData;
```

Now, instead of iterating on structures and picking single elements out, we can just iterate on objects of type A, B, and int efficiently.

Polymorphism avoidance

A related technique replaces a single array of polymorphic object pointers, or worse, a big ad hoc graph structure of them, with several arrays, one for each specific static object type.

We first get rid of polymorphism, sparing us a vtable indirection, and second, manually ensure a nice contiguous placement of data. Now instead of iterating over a single data structure we have several arrays to be considered. Well, the code gets somehow uglier, but this inconvenience is the price paid for better performance. Remember—it's a trade-off.

This technique is also known as **data-oriented design** (**DoD**) and an implementation of the CSS animation system was reported to run six times faster than an original OO implementation after a rewrite took place along these lines.

Hot-cold data separation

Another somehow-related technique solves the problem of the following class:

```
struct FileData
{
  int fileDesc;
  std::string filePath;
  ~FileData()
  {
    close(fileDesc);
    unlink(filePath.c_str());
  }
};
```

You have many files open in your program and you store these structures in a big array. The problem is, the file descriptor will be used quite often, but the path is only needed in a destructor, clobbering the cache. We can solve that problem in two ways: First, we can use our trusty **structure of arrays** technique, hold two arrays in parallel, and associate the path to the file descriptor using their indexes in the array. In that case we will lose the destructors and object orientation, which may be acceptable, but isn't very pretty.

The second solution which was proposed is to put the cold data **out of line** (accidentally, it is also the name of this pattern) with a global data map, as in the following code:

```
struct FileDataFast
{
    static std::map<const FileData*, std::unique_ptr<std::string>> globalMap;
    int fileDesc;

    FileDataFast(int fd, const std::string& fpath)
    {
        fileDesc = open(fpath.c_str());
        globalMap[this] = std::make_unique<std::string>(fpath);
    }
    ~FileDataFast()
    {
        close(fileDesc);
        unlink(globalMap_[this]);
        globalMap_[this]->reset();
    }
};
```

Now, the cold data is shuffled away and is **out of the way** of the hot data but is still accessible over a pointer. We could capture this mechanism as a CRTP template, a technique we discussed in `Chapter 3`, *Deep Dive into C++ and Performance*.

Use a custom allocator

I know, I said the list would be one of the bad guys, but sometimes the default vector container just isn't good enough. If we are constantly adding elements in the middle of the vector, that's the worst use case for array-based containers! In this case we can fall back to the list, as it offers constant time element insertion. We only have to provide it with a custom allocator to improve its memory locality in a manner we already discussed.

Fixed size containers

As with strings, the EASTL library offers fixed size containers, which won't allocate any additional memory. They hold all of their memory locally, which tends to be cache-friendly due to its contiguity and proximity to the container's housekeeping data. The following containers are implemented: `fixed_list`, `fixed_vector`, `fixed_set`, `fixed_map`, `fixed_hash_set`, `fixed_hash_map`, plus their multivalued variants. Many users view the non-allocating containers as the most important part of EASTL.

We could also title this section **Use a better data structure**, as this is an example of the classic **use a better library** optimization pattern. By the way, it is possible that fixed strings will be part of C++20.

Write your own

After we finish the memory locality topic, we will close this section with a more general consideration - should we write our own data structures?

As we have seen in the discussion of hash table implementations, STL design might sometimes be a compromise as it has to support a wide array of usage patterns. Sometimes, we can capitalize on that and can write a custom implementation of an algorithm or data structure that are constrained to a specific task's requirements and thus can achieve better performance.

Summary

This chapter has shown you the basic building blocks of programs, namely algorithms and data structures, at work in the Qt environment. More specifically, we learned about algorithms and data structures, in particular about algorithm classes, the *O(n)* notation, array and vector containers, lists, trees, and hash tables. We saw also how the Qt containers look internally and how to use them, as well as the dangers of using COW containers, and Qt's standing in respect to algorithms and iterators, along with Qt string classes and how to use them efficiently. Some general string optimization techniques, some pointers about how to optimize your algorithm, and the techniques to improve the locality of your data structures were also addressed.

In the next chapter, we will turn our attention to another big building block of performant programs—concurrent, parallel, and asynchronous processing. Let's unleash the power of your computer's cores!

Questions

Once again, here are a couple of questions to test your understanding of the material from this chapter:

1. If a better algorithm uses knowledge about the structure of the data, how does that apply to sorting? Is the data to be sorted, by definition, devoid of any structure?

2. Is using the `QStringList` class a good idea? Or should you use `QVector<QString>` instead?

3. Is there any chance that Qt will start using the standard library containers in their APIs?

4. What is SSO? What is SVO? Where are they used?

5. Consider the following code:

```
Q_FOREACH(auto const& v, qvector) { ... }
```

Is it dangerous?

6. Do you know now why back in time the COW containers were also known as **mad COW** containers?

7. Who were the Gang of Four? Are they relevant for performance?

8. What seems to have the greatest improvement potential when implementing data structures?

9. Talking about strings, what can you say about the performance of the following code:

```
bool hasTwoDigits(const QString& numberStrg)
{
    QRegExp rx("^\\d\\d?$");
    return rx.indexIn(numberStrg) != -1;
}
```

Further reading

I highly encourage you to have a look at *5 Rules of Programming*, written by *Bob Pike* (https://users.ece.utexas.edu/~adnan/pike.html)—short and succinct, alas I cannot quote all of them here.

If you want to learn more about algorithms, data structures, and the $O(n)$ (big O) notation, there is the classic academic reference book, *Introduction to Algorithms* by Cormen, Leiserson, Rivest, and Stein (MIT Press, 3rd edition, 2009), but it could be a little heavy going, though. A lighter read is *The Algorithm Design Manual* by Steven Skiena, (Springer, 2nd edition, 2008).

A classic example of algorithmic optimization in action is the HashLife optimization for the *Game of Life* and you might like to read it. One of the descriptions can be found here: *An Algorithm for Compressing Space and Time* by Thomas Rokicki (2006) `http://www.drdobbs.com/jvm/an-algorithm-for-compressing-space-and-t/184406478`.

The *Optimized C++* book by Kurt Guntheroth (O'Reilly, 2013) describes the usage of the standard STL algorithms and their performance in detail.

5
An In-Depth Guide to Concurrency and Multithreading

In this chapter, we will focus on performance improvements that can be achieved with threads and concurrency. We will learn about different concurrency mechanisms, thread usage, communication between threads, and guidelines for good concurrent performance.

As this is a mid-level book, we won't present the basic thread usage but will rather concentrate on the performance aspects of multithreading and parallel processing.

This chapter will discuss the following topics:

- **Concurrency, parallelism, and multithreading**: Introducing the basic concepts and classic problems
- **Threading support classes in Qt**: Overview of the classes we can work with
- **Threads, events, and QObjects**: How the `QObject` and `QThread` fit together
- **Higher-level Qt concurrency mechanisms**: How not to worry about locking
- **Multithreading and performance**: How to speed up programs with threads
- **Beyond threads**: A look into the future

Let's start with some general discussion of basic concurrency concepts.

Concurrency, parallelism, and multithreading

As you are a mid-level programmer, I assume you have at least some basic idea of what threads are, how they are different from processes, how and why we synchronize threads, mutexes, and what an atomic variable is.

Nonetheless, we will first have a quick overview of the basic concurrency concepts, namely:

- **Thread**: This is an independent unit of computation your **operating system** (**OS**) can run in parallel. It is different from a process in that it shares common memory with other threads. In fact, a process can contain several threads.
- **Mutex**: This is an abbreviation of "mutual exclusion," also known as a **lock**. It is a mechanism of the OS, which will block a thread if another thread has already marked the mutex as taken, or in other words, locked or acquired it.
- **Synchronization**: C++ standard says that a simultaneous access of two threads to the same memory location is undefined behavior. Remember scary UB from `Chapter 3`, *Deep Dive into C++ and Performance*? We can take care that this won't happen by acquiring a mutex before we use that shared object, thus precluding other threads from synchronously accessing it. The piece of code guarded by a mutex is called a **critical section**.
- **Atomic variable**: This is a variable that can read and write with a single (that is, atomic) machine instruction. As we will see later, this is as good as a mutex but much cheaper because no OS call is needed in this case. Also, it is worth noting that volatile variables cannot be used to prevent race conditions in C++.

There is one last confusion to be cleared up, namely the question of whether concurrency, parallelism, and multithreading are all one and the same thing, or are they maybe somehow different?

In day-to-day usage, they are often used interchangeably but, strictly speaking, they denote slightly different concepts:

- **Concurrency**: This is the case when parts of a program are executed at the same time, even in an old, single-processor, time-sharing manner, or cooperative multithreading.
- **Parallelism**: This takes place when parts of your program are running truly in parallel using multiple cores or processors at the same time.
- **Multithreading**: This will always be the case when you are using threads. We can then have parallelism between threads and concurrency inside them.

Problems with threads

Threads are a super-easy way to make use of the multiple cores and processors of modern computers. They are easy to use because, in contrast to an older concurrency technique of installing asynchronous callbacks, they give you the illusion of continuous execution and ease of reasoning about code. The only thing we have to take into account is locking, but it doesn't seem so difficult a concept at first sight. So, why does the *Multithreading is hard* mantra get repeated over and over?

The main problem is that using several mutexes in parallel is pretty error-prone. The scientific name for that fact is the noncomposability of mutexes and it shows itself in problems like:

- **Deadlock**: This is the most typical and the deadliest of the problems, as your program will just freeze dead! It occurs when one thread is holding a mutex X and is trying to acquire the mutex Y, while another thread is holding the mutex Y and trying to get mutex X. Clearly, no progress can be achieved here. A simple countermeasure is for every thread to acquire the locks in the same order. An example implementation of this strategy could be to order the locks by their IDs or even addresses.

  Now, we can see the dreaded *noncomposability* in action—if we are using some function which may be using mutexes, we have to know what mutexes it uses so that we can insert them in our lock ordering. Thus, we cannot simply use two pieces of software which would then internally implement locking and be sure that no deadlock can occur! This is also the reason for the old advice of not holding any locks when invoking a callback.
  There is still a lot of ongoing research about deadlock prevention and avoidance on the OS level, but we won't discuss it here leaving it for the reader to discover. Another possibility to solve this and the following livelock problem is the formal verification of the algorithms using tools like SPIN or TLA+.

- **Livelock**: Livelock is somehow like deadlock, but is different from it because both threads will acquire mutexes but won't make any progress nevertheless. A good illustration of it would be—two people trying to go through the door at the same time and both trying to let the other one go first.

- **Starvation**: In this scenario, one thread is trying to acquire a lock and is waiting endlessly for its turn, but that will never get scheduled, even without any deadlocks. How can this be? Hypothetically speaking, if there are several threads always contending for a resource, there is no guarantee that each one will access it. For that to be true, the lock implementation of OS has to be *fair*. Why should that be a problem? Unfair lock implementations can be much more performant. Statistically, a thread will finally get the mutex in the long run, but it could be waiting for it for quite a long time. For example, Windows changed its lock implementation from fair locks used in the older versions to unfair locks exactly because of the performance considerations.

- **Convoying**: This describes the situation when a number of threads are waiting on a lock, and the thread which actually holds it is descheduled, for example, because of a time-slice interrupt. In this case all the other threads cannot proceed too and have to wait for the lock's holder to be scheduled again, thus remaining passive and convoying on its way to and from the kernel lands.
  To minimize convoying, try to hold the lock as briefly as possible. Note that fair locks will make this situation even worse! There is some research on this **lock holder preemption** (**LHP**) problem in the context of virtualization platforms which could be interesting, but we will leave it for the reader to discover.

- **Priority inversion**: Here we encounter a new concept, which is that of thread priority. We can tell the OS that some threads are more important than other ones and that they should be scheduled accordingly. This is especially relevant in real-time systems.
  Now if a low-priority thread holding a common lock is descheduled, it can prevent high-priority threads from proceeding! In the real-time community, there are some well-established techniques to deal with this problem, such as priority ceiling, priority inheritance, or random boosting. The latter is used in the Windows OS and works by randomly boosting the priority of ready threads holding locks as they exit the critical section.

More problems – false sharing

On the lower, but all-important level of CPU caches we have one more problem to deal with, namely so-called false sharing.

This problem surfaces when threads on different processors or cores modify variables that reside on the same cache line. It is called false sharing because the threads are not consciously sharing any data, but are instead sharing the underlying unit of information exchange between processor caches, that is the cache line. Look at the following picture for visualization:

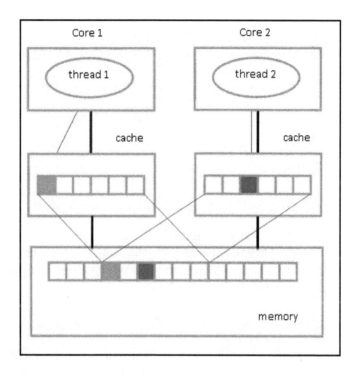

We see now why false sharing is also known as cache-line ping-ponging. The first core is repeatedly invalidating the caches of the other cores, which forces the other cores to read data from main memory instead of their local cache! As we already learned, this will be a real performance downer!

As this problem isn't easy to spot in code, tools like Intel VTune Performance Analyzer offer support for detecting false sharing in your program.

We can avoid false sharing if we ensure that variables causing the problem are spaced far enough apart in memory that they cannot be contained in the same cache line. We can achieve it in a simple way if we allocate the variables using a big enough alignment. This can be done in a number of ways:

- Using compiler directives such as the following:

```
// Visual Studio
__declspec (align(64)) int variable1;
__declspec (align(64)) int variable2;

// gcc
int variable1 __attribute__ ((aligned (64)));
```

- Using standard C++ support, such as the `alignas()` specifier:

```
alignas(64) int variable; // since C++11
```

    Or, for dynamic allocations, using the following:

```
int* p = std::aligned_alloc(64, sizeof(int)); // since C++17
```

- Using library helpers is also an option:
  For example Intel's **Thread Building Blocks** (**TBB**) library offers the `cache_aligned_allocator<T>` template, which always allocates data on separate cache lines, to be used like that:

```
std::vector<int, tbb::cache_aligned_allocator<int>>;
```

We have also to take care when using an array of data structures. To avoid false sharing in this case, we will have to pad the structure to the end of a cache line manually to ensure that all array elements begin on a cache line boundary. C++17 provides us with the means to query the cache line size by using the `std::hardware_destructive_interference_size` constant.

Now we have set up a common vocabulary and learned about the classic problems with concurrency, let's look at Qt's support in the matter of threading.

Threading support classes in Qt

In the following, we will briefly describe implementations of basic concurrency concepts, starting with the most important of them, namely threads.

Threads

The class that offers a thread abstraction in Qt is unsurprisingly named QThread. We start an OS thread by subclassing the QThread class in the following manner:

```
class MyThread : public QThread
{
public:
  void run()
  {
    // thread working...
  }
};
```

Then, we instantiate this class and call its start() method. This will start a new OS thread instance and execute the run() method in this new thread's context. The second possibility is not to subclass the QThread but just to call its start() method, which will in turn start its event loop, but more on that later.

Compared to a standard C++ thread class, it must be said that QThread implements thread interruption, which isn't available in C++11 and later.

Mutexes

We synchronize threads using the QMutex class, preferably through the QMutexLocker class, which implements automatic unlocking in its destructor, as in the following code:

```
void MyThread::run()
{
  QMutexLocker guard(&myMutex_); // locked
  ...
} // unlocked
```

Another locker class is the QOrderedMutexLocker, which can lock and unlock several mutexes at once, making sure that their ordering is preserved so as to prevent deadlocks.

Compared with Qt lock managers, the corresponding standard C++11 classes are much more flexible and convenient, and offer more functionality. However, since Qt 5.8, QMutex has implemented the *TimedLockable* concept and can thus be used with STL lock managers.

QMutex can be used in recursive mode (that is, locked again if the current thread already holds it) but it is more expensive to use than a nonrecursive mutex. Moreover, QMutex is not fair. QBasicMutex is the base class of QMutex, which is designed to be used as a global static object because it doesn't have a custom constructor and thus does not incur any additional initialization costs in the startup phase. QBasicMutex only supports nonrecursive mode and so can avoid a custom constructor. Sadly, this class is missing in the Qt documentation.

A **semaphore** is a counting mutex, that is, a mutex which can be acquired *N* times. It can be used if we want to have the maximum *N* threads in a critical section, because we have exactly *N* copies of a shared resource available. QSemaphore is the Qt implementation of this concept. As of C++17 the C++ standard library doesn't have a semaphore implementation.

Condition variables

There is another class which can be used with implementing mutexes, a mechanism we haven't yet introduced—the QWaitCondition class. It can be used by a thread to tell other threads that some condition has been met. Other threads can block on a condition variable and be notified when wakeOne() or wakeAll() is called on this variable. For example:

```
void waidForCondition(QWaitCondition& cond, QMutex mutex)
{
  mutex.lock();
  cond.wait(&mutex);
  // ... do work
  mutex.unlock();
}
```

We see that the wait condition is used in conjunction with a locked mutex—after wait() was called, the mutex will be unlocked and when the condition will be met, it will be locked again before the thread is woken up.

The preceding code would be correct, if there weren't such a thing as a spurious wake! **Spurious wake** is the condition variable that will return from a wait() call without wakeOne() or wakeAll() even having been called! The first time I encountered that in a *pthreads* context, I thought it must be a bug, but then I checked the documentation and there it was, in its full glory! The correct code should then double-check that the condition we were waiting for was really met, as in the following code:

```
QMutexLocker locker(&mutex);
while(thereIsAFreeSlot() == false)
```

```
{
    cond.wait(&mutex);
}
```

Compared to standard C++ classes, we must again say that the `std::condition_variable` class is more generic and convenient than the `QWaitCondition` class. For example, one can pass a predicate to test for spurious wakes to the `wait()` call, instead of writing the test loop by hand.

Atomic variables

Qt offers two atomic variable types, namely `QAtomicInteger<T>` and `QAtomicPointer<T>`. These variables implement operations like `test` and `set` (also known as CAS, the acronym for "compare and swap"), `fetch` and `store`, or `fetch` and `add` for different memory orderings. For starters, we will only use the ordered memory ordering semantic. Look in the *Further reading* section for resources on the C++11 memory model.

Starting with Qt 5.7, Qt's atomics actually use the C++11 atomics under the hood, except for platforms or compilers, which don't implement them properly. Their API is more restricted than the C++ API, so for more advanced use cases you should probably employ their **Standard Template Library (STL)** counterparts.

Thread local storage

`QThreadStorage` provides the same functionality as `std::thread_local`. It implements local thread storage, which isn't accessible from other threads.

Q_GLOBAL_STATIC

The `Q_GLOBAL_STATIC` macro will create an object that initializes itself on first use in a thread-safe manner on all supported Qt platforms. This means that if multiple threads try to initialize the object concurrently, only one thread will be allowed to initialize, while all other threads wait until initialization is completed.

```
Q_GLOBAL_STATIC(MyGlobalData, globalState)
// usage
auto globalValue = globalState->valueX;
```

This macro should be used as a fallback option because C++ introduced thread safety guarantees for function-local static variables, as shown in the following implementation of Meyer's singleton:

```
static Singleton& instance()
{
  static Singleton instance_;
  return instance_;
}
```

Alternatively, we can use the C++11 `std::call_once` function, which executes a callable exactly once, even if called from several threads:

```
Singleton* instance_ = nullptr;
std::once_flag flag;
std::call_once(flag, [](){ instance_ = new Singleton(); });
```

For now, we have seen that the thread support classes in Qt roughly correspond to the standard C++ classes. However, there are some Qt specifics which could easily trip you up if you are used to the `std::` classes. Let's look at what these are.

Threads, events, and QObjects

If it wasn't for the `QObject`, we could probably just use the C++ standard thread class. However, a `QObject` can emit and receive signals and Qt offers infrastructure to do so in a **multithread-safe** (**MT-safe**) way. In order to be able to understand this mechanism, we have first to take a look at signals, slots, and asynchronous processing in Qt.

Events and event loop

Qt is an event-driven toolkit and this means that we are always reacting to some events occurring in the system. Thus, we are doing all things asynchronously—we will be notified of something, then we react to it in some specific callback, and then we are done. So, our program isn't one single code strand, it's rather a collection of decoupled callbacks.

When Qt program is launched, it will run in the main thread and will have its main event loop started there. The event loop will get events out of its event queue and call their handlers (that is, their respective callbacks). The basic cases where the system events are driving a Qt application forward are:

- Keyboard, mouse, and window manager events (for widget painting and interaction)
- Timer events
- Network events

Internally generated Qt events are also active in this, such as:

- Signals

As you'll certainly know, signals are custom events which a `QObject` can emit and other objects can subscribe for.

So, the first performance guideline we receive as Qt programmers is never to block the main event loop! Otherwise, widgets won't repaint themselves, timers won't fire, and networking will slow down or stop completely. And what does **blocking the event loop** mean exactly? It means performing computation or I/O intensive actions in the event loop callback.

Thus, if such actions have to be done, we'd be better off if they were made outside of the main event loop, which gets us directly to our next topic, namely `QThreads`. Admittedly, we can force event dispatching in our compute-intensive event handler using the `QCoreApplication::processEvents()` method, but this technique can lead to subtle bugs in unexpected places. So, be very careful if you do use it. But, we digress. Let's go back to `QThreads` and their idea of event handling.

QThreads and object affinities

We have already got to know the `QThread` class and its basic usage, that is, overriding its `run()` method and running this thread's actions there. However, as we have already hinted at, there's a second possibility to use a thread, and that is just starting it without any subclassing. In this case, the default implementation of the `run()` method will call the `exec()` methods starting `QThread`'s own internal event loop. Now, we can additionally process events in the context of the new thread, parallel to the main thread's event loop.

But, to see the whole concept we have to introduce one last concept: that of an object's thread affinity. As we have already mentioned, a QObject can emit signals which will then be put into the event queue and dispatched when the event loop resumes running. Now, the important thing to understand is that the events destined for a QObject will be delivered to the event queue of a thread with which it has an affinity relation! By default, an object's affinity is set to the thread in which context it has been created. But, you also may change an object's thread affinity (that is, the thread where it *lives*) by using the QObject::moveToThread() method.

Thus, we have a general situation of a kind shown in the following figure:

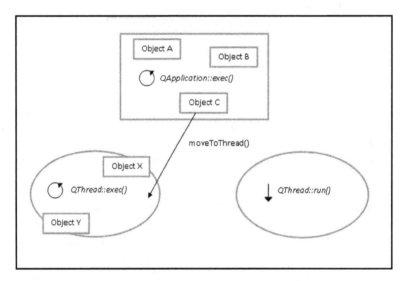

First, we have the main thread and the main event loop, some threads running event loops themselves, and some threads without event loops. As you will already know, it is possible to send signals from objects in one thread to objects in another one. A metacall event for the sent signal will be put into the event queue of another thread and then processed in its event loop.

The following code will illustrate the difference between threads with and without an event loop, using a common example of a thread which should periodically check for some condition:

```
class MyThread : public QThread
{
public:
  void run() override
  {
    while (!isInterruptionRequested())
```

```
    {
      if(checkCondition() == true) ... // do something
      QThread::currentThread()->sleep(oneSec);
    }
  }
};

auto mythread = new MyThread();
mythread->start();
```

Now, without subclassing, the code would look like the following:

```
class WorkerObject : public QObject
{
  Q_OBJECT
  // ...
public slots:
  void doWork()
  {
    if(checkCondition() == true) ... // do something
  }
  void startTimer()
  {
    timer_.start(oneSec);
    connect(&timer_, &QTimer::timeout, this, &WorkerObject::doWork);
  }
private:
  QTimer timer_;
};

auto thread = new QThread();
auto worker = new WorkerObject();
QObject::connect(thread, &QThread::started, worker,
&WorkerObject::startTimer);

worker->moveToThread(thread);
thread->start();
```

Additionally, we could observe a peculiarity in Qt's timers—it's not enough to move them to a thread, they have also to be started in the context of the thread where they are living. Thus, we have the additional WorkerObject's method startTimer().

There is another method, which is looked down upon as confusing and misleading, but we will show it here nevertheless just to make sure we understand the usage it makes of Qt mechanisms:

```cpp
class MootThread : public QThread
{
  Q_OBJECT
  // ...
public slots:
  void doWork()
  {
    if(checkCondition() == true) ... // do something
  }
  void startTimer()
  {
    Q_ASSERT(timer_);
    timer_->start(oneSec);
  }
 private:
   QTimer* timer_ = nullptr;
};

auto thread = new MootThread();
auto timer = new QTimer();

QObject::connect(timer, &QTimer::timeout, thread, &MootThread::doWork);
QObject::connect(thread, &QThread::started, thread,
&MootThread::startTimer);

timer->setInterval(oneSec);
timer->moveToThread(thread);

thread->moveToThread(thread); // controversial!
thread->setTimer(timer);
thread->start();
```

The controversial point is the line moving the thread object to its own thread context. As controversial as it seems, this only ensures that the slots of the thread won't be executed in the context of the current thread, but rather in the newly created thread context behind the MootThread class. This spares us the definition of a worker object for the price of being clever. But, we had to define an extra QThread subclass so we didn't spare anything. Thus, I wouldn't recommend it, but you could see it in some older, clever code, so don't be confused by it.

Getting rid of the QThread class

We said that we cannot use the `std::thread` class because it does not provide the event loop. Well, that's not entirely true. In fact, we could mimic `QThread` inside of the regular `std::thread` by using a `QEventLoop` instance to run a thread-local event loop. We could even move a `QObject` into that thread's context because the static `QThread::currentThread()` function will give you a `QThread*` we can use for this purpose.

But, why should we want to do that? Just look at this as an exercise, testing your understanding of Qt threading mechanisms.

Thread safety of Qt objects

There is one last topic we have to discuss in relation to `QThreads`, namely the multithreading safety of the Qt classes.

The Qt documentation states that some classes and functions are MT-safe, and thus they can be used without any precautions from several threads, for example, `QMutex`, `QObject::connect()`, and `QCoreAplication::postEvent()`.

Container classes, `QString`, `QImage`, and others are reentrant, which means that they can be used from several threads if the access to them is guarded by a mutex.

However, the `QWidget`, `QQuickItem`, `QPixmap`, and generally the GUI classes are not reentrant, which basically means that they can only be used in the main thread, and for this reason it is also called the GUI thread.

Higher level Qt concurrency mechanisms

Because usage of the low-level threading constructs is known to be error-prone (we have seen a list of the problems earlier in this chapter), there is an ongoing quest in the concurrent community to provide better and higher level abstractions. Qt also implements a couple of such mechanisms and groups them in the `QtConcurrent` module. Let's have a look at it.

QThreadPool

A thread pool preallocates a number of worker threads and then allows the user to use them for their `run` computations. Each Qt application has one global `QThreadPool` object, which can be accessed by calling `globalInstance()`. `QThreadPool` allows running instances of `QRunnable` (also known as tasks) by calling `QThreadPool::start()`, as in the following example:

```
class DoSomethingTask : public QRunnable
{
  void run() override { ... do something  }
};

auto taskPtr = new DoSomethingTask ();
QThreadPool::globalInstance()->start(taskPtr);
```

Note that `QThreadPool` will take ownership of the task and will delete it automatically on completion. You can disable this by using the `QRunnable::setAutoDelete()` function. We can control the number of threads in the pool by using `setMaxThreadCount()` and `setExpiryTimeout()`. We can also reserve a thread from the pool using the `reserveThread()` function. `QThreadPool` will start with the optimal thread number for the hardware, that is, as many threads as there are cores.

It must be noted that `QRunnable` objects are not subclassing forms of `QObject`, thus queued signal-slot connections cannot be used to communicate with `QRunnable`-based workers. We could use `QWaitCondition` for that purpose, but the thread pool is best used for one-shot tasks that have to be done asynchronously.

All things considered, `QThreadPool` is still something of a low-level construct compared with `QtConcurrent`, as it only encapsulates thread creation and reuse. It isn't a part of `QtConcurrent` proper either, but is used by it internally to run computations in the background.

QFuture

A future is a handle to a computation, which will be finished some time in the future. While in the C++11 standard library this functionality is split up between `std::promise` (for producers) and `std::future` (for consumers), in Qt it is implemented in a single class.

We can start asynchronous computations with `QtConcurrent::run()`, which returns a `QFuture` that can be synchronously waited on or used in an asynchronous manner by using the `QFutureWatcher` class as shown in the next example:

```
// schedule an action
QFuture<QImage> readImage(const QString& fileName)
{
  auto readImageWorker =
      [](const QString &fileName)
      {
        QImage image;
        image.load(fileName);
        return image;
      };
  return QtConcurrent::run(readImageWorker, fileName);
}

// usage
ImageReader reader;
auto future = reader.read("....");

QFutureWatcher *watcher = new QFutureWatcher<QImage>();
connect(watcher, &QFutureWatcher::finished,
        [=]() {
          showImage(future.result());
        });

watcher->setFuture(future);
```

You can have a look at a program contained in this book's resources, which uses `QFutures` to load images outside of the main GUI thread, if you'd like to see a more complete example.

We can also group a couple of futures and wait till all of them will finish using the `QFutureSynchronizer` class:

```
void fetchImages()
{
  QFutureSynchronizer<void> sync;
  sync.addFuture(QtConcurrent::run(fetchImage("image1")));
  sync.addFuture(QtConcurrent::run(fetchImage("image2")));
  ...
  return; // QFutureSynchronizer waits for all futures!
}
```

As QFuture supports cancelling, QFutureSynchronizer can also cancel all its futures using the cancelOnWait() method. Unfortunately, this doesn't apply to any QFuture returned by QtConcurrent::run().

QFutureInterface

Remember when we said that QFuture doesn't have the *promise* and *future* parts known from the standard C++ library? Well, that's not entirely true. Officially, a QFuture instance can only be created by calling a method of the *QtConcurrent* framework, but unofficially there's an undocumented class called QFutureInterface that can be used as the *promise* part of the QFuture. This means that we can write our own method, returning QFuture and communicating work's status back to the invoker using QFutureInterface as shown in the following example:

```
QFuture<QImage> loadImage(const QString& filePtah)
{
  QFutureInterface<QImage> futureInterface;
  futureInterface.reportStarted();

  // start asynchronous processing, for example:
  imageWorker_->sendRequest(futureInterface, filePath);

  return futureInterface.future();
}

// in the worker ....
... work
// on success:
futureInterface.reportResult(&image);
// or, on error:
futureInterface.reportException(MyImageErrorException());
futureInterface.reportFinished();

// in the invoker:
auto future = loadImage(",/image.jpg");
while(!future.isFinished()) { ... wait ...  }
QImage result = future.result();
```

As we see, a `QFutureInterface` object can be sent a with an asynchronous signal from one thread to another while passing the future provided by the `QFutureInterface` to the invoker, which will wait for the result. This is possible because a `futureInterface.future()` call sets a copy of the `QFutureInteface` as `QFuture`'s internal data and `QFutureInteface` is only a wrapper over `QFutureInterface`'s private data, which will be reference counted. These interdependencies can be seen in the following figure:

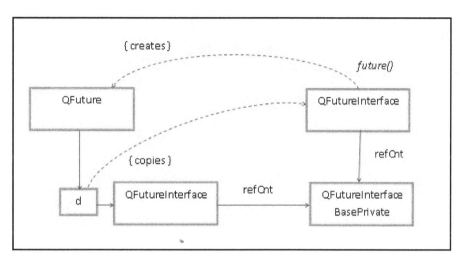

The `reportResult()` takes a pointer to the result data and makes a deep copy when storing it. Note that, when reporting an error, `reportException()` requires a subclass of Qt's custom `QException` class. The previous code uses the `QFuture` directly, but you could just as well set up an asynchronous callback using `QFutureWatcher`. If you are interested, you will find a longer example program using `QFutureInterface` in this book's resources (https://github.com/PacktPublishing/Hands-On-High-performance-with-QT/tree/master/Chapter%205).

Should we use it?

Strictly speaking, `QFutureInterface` is an internal Qt class that shouldn't be used externally and it even lacks any official documentation! However, its usage isn't unknown in the Qt community and, when you look at Qt Creators's source code, you will see that it is used quite pervasively there. Thus, the chances are good that it won't vanish all of a sudden, at least in Qt 5. In Qt 6, this area could perhaps be refactored, but major versions break code compatibility anyway.

Map, filter, and reduce

QtConcurrent offers the classic map and filter algorithms for sequences which will however be processed in parallel using several threads. First, we have two basic operations: `filter()` and `reduce()` which will operate in place on the sequence. These operations have variants which do not modify the sequence, but instead return a new one as a result, namely `filtered()` and `mapped()`. These functions return a `QFuture` object but they also have their blocking variants, namely `blockingMap()`, `blockingMapped()`, `blockingFilter()`, and `blockingFiltered()`. Let's have a look at an example of their usage for the map family of functions:

```
void scaleImage(QImage &image)
{
   image = image.scaled(100, 100);
}
QVector<QImage> imageList = ...;

// blocking in-place
QtConcurrent::blockingMap(imageList, scaleImage);
// async in-place
QFuture<void> future = QtConcurrent::map(imageList, scaleImage);

// blocking with copy
QVector<QImage> scaledImages =
QtConcurrent::blockingMapped(imageList.constBegin(), imageList.constEnd(),
scaleImage);
// async with copy
auto future = QtConcurrent::mapped(imageList.constBegin(),
imageList.constEnd(), scaleImage);
```

These functions will apply an operation or condition to every element of a sequence. Internally, they will use a thread pool and futures to distribute the work over the threads available in the pool. The work will be automatically partitioned in chunks whose sizes will be rebalanced during execution, depending on the processing time for the single elements.

Many parallel computing frameworks, such as the *OpenMP* framework on the Intel TBB library, implement a so-called *fork-join* model of parallelism in as much as that execution branches off in parallel at some points of the program (*fork*) and then the branches meet again (*join*), combine their results, and resume sequential execution.

QtConcurrent provides some support for that model, in that it implements a fork-join version of the previous algorithms, namely `filteredReduced()` and `mapedReduced()`, as well as `blockingFilteredReduced()` and `blockingMapedReduced()`. Look at the following example:

```
QStringList strings = ...;
int countWords(const QString& s) { ... }
int countWords(int& total, const int& count ) { total += count; }

int wordCount = QtConcurrent::blockingFilteredReduced(strings, coundWords,
addCounts);
```

We can see that there is a progression of abstraction levels to be observed here. `QThreadPool` abstracts away thread creation and execution of tasks in thread context, `QFuture` and `QtConcurrent::run` encapsulate asynchronous result delivery, while `QtConcurrent::map` and `QtConcurrent::filter` functions relieve us of the task of partitioning the tasks to available threads and waiting for the result of the entire computation.

You might be tempted to say that the C++17 **Standard Template Library** (STL) algorithms using the `std::execution::par` execution policy are doing exactly the same, but they aren't. Consider the following example:

```
std::vector<int> vec;
std::for_each(std::execution::par, seq.begin(), seq.end(), [&](int i) {
    vec.push_back(i*2+1); // error: data race!
});
```

The standard states explicitly:

When using parallel execution policy, it is the programmer's responsibility to avoid deadlocks!

Summing up, we can say that Qt provides some basic support for higher level concurrency constructs, but it is not very advanced. As the `QFutures` cannot be chained, nor can the *QtConcurrent* algorithms be combined. But they are at least a starting point.

Which concurrency class should I use?

Now, we have seen an array of different Qt classes supporting threading in addition to the C++ standard library ones. That's a lot, so how can we decide which class to use in our application? Let's have a look:

- QThread

  We can use QThread with a reimplemented run() method to perform one-shot computation and emit signals to update progress from it. We can also use a QThread with a worker object, which can perform different tasks upon request. We will send commands and receive updates over queued signal-slot connections in this case. A third possibility is a thread which will periodically perform an expensive operation and doesn't need to receive any signals or events. We will use QThread with a reimplemented run() method and will emit signals to send result data back.

- QRunnable

  We can use QRunnable with a reimplemented run() method to perform one-shot computation as in the QThread case, but in order to communicate progress updates, we will have to use a thread-safe variable.

- QtConcurrent::run

  As in the case of QRunnable, we will perform one-shot computation and communicate progress updates by using a thread-safe variable. However, we can additionally return result data from the computation using a future, and be notified of its completion using QFutureWatcher.

- QtConcurrent::map and filter

  We use it to select container elements or to apply an operation to each element. We can fold the results together using the *Reduced* variants of the operations.

- std::thread and std::async

  As Qt thread classes are interoperable with standard library threading classes, we can mix and match both of them. However, if we want to communicate over signal and slots, we will prefer the QThread class out of convenience. C++11 std::async also provides thread pool support, but the returned std::future cannot be integrated in Qt's signal and slots mechanism.

As a general advice, we should always prefer higher level concurrency mechanisms whenever possible.

Multithreading and performance

Multithreading is hard is the mantra you will hear very often. But, as we learned in Chapter 1, *Understanding Performant Programs*, if we want to use the advances in processor design, we must parallelize our programs! Otherwise, we will only use a single core, which will normally utilize only a fraction of our computer's CPU.

So, how can we speed up our programs? Well, before we can answer this question, we will first have a look at the costs of several concurrency constructs. Not again, you say? We have discussed so much of that stuff, Qt or not, already, you say? We have to see some cool techniques at last, you say? Sorry to disappoint you, but success in performance optimization comes from deep understanding. So, let's have a look at those costs, shall we?

Costs of multithreading

We will start with the costs inherently bound to OS-level thread implementation.

Thread costs

Threads are kernel-level constructs, so each operation on them requires a context switch from the user land to the kernel context (also known as a kernel trip). This is rather expensive because we are changing the privilege level of code and also switching all the context data of the current thread. An often-given estimate for crossing the kernel boundary in a syscall is 1,000-1,500 CPU cycles. By comparison, the dreaded reading from main RAM needs 100-150 CPU cycles.

One big cost, which we do not want to pay too often, is the thread creation and deletion overhead. Creating and deleting threads each time we have some operation to be run in parallel with another would be a great waste of resources. This problem can be solved using a pool of preallocated threads.

Another problem is that OS-level threads are a pretty heavy abstraction. We can have maximally a couple of thousand OS threads, but literally millions of Erlang processes or hundreds of thousands of Go's goroutines. The difference is that the latter are user-space constructs and that they are using dynamic stack sizes. Compared to that, an OS-level thread is a very heavy object.

Other often overlooked overheads are the costs of switching between threads. It is more expensive than a system call, which can be better optimized, and it can be estimated with 2,000 CPU cycles, but the total cost, including cache invalidation, can be as high as 10,000 and more CPU cycles!

Synchronization costs

When a thread is trying to acquire a mutex it will have to invoke an OS call, and thus switch to the kernel context. While in the kernel, when the mutex is already taken, the thread will be put to sleep and woken up when the mutex is released.

However, modern OS platforms offer low-overhead locking mechanisms, such as a *futex* on Linux or *CriticalSection* on Windows. The basic idea is to check an atomic counter in the user space and spare the switch to the kernel context, if the mutex is free (also known as uncontended). In this way the uncontended case might be highly optimized!

So, remember—mutexes aren't slow *per se*, it is the contention that slows things down!

You might sometimes still see the *thundering herd* problem mentioned in conjunction with thread synchronization, but modern platforms do not suffer from that anymore. "Thundering herd" used to describe the situation where several threads were waiting on a lock and then all of them were woken up, although only one could acquire the lock and proceed.

QMutex implementation and performance

The Qt 5 mutex class internally employs the CAS optimization by using a pointer to internal mutex data in a special way. If that pointer is set to `0x00`, the mutex is unlocked. If it is set to `0x01`, the mutex is locked and there's no contention. Only in cases of contentions will a `QMutextPrivate` object be created, which will then put the thread to sleep using a `WaitForSingleObjectEx()` system call on Windows and a futex on Linux. Note that for recursive mode, the `QMutextPrivate` is always created, which explains its slower performance.

An interesting fact is that the `QMutextPrivate` will be detached when the contention has finished and will be stored in a global list to be reused later. So, we have the object pool optimization pattern here. The global list is again implemented as a lock-free stack, as it is assumed that there will only be a few `QMutextPrivate` objects in the system! We will have a look at lock-free structures subsequently.

A thing to be noted is that, because of this optimization, `QMutex` is faster than `std::mutex`! The explanation is that the latter always requires an underlying OS primitive to be used due to some wording in the standard.

Atomic operation costs

At least on the Intel architecture, atomic operations, also called **Cache Acceleration Software (CAS)**, are implemented by using the `LOCK` instruction prefix. In older Intel architectures, this would block the bus and thus all memory operations on all cores, incurring rather a high overhead on atomics. However, newer Intel processors will only block the relevant cache line, significantly reducing the costs.

Additionally, if we require a sequential memory ordering, a memory fence will be needed, flushing all the pending writes and stalling the pipeline. We can work around this in C++ using relaxed memory orderings, but we won't discuss this advanced topic further in this book.

As may be seen, atomic operation on modern systems is not very costly, but it isn't cost-free either.

Memory allocation costs

As we have already mentioned, in the old days the memory allocator's global lock was a single point of contention for all threads in systems. However, in all modern systems this is no longer a problem, as state-of-the-art allocators using local thread memory pools are used. Consult `Chapter 3`, *Deep Dive into C++ and Performance* for details on memory allocators.

Qt's signals and slots performance

In the Qt environment, we will often use signals and slots to communicate between threads, so let's take a closer look at the implementation and performance of this mechanism.

The signal slot mechanism use tables generated by the *moc* compiler. These tables are stored in `const` arrays that are placed in the shareable read-only data segment. The *moc*-generated code avoids dynamic allocations and tries to reduce relocations. Because of that, tables are static and there is nothing to be done on startup in order to set up the signal slot mechanism.

When sending a signal to a `QObject`, the connected slot will either be invoked immediately if the object lives in the same thread, or a so-called queued connection will be used to send the signal to a different thread.

When sending signals over a queued connection, an event will be put into the event list (a `QVector`) of the target thread, which is guarded by a `QMutex`. The receiver thread waits for new events arriving in that queue by using a `MsgWaitForMultipleObjectsEx()` system call on Windows and `ppoll()` on Linux. This means the receiver thread is put to sleep by the OS if there are no messages for it to process.

What about of the costs of emitting a signal in a synchronous connection? As the Qt documentation states (`http://doc.qt.io/qt-5/why-moc.html`):

> *While emitting a signal is approximately the cost of four ordinary function calls with common template implementations, Qt requires effort comparable to about ten function calls.*

We see that sending signals is not as fast as it could be! This is partly because their implementation focuses on safety and partly due to avoiding inlining in order not to leak internal implementation details in Qt's abstract binary interface (ABI). So, for a tight loop in a performance-critical portion of your code, signals and slots in the same thread could be a bad idea. Just use a direct function call instead.

Speeding up programs with threads

Now, we have N cores and would naturally expect that our program can be made to run N times faster. However, Amdahl's law sensibly states that this isn't possible, as the total speedup will always be limited by this part of the program that cannot be parallelized. Gustaffson's law somehow refutes this pessimistic outlook, stating that bigger systems will be able to solve bigger problems, while Amdahl's law assumes fixed problem sizes. We will spare the reader the exact formulas, but the conclusion from this theoretical work is that the possible speedups depend on the structures of the problems at hand.

After that theoretical underpinning, let's turn our attention to more practical matters and look at how we would go about speeding our program with threads, being well aware of this method's limitations.

Do not block the GUI thread

We already mentioned the first commandment of Qt programming, namely *thou shalt not block the GUI thread*. We can easily achieve that by starting a thread in the background every time we have an operation which would block the main event loop. That is easy, simple, and effective. Even better for the performance is to use `QRunnable` or `QtConcurrent`, which use one of the threads from the global pool.

Use the correct number of threads

The previously described scenario constitutes the very simplest of concurrency. What if we don't have an odd costly operation, but rather the total computational load is to be spread evenly over the available processor cores?

The optimal number of threads we can use is equal to the number of cores, because we will have to pay the price of thread context switches for any additional thread. The `QThreadPool` already allocates this number of threads, but if we do not want to use it, we can query this number by using the `QThread::idealThreadCount()` method, an equivalent to C++11's `std::thread::hardware_concurrency()` function.

However, if we are doing I/O, we can afford an additional I/O thread per core (that is, oversubscribing), simply because the thread will mostly be idle waiting on the triggered I/O operation to be finished.

Avoid thread creation and switching cost

As threads are heavy kernel-level objects, we'd like to avoid the costs of creating a thread for the execution of a single operation and dispose of it afterwards. For load-uncritical applications however, this might be acceptable (see the *Do not block the GUI thread* previous topic). As the reader probably already knows, we use thread pools for that purpose and Qt already provides us with its own `QThreadPool`.

However, another big cost that tends to be overlooked is the thread-switching overhead. To illustrate that, let's recount the story of Apache and NGINX web servers. In Apache's design, there was a thread-per-client connection which was serving all the communication with that client. NGINX could improve on Apache's performance by using a thread pool and multiplexing the handling of client interactions over the threads from the pool. In game programming, this idea is known as **task-based parallelism** and it can significantly improve performance by reducing the number of thread context switches. Because of that, it is sometimes also called **coarse-grained parallelism**.

Avoid locking costs

We already know that we shouldn't fear locks, but we'd like to avoid the costs of contentions. Let's look at a couple of techniques for doing that.

Fine-grained locks

We can decrease contentions between threads if we can minimize the time a thread spends keeping a lock. An example from the database programming is the difference between the locking of a whole table and the locking of single rows in that table.

A motivating example for this technique is the change of Windows OS kernel's Dispatcher database lock. This lock protected access to objects that needed to be scheduled such as threads, timers, I/O completion ports, and other waitable kernel objects. In Windows 7 the dispatcher database lock was replaced with fine-grained per-object locks. This resulted in one of the biggest performance boosts in Windows history, showing up to a 290% improvement on the SQL database TPC-C benchmark!

One example of how lock-keeping time can be optimized is a technique sometimes called shadow paging, as shown in the following code snippet:

```
QMap<QString, Employee> dataCopy;
{
  QMutexLocker guard(&mutex_);
  dataCopy = userData_;
}

// give raise to each employee, and so on...

{
  QMutexLocker guard(&mutex_);
  userData_ = dataCopy;
}
```

We see that first we acquire a lock, then we copy the data, and then release the lock. Now, any long-running operation can be done without blocking out other threads. At last, we can swap the old and new data under lock.

Lock coarsening

This looks like a contrary advice to the fine-grained locks previously. But it's not. It refers to a situation when we have two or more adjacent operations using locks on the same object, just as in the following example:

```
void appendData(const Data& d)
{
  QMutexLocker guard(&mutex_);
  collection.append(d);
}

void someOtherFunc()
```

```
{
  appendData({"aaa", ....});
  appendData({"bbb", ....});
  appendData({"ccc", ....});
}
```

It is only natural that we can replace the fine-grained lock with a more coarse one placed in `someOtherFunc()`. Sometimes, it is even applicable to different data, which is often used together.

But, there is also a general remark to be made at this point. Lock coarsening and the lowering of lock granularity are both sides of one coin—if your locks are too coarse, you have too much contention between threads, but if they are too fine-grained, you first risk producing deadlocks as you lose the overview over the composition of your locks. Also, you will induce too much overhead, decreasing the overall performance. The right path is rather narrow, and that is why coming up with a good locking scheme is hard!

Duplicate or partition resources

We can avoid contention on a single resource if we simply duplicate it! The idea is that at some point we will than merge them back again if we need a unifying view.

An example of such a design is the `ThreadCachedInt` multithreaded counter class implemented in Facebook's Folly library. The idea is that every thread holds an integer counter locally and the global counter is updated periodically. It has two read methods: `readFast()` returns a potentially stale value with one load, and `readFull()` gives the exact value, but is much slower as it has to synchronize with all threads' local counters. So, we sacrifice the accuracy of the counter for fast updates in the threads, opting for eventual consistency. If you can live with such a trade-off, then this may be a technique you can use.

Sometimes, however, we could truly partition some resource, taking inspiration from *sharding*, a technique used in the database field. Sharding works by physically partitioning database tables over several machines and defining a hash function, converting user names or IDs to the shard number. In that way, the requests get distributed to several physically independent machines. If there are no dependencies between data elements we could just as well partition it between parallel threads and spare us a mutex.

Another example could be duplicating some read-only data in several parallel structures to avoid lookups in a global table. On one side, this is a technique for improving the data locality, but if that global table had a mutex, we would also optimize away locking. In the field of database design, this is called **denormalization**.

Use concurrent data structures

Concurrent data structures are thread-safe data structures, which implement synchronized access to their data internally. There are several libraries implementing concurrent data structures such as Intel's TBB library or Microsoft's **Parallel Patterns Library** (**PPL**), which have already been mentioned several times. Typically, such implementations will use fine-grained locks internally. As Qt containers are not thread-safe, we could lower lock granularity using such libraries—a classic case of a *use a better library* optimization pattern!

However, notice that concurrent data structures come with an additional cost of locking! Therefore, as always, use concurrent data structures when the speedup from the additional concurrency outweighs their slower sequential performance!

Know your concurrent access patterns

As always, if we can somehow find a special case in our program, we can than optimize it against the general case using that extra knowledge. One such case is when a lock is accessed by threads in two different ways—either read-only or write-only.

If there are many readers and only a few, or maybe just one writer, we can optimize synchronization by using a reader-writer (also known as read-write) mutex, implemented in Qt by the QReadWriteLock class. This lock type will allow every reader to acquire it. If only other readers are holding it, though, the writer has to wait until all of the readers release it before it can get hold of it. In that manner, the readers won't block themselves on read-only operations.

If we have many more readers than writers, we can apply the big read lock (also known as the distributed lock) pattern to optimize the synchronization further. Each reader thread gets its own read-write lock and it takes its own lock for reading. A writer, however, has to take all the read-write locks if it wants to write. This favors the readers and makes the code less elegant, but all the reader threads will then work on their local lock cache line (if we are using atomic counter optimization) and the lock latency will be minimal in common cases!

As an aside note, QReadWriteLock has been optimized along the lines of QMutex since Qt 5.7.

Do not share any data

This is the simplest and best technique for lower locking costs because it does not need any locks at all! Always try to achieve this goal. We will discuss a variant of this approach in the section on sharing-nothing architectures.

Double-checked locking and a note on static objects

This is the original lock optimization pattern, which was then shown to be flawed due to compiler and CPU instruction reordering. In C++11 (and Qt), it can however be fixed. The original field where it emerged was the singleton implementation. The idea was that before we use a costly lock operation to initialize the singleton, we first peek to see if the initialization is needed at all. A naive implementation fails in general because of memory-ordering subtleties. Without much ado, the correct code would be as follows:

```cpp
class Singleton
{
  static QAtomicPointer<Singleton> instance_;
  static QMutex mutex_;
public:
  static Singleton *instance()
  {
    Singleton* inst = instance_.loadAcquire();
    if (!inst)
    {
      QMutexLocker guard(&mutex_);
      if (!instance_.load())
      {
        inst = new Singleton();
        instance_.storeRelease(inst);
      }
    }
    return inst;
  }
};
```

We check if there is already a singleton created using an atomic pointer operation. Note that we optimized the atomic access to the instance_ variable using the acquire-release memory ordering, which results in weaker memory fences. Confused? That's normal, since memory orderings in the context of multithreading are an advanced topic, which is full of pitfalls. Because of that, prefer correctness and use Meyer's singleton, std::call_once or Q_GLOBAL_STATIC, which we have already discussed in this chapter. However, if you are keen to learn more about the C++ memory model, the *Further reading* section provides some pointers.

Also note that function-local static variables, as employed in Meyer's singleton, are burdened with a synchronization overhead even in a single threaded case! Depending on the compiler, it can be as high as 5-10%, because the accesses must be guaranteed to be thread-safe. So, don't use it out of convenience on performance-critical paths!

Just switch to lock-free and be fine?

This is advice which will often be heard, but is it really a cure-all? There are stories to be heard about dramatic performance improvements when using lock-free algorithms! Let's first explain what lock-free techniques are and then analyze their performance implications.

The simplest example of a lock-free construct is a spinning lock: we are using a **compare and swap** (**CAS**) atomic processor instruction and trying to set an integer to some value. The CAS instruction will return the previous value of the integer and, if it was the same value we are trying to set, we know that the other thread already set the value and thus *acquired* it. In that case, we simply spin:

```
QAtomicInt val = 0;

// try to acquire
for(;)
{
  if(!val.testAndSet(0, 1))
    continue;
  else
    break; // acquired
}
```

In the example, we expect that the `val` variable has a value of zero and then change the value to reserve it for our use. We could even make it more performant by taking advantage of relaxed memory orderings. As we can see, this has the same functionality as an acquisition if it is a mutex, but we spare ourselves a kernel trip.

We can use this type of technique to implement lock-free, thread-safe data structures. For example, a simple queue would use two such spin locks for head and tail operations. However, before you start implementing your own lock-free data structures, we have to say that it has proved to be an extremely difficult and nonintuitive undertaking. One of the hardest problems in languages without garbage collection, such as C++, is the reclamation of unused memory, with solutions using fine-sounding names such as hazard pointers, **read-copy-update** (**RCU**), or Left-Right. And I didn't even start talking about the ABA problem. So, don't write your own, use a ready implementation like Boost's Lockfree library.

Lock-free performance

If we are sparing a kernel trip, this is a clear win, so we want to use it everywhere!

No so fast. First, we already mentioned that taking an uncontended mutex is a fast operation and the kernel trip is only needed if there is a contention. Second, the attentive reader will surely notice one big problem with CAS—yes, we are spinning, thus burning CPU power and exacerbating the contention even more!

We must mention that modern Intel processors have a special PAUSE instruction which can be added to the body of the spin and provide a hint to the CPU that the code being executed is a spin-wait loop. This will improve the performance of the spin somehow. We could further reduce spinning costs by using an exponential back-off strategy with a sleep() system call when waiting.

However, the advantage of the classic lock is that in such a case one of the contending threads will be put to sleep, thus diminishing contention, sparing CPU resources, and reducing cache pressure.

On the other hand, if we want to optimize latency, which refers to the reaction times for some events in the system, which may be necessary in real-time applications, we could spend some CPU power for CAS spinning to spare the kernel context switch on thread wake-up. This is the reason why some high-performance databases are using lock-free data structures as work queues (for example, in the way Scylla uses boost::lockfree::spsc_queue, that is as a single producer, single consumer queue).

In general though, if we want to optimize for throughput, concurrent data structures are the default choice.

Having said that, on some older systems where the OS mutexes aren't optimized for the no-contention case, we could earn some performance gains by wrapping it in an atomic variable. Also, the case where there is high contention but the contention periods are rather short (less than 1,000-2,000 cycles) would favor lock-free techniques as with, for example, a reader-writer scenario with lots of writes and short lock hold times.

In any case, the advice is to perform benchmarks with different data structures for a specific workload.

Progress guarantees

So, there is no clear winner performance-wise. The really big advantage of lock-free data structures is, however, a different one, namely the progress guarantees. Because every thread is in control of its own spinning, if we are clever, we can always avoid deadlocks and prevent priority inversions.

There are several levels of progress guarantees, which are sometimes also used as synonyms for the colloquially named lock-free algorithms: *non-blocking* (or *obstruction-free*) if the failure or suspension of any thread cannot cause the failure or suspension of another thread, *wait-free* if every operation in a program is guaranteed to complete in a finite number of steps, and *lock-free* if this guarantee also applies to single threads.

Messing with thread scheduling?

Normally the OS scheduler does a pretty good job scheduling our threads. However, operation systems offer possibilities to change their default scheduling, such as:

- **Changing thread priority**: If a thread has a higher priority, then it will be scheduled more often than other threads and therefore can use more CPU time. This can be important on real-time systems when we have to react to some event very quickly. However, with priorities comes the already mentioned priority inversion problem we have to cope with. The simplest remedy is not calling any other function which could use locks. For example, if your memory allocator uses a mutex at some stage, it can cause priority inversion! Thread priority can be changed in a portable manner with the `QThread::setPriority()` method.

- **Changing thread affinity**: Setting thread affinity tells the operating system that we want to *pin* a thread to a specific processor or core. Why would we like to do it? Because we can improve the cache usage in that way—by placing two threads operating on the same memory on the same core, we could ensure that the cache will stay warm and get reused in both threads.
  However, there is a downside to pinning threads to cores as it can result in threads receiving less CPU time, because (at least on Windows) the scheduler is then restricted from running them on certain processors or cores. So, in general, it is better to let the kernel select the core to run on.
  Thread affinity can be changed with `SetThreadAffinityMask()` on Windows and `sched_setaffinity()` on Linux. There's no portable Qt or C++ STL function for that.

Although these techniques do look really cool, they are reserved only for rather a few special cases. Start by trusting that your OS will optimally schedule your threads.

Use a share nothing architecture

As we already know the best method for reducing synchronization costs is not needing any synchronization at all. This can be easily achieved by not sharing any data between threads. Simple? But, is it also realistic? In a real program we have dependencies between its parts, so we have to share some data in any case!

We can solve that conundrum using a method we already introduced—duplicating resources. This means all the data which one thread needs from another will be simply copied and then given to that thread. In that manner, both threads won't share any data, and won't need to use locks!

The **share nothing principle** is borrowed from the Erlang programming language and ecosystem, which in turn implements the **actor model** of parallel programming. Actors are independent objects running in their own threads of control, communicating with other actors over messages.

What makes this model so appealing is its lack of data sharing, and thus the absence of synchronization and locking! However, there are other overheads to be taken into account—that of copying data and of communication between objects. Another problem is the heavy nature of threads—we can only have a couple of them in a program and that's not enough to give one to each actor. But, we could take this as an inspiration and partition our application using worker threads with input queues.

Maybe not always, but sometimes you can structure your application in that manner as, for example, in the already mentioned *task-based parallelism* technique from the field of game programming.

Implementing a worker thread

There is some good news—Qt already has all we need in that respect. Just use a `QThread` with an event loop!

If we refuse to use the thread event loop then we have to implement it using a `QThread` or `std::thread`, using one of two alternatives for its input queue:

- **Traditional container guarded by a mutex**: This is what the Qt event-dispatching mechanism already provides! We would have the worker wait for new requests using a `QWaitCondition`, which internally would probably also use some `MsgWaitForObject` call, so there would be no big difference here. However, we could replace `QVector` by `QList` or another data structure which would be more performance-friendly in this case.

- **A lock-free data structure**: A lock free data structure could work better than `QMutex`, because the latter does not spin on the atomic value and only does a single check. But this depends on your workload. Note that a single-reader, single-writer, lock-free queue is an often-seen suggestion these days.

We see that there are some performance gains to be earned but, as a default, a `QWorker` running an event loop is a solid choice.

On the other hand, even using a custom lock-free queue data structure could be suboptimal because of the contention encountered on the head and tail of the queue. An advanced design for a worker thread input queue is offered by the *LMAX Disruptor* pattern. It is a ring buffer structure additionally using sequencing to achieve better performance than the traditional queues. You might like to look it up to expand your horizons.

Active object pattern

Active object pattern wraps an asynchronous operation in an object containing a worker thread and a request input queue. Thus it can be seen as another name for the actor pattern. A known example is the wrapping of asynchronous writes to a log file with an active object to offload logging to a background thread as in the following example:

```
class AsyncLogFile
{
public:
  void write(const QString& str)
  {
    // we use a lambda taking a copy of the data with it
    a_.send( [=] { log_.write(str); } );
  }
private:
  SyncLogFile log_; // log file
  ActiveObject a_;   // helper (queue+thread)
};

AsyncLogFile logFile;
logFile.write(" text text text ... ");
```

A drawback of this technique is that we waste one whole thread for a single type of task, but for I/O operations this can be justifiable because that thread would be mostly sleeping. Also, note that sending a lambda through `std::function` incurs a cost of one memory allocation (type erasure used in `std::function`)—this is the cost of a general implementation in this case.

Command queue pattern

In the previous technique, we have one dedicated tread doing all the work posted to its input queue. A variant of this scheme would be an active object without a dedicated thread.

When a thread would like to do some operation on the object it would insert a command into the input queue of the object (in this case called command queue), lock it, and start processing the command. When another thread wants to access the object but sees that its command queue is not empty, it will just enqueue its command and finish processing. The first thread would then look up the command queue and if it's not empty it would process the next command.

In that way, we avoid the other threads waiting on a mutex, but also avoid a single dedicated thread working on that object. It can, for example, be applied in the case of network communication where the object worked on could be a connection.

Beyond threading

We have seen that concurrency is a rather deep and difficult topic and it rightly deserves the *Concurrency is hard* label. Can we not do any better? Are threads the last word in concurrency?

Well no. There are a couple of other approaches and we will have a brief look at them just to give the reader some broader perspective of what to expect in the future.

User-space scheduling

As we already said, threads are a rather heavy abstraction! The alternative is to use lightweight threads, that is threads which are scheduled in user space to avoid the thread context switch costs. Languages such as Erlang and Go use that approach and can achieve massive concurrency which makes implementations of actor-based *share nothing* models feasible.

At the OS level Windows offers fibers, which are units of execution that must be manually scheduled by the application. There are also libraries implementing fibers for C++, for example, Boost.Fibers.

Transactional memory

Because locks do not compose (remember the composability problems?), researchers were trying to provide synchronization mechanisms that would be composable. One such proposal that obtained some traction was the concept of transactional memory. It is best explained with an example from the relevant C++ proposal:

```
int f()
{
  static int i = 0;
  atomic_noexcept
  {
    // begins transaction
    ++i;
    return i; // commits
  }
}
```

As we may see, a transactional memory clause allows a group of load and store instructions to execute in an atomic way, and thus either succeed or fail. If another transaction updates some of the variables used by this transaction, changes will be silently retried. The abstraction of atomicity in transactional memory requires a hardware mechanism to detect conflicts and undo any changes made to shared data.

Tansactional memory programs produce a deadlock, but may still suffer from livelock or starvation. This is not a cure all but it is definitely a great help.

Continuations

At the moment, we cannot compose and chain the futures either in the C++ standard library or in its Qt implementation. However, there are implementations allowing this, such as Microsoft's Concurrency Runtime for C++. Here is a usage example from C++ REST-SDK, which uses it to implement asynchronous network and file processing:

```
auto fileStream = std::make_shared<ostream>();
// open stream to output file
pplx::task<void> requestTask =
  fstream::open_ostream(U("results.html"))
    .then ([=](ostream outFile)
```

```
    {
        *fileStream = outFile;
        ....
        return client.request(methods::GET, .... );
    })
    .then ([=](http_response response)
    {
        // save reponse data to file
        return response.body().read_to_end(fileStream->streambuf());
    })
    .then ([=](size_t)
    {
        return fileStream->close();
    })
    );

    // wait for complete operation
    requestTask.wait();
```

We see, each operation is executed as a separate task and returns *n* future, which can be forwarded to a next `then()` clause. Tasks are then internally scheduled on a thread pool and executed asynchronously.

This is very handy for chaining simple sequences of operations but with alternatives and exceptions being thrown, it can get complicated quickly. Nonetheless, it's a nice improvement over manually connecting features and dispatching them for execution.

Coroutines

Coroutines are an old concept from mainframe days that have pulled off a kind of comeback recently. Coroutines, formerly known as **C++ resumable functions**, offer a possibility to suspend a function and than reenter it. You can see that this is similar to manually scheduled fibers or lightweight threads. In the C++ proposal, we have keywords like: `co_yield` to pause and publish some computed value, `co_return` to finish the coroutine and return a result, and `co_await` to wait for a result from another coroutine.

Coroutines with `co_await` offer a possibility to escape the *continuations hell* and to arrive at a much more readable code, as in the following example:

```
std::future<unsigned> dummyReadFromTcp(unsigned size)
{
    std::array<char, 4096> buffer;
    auto conn = co_await connectTcp("127.0.0.1", 8018);
    for(;;)
    {
```

```
      unsigned = co_await conn.read(buffer.data(), buffer.size());
      total-= bytes_read;
      if (total<= 0 || bytes_read== 0)
        co_return total;
  }
}
```

Here, the other asynchronous code invoked is cleanly placed behind `co_await` and looping is no problem either. The scheduling of the coroutines is done by the runtime system. I must say this looks rather promising!

Summary

In this chapter, we covered a lot of stuff, but concurrency is one of most important and, sadly, one of the most difficult and error-prone topics in programming.

We started with the basics, namely with what threads, mutexes, and atomics are. Then we learned the unfortunate fact that the use of mutexes can lead to several problems such as: deadlocks, livelocks, starvation, priority inversion, convoying, and false sharing. Fortunately, these problems can be avoided with some care. We then progressed to evaluating the performance costs of using threads and mutexes and of their alternative, namely lock-free data structures. In the next section, we learned what thread support classes Qt provides and how they integrate with its signal-slot mechanism. After that, we proceeded to multithreading optimization techniques—first, we learned how to decrease thread construction and context-switching costs and then how to decrease synchronization costs by the clever usage (or absence) of locking.

With this chapter, we have finished the first part of this book, which was intended to give the reader an overview of the generic performance principles as applied to the Qt framework.

In the next chapter, we will tell some stories about performance fails seen in the wild in order to illustrate and corroborate the general performance principles we have learned in the first chapters. After that, we will at last delve into a performance evaluation of the most important Qt modules.

Questions

As usual, here are some questions to test and maybe deepen your understanding of the material in this chapter.

1. Why is a data race an **undefined behavior** (**UB**) in C++?
2. What does **resource acquisition is initialization** (**RAII**) mean? (we have seen it already in `Chapter 3`, *Deep Dive into C++ and Performance*) and how it can be used in `QAtomicLocker`?
3. Why can `volatile` variables not be used to prevent race conditions?
4. What are spurious wakes and why aren't they banned?
5. Assume you are an OS (or some tool) and have just detected a deadlock. What could you do to resolve it?
6. What is cache ping-pong?
7. If you define slots in a `QThread` subclass, what do you think will happen when they get invoked by a signal?
8. What do you think, the Windows system call `InitializeCriticalSectionAndSpinCount()` could do?
9. What do you understand about using `QProcess` instead of `QThread`?
10. What does the phrase *flushing all the pending writes and stalling the pipeline* from the subsection on atomic instruction costs really mean?

Further reading

Is Parallel Programming Hard, And, If So, What Can You Do About It? by *Paul E. McKenney* (2017) is a comprehensive free PDF book available from `http://kernel.org/pub/linux/kernel/people/paulmck/perfbook/perfbook.html`. It discusses the low-level parallel techniques from the Linux and C-language angles, including atomics, mutexes, and **read-copy-update** (**RCU**) synchronization.

What really happened on Mars by *Glenn E. Reeves* (1997) is a short write-up available at `https://cs.unc.edu/~anderson/teach/comp790/papers/mars_pathfinder_long_version.html` and is a description of a real-life case of priority inversion in the Mars Pathfinder's software.

C++ Concurrency in Action by *Anthony Williams Manning* (2012) is a detailed guide to C++11's concurrency and multithreading support. It discusses language level constructs such as C++ memory model, memory orderings, and atomic operations, and also standard library thread and concurrency classes. A discussion of the design of lock-free and concurrent data structures is also included.

If you'd like to delve deeper into memory orderings and lock-free data structures, Jeff Preshing's homepage (`https://preshing.com/`) is a good starting point as well.

And last but not least, just read the Qt code! It's open source and there is a good code browser for Qt 5 at `https://code.woboq.org/qt5/`, so do not be afraid to consult it.

6
Performance Failures and How to Overcome Them

In this chapter, we will go through an array of performance problems that have been encountered recently by the author in his programming work—either caused by himself or by others. They all seem to fall under the same label of being basic, but that's what most performance problems are like in the real world – trivial, once you've spotted them. These problems are those that the author can recall because he either had to correct them or has heard about them in more detail.

This isn't a catalog of all possible performance fails (can such a thing exist?) but rather a list of real-life problems as opposed to artificial examples that we could set up as an alternative. I believe that a real-life touch is more important than any attempt at an exhaustive catalog. These problems will also show you in which unexpected places performance problems can crop up.

This chapter will discuss, among other, the following examples of performance fails:

- Wasting CPU time for ineffective searches
- The case of slowly opening windows
- HTTP file transfers slowing down
- Slow program startup times
- Display stalls with Qt Quick and Qt Widgets
- Overly academic system design

Linear search storm

This problem was encountered while working on a carefully designed multithreaded program, but it didn't have anything to do with the **multithreading is hard** mantra.

Context

I encountered this problem in a project that decoded satellite stream data and saved the detected contents to files. The system was supposed to be running 24/7 and to cope with the live data streams, they were delivered directly from a rather big satellite antenna. The program was supposed to run on a well-equipped Windows server, so machine power shouldn't have been a problem. The Qt framework was chosen for this project as a kind of portability layer.

I designed the architecture according to the *share nothing* principle. The program was structured as a graph of worker threads, which would read data from two separate input streams: data in the up and down direction. The idea was to decode transport protocols, combine the streams, decode the application layer protocols, and finally save the extracted contents to disc.

According to the optimization hints we learned about in the previous chapter, the program had two reader threads, two decoding threads – one each for the transport and application layer protocols – and a single content saving thread, thus oversubscribing on I/O threads. All the workers had a bounded input queue (synchronized on a mutex first), where the data to be processed was inserted by the preceding worker using a pointer to avoid copying the data. The thread graph per satellite input stream pair would look like this:

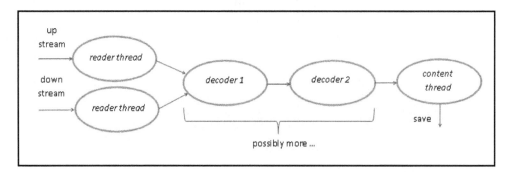

As we can see, I had set up a *shared nothing* message passing system, implemented coarse-grained parallelism for several decoding stages, and the protocols were being shared in the same worker thread context according to the number of cores. What could possibly go wrong?

As an aside, I tried to pin the reader threads to a specific CPU, but it didn't improve performance. Instead, the results even got slightly worse, so in the end it turned out that leaving the scheduling of workers to the OS was a better decision.

Problem

When I tested the ready system with the live data from the satellite antenna, there were no apparent problems – the system was able to hold pace with the data and the contents were saved to the disk without much contention. As I mentioned earlier, the machine we used was a nice middle-class server blade and it coped with the load fine.

Because there weren't any evident problems, I decided to have a closer look at the system and find out where its bottlenecks were. When I attached a profile (I think it was GlowCode back then) to the program, I was surprised, and somehow horrified to discover that most of the system's time was spent in the std::find() function. The program was clearly burning CPU cycles doing some needless and repetitive work!

An analysis of the problem yielded the following results:

- The lookups happened to concentrate on the vector storing descriptions of the **Transmission Control Protocol (TCP)** and **User Datagram Protocol (UPD)** connections in the application layer decoder
- The transport layer decoder sent data it retrieved for a pair of IP endpoints, and then this data had to be associated with a running TCP or UDP data stream to be decoded further

However, the connection descriptions were stored in a vector, which was then searched linearly!

Why's that a problem? In Chapter 4, *Using Data Structures and Algorithms Efficiently*, we said that the $O(n)$ complexity is one of the good guys! (Well, not always.) In our case, it dominated the runtime instead of the actual workhorses – the decoding methods!

Solution

The reason for choosing a linear algorithm was that in the recorded test data that I started the implementation with, there were only a few connections present. However, with live data streams, there were suddenly hundreds and thousands of them! Where did they record the test data? I don't know, but the real data was anything but that! That amount of connections was far too much for any linear algorithm to cope with.

The solution was, of course, simple – just to use a better data container. At first, I considered something fancy like a priority tree that keeps the last recently used data item close to the top, but then I renounced that idea following the guideline that we already learned about –avoid fancy data structures most of the time. Instead, I just used a `std::map` to reduce lookup times to *O(log n)*. We won't use a hash table because of the **keep it simple, stupid (KISS)** principle – at that time, C++ didn't have a standard hash table, and I didn't want to use Qt containers in the system.

This change resulted in an instant drop of lookup costs, and then the functions that showed up on top of the CPU profiler data were those that had to do the most work – the real decoding functions!

Conclusion

Linear algorithms are OK with small data collections. For bigger problems, try to go down to *O(log n)* or, even better, *O(1)*. The second insight is that even if there's no apparent problem, it is always worth taking a look at the performance profile of the program, just to make sure that it is working as expected.

Last but not least: a programmer can be easily misled about where to expect bottlenecks and performance problems. Because of that, measure your program's behavior!

Results dialog window opening very slowly

This problem wasn't very complicated but it was rather serious and its solution was somehow embarrassing, so let's have a look at it.

Context

I was developing a program for migrating some application's data from the legacy format to the format used by its newest version. Needless to say, I had to provide a UI for it as well, so I wrote a modern-looking slim GUI using QtWidget. There was a start screen where the migration process could be parameterized and started, the status screen where the progress of the operation was visualized, and the result window where detailed information about each of the migration subtasks would be given.

Problem

The application ran very well; I only had to do some GUI cosmetics and solve one annoying problem: when opening the results window, it sometimes froze for an annoyingly long time. In the results, the program showed the newly constructed resources, as well as the logs that were written during the migration process. All of this data was visualized as tables using the basic `QTableWidget`. For simplicity's sake, we didn't use view and model classes of Qt, because once the migration was done, all the data would be static.

Solution

At first, I suspected that the usage of the rather inefficient `QTableWidget` class and manually inserting widget items instead of using `QTableView` would be the culprit, but it turned out to be a totally different problem.

I asked my buddy to make the last few changes to the UI cosmetics and to have a quick look at the slow window loading times. Guess what? The problem didn't even need a profiler. Using the *poor man's profiling* technique (see `Chapter 2`, *Profiling to Find Bottlenecks*, for details), namely, getting a couple of stack traces manually using Process Explorer, the reason for the problem became clear – the `resizeToContents()` method was being called for the table after each new row had been added. As we can recall from our discussion of algorithms, this turned filling the log table into an $O(n^2)$ problem.

After the problem had been identified, the solution was trivial – just move the call to `resizeToContents()` out of the loop.

Conclusion

Sometimes, it's just a simple bug, a moment where you don't pay attention. Well, *errare humanum est* – to err is human. From this, we can also see that it became once again apparent that a programmer's intuitions about the causes of performance problems cannot be trusted.

Increasing HTTP file transfer times

This was a very hard problem to diagnose and find out about. I have to admit that the other problems may be unexpected, but they aren't very hard to solve – however this one was. It was only down to my persistence at finding a solution that led me to cracking it in the end.

Context

I was implementing a HTTP server for an application written in Qt that would add a **Representational State Transfer (REST)** interface to a redesigned product for my customer. The new release should have transformed their, as yet desktop-only and Windows-only application into a cross-platform, distributed, client-server application using an HTTP API for communication.

The specifics of my customer's application domain was that it repeatedly required several big file transfers to the HTTP server. I chose an open source HTTP framework containing server and client code that used Windows completion ports internally, thus promising good performance in that respect. After we had used it for some time, we were quite happy with its performance and reliability.

Problem

The problem that hit us came quite unexpectedly after we let the program run some long test scenarios to stress the server.

The trouble was that, after a couple of thousands of file uploads or downloads, the server's performance tumbled into a free fall. The same basic HTTP polling scenario that had normally taken 2-3% of the CPU time surged to 20-30% after that! That was a real showstopper at first because our customers would use the server exactly like that. And of course, it wasn't our code that showed up in the profiler – it was some of the used open source framework's internals.

It was the ultimate worst-case scenario – do we have to rewrite all of the HTTP and REST stuff now? After all, we wanted to ship in a couple of months!

After I ran some tests myself, I could observe that, upon taking a closer look, after every file transfer, the next one took a little longer. Due to this, I just commented out all of our processing and only left the naked file transfer since this was done in the framework. See the following performance profile of a test run to see what we mean:

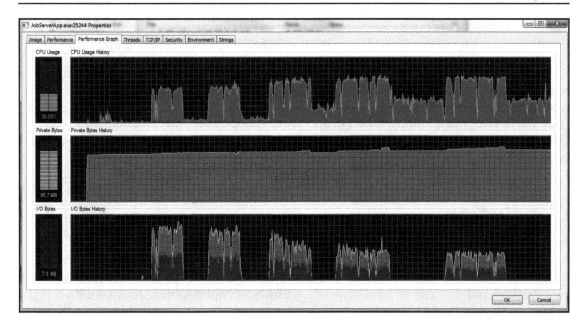

The shown performance profile was created with an older version of the Process Explorer tool that we introduced in Chapter 2, *Profiling to Find Bottlenecks*. In the uppermost pane, we can see that the CPU usage continuously increases for each set of transferred files.

Solution

It took me about 2 weeks to investigate this thoroughly using Visual Studio profiler and thread visualization tools, but in the end, it was just a question of starting the debugger and finding out things about the implementation. Fortunately, I had the source code of the framework and libraries it used.

The framework in question used Windows Concurrency Runtime, which at the time was the native, task-based implementation of Windows' **Parallel Patterns Library** (**PPL**). Do you remember task-based parallelism from Chapter 5, *An In-depth Guide to Concurrency and Multithreading*? It turned out that the Concurrency Runtime was left with an ever-growing internal list, which was sequentially scanned with each tick of the scheduler. This, of course, killed performance when there were a couple of thousand entries in the list. Remember the linear search storm case we discussed previously? Sounds similar, doesn't it?

Frankly, I didn't figure out there may be an error in the Concurrency Runtime or if it simply wasn't designed for use cases such as ours, that is, for long-running server applications.

I reported it to the tech giant that authored the framework, and they reacted pretty quickly – the next release included the option to disable Concurrency Runtime usage and to switch over to the Windows Thread Pool-based implementation of the PPL. I got the latest version from the development branch, tested it, and voilà! Our performance problems vanished into thin air. We then waited for the next release and, when it came out, we upgraded our code to it and suddenly everything worked like a charm.

Conclusion

Sometimes, there isn't a simple solution; for example if the library – or worse, your operating system – has a bug! In such a case, you either file a bug report and hope for a quick reaction or you must choose a different implementation. If you are lucky, there might be a workaround. Life can be hard sometimes! However, open source software allows you at least to diagnose your problems.

Secondly, you have to test your product extensively because problems can lurk in places you wouldn't expect them to! Last but not least, performance problems may be hard sometimes, and can only be solved with equally hard work!

Loading SVGs

This problem is an example of applied creative problem solving and thus one of my favorites. Although the optimal solution wasn't viable under the given circumstances, some satisfactory measure could still be found and applied with relatively little effort.

Context

In an embedded project I was working on once, we had a problem with startup times, which is quite normal in embedded development. Besides the usual Linux kernel and *uboot* optimizations, we noticed that the SVG images we were using were slowing down the startup phase.

Let me spend a few words on this project's history first. At the beginning, the requirement for this project was that we should seamlessly scale the screen to different device sizes. Later, that was changed and the project was set up on a fixed sized screen device, thus rendering (no pun intended) this requirement useless. However, a bulk of code was already written and the used icons had already been ordered and paid for.

Problem

The SVG images alone weren't the problem; instead, the overall setup of the application was, so to speak, somehow inefficient. The embedded device could be operated in a number of modes, and each of the modes had several swipeable screens. As the application didn't use QML, the swiping was implemented manually on top of a *QtWidgets* UI by composing all screens of a mode in one long widget, of which only a part would be visible at a given time. Even worse, all the screens for all the modes were created at startup and hidden, except for the one for the current mode!

When we added the usage of SVG images, which are stored as an XML description of the contents and must be read from a file and parsed before they can be displayed, all of these screens with all of their icons and images were too much for the embedded hardware that the project had at its disposal. To boot, the competitor's device was a couple of times faster and the date of an important fete was approaching quickly!

Solution

The obvious solution, that is, replacing all of the images with fast-loading bitmaps, was out of the question due to a lack of time and also because of the sunken costs fallacy. Thus, *the better algorithm/data structure* strategy was not possible. The next strategy that offered itself up was *caching* the already rendered SVG icons. Due to this, we employed the caching technique and avoided needless repetition of work, that is, opening and parsing the SVG icon files:

1. First, we created a cache for the SVG icons using the `QSvgRenderer` class for reading and parsing the XML files:

    ```
    QMap<QString, QSvgRenderer*> svgMap_;

    auto iter = svgMap_.constFind(path);
    if (iter == svgMap_.constEnd())
    {
       iter = svgMap_.insert(path, new QSvgRenderer(path));
    }
    ```

2. The SVG widget got subclassed to use the loaded and parsed data for painting:

```cpp
class MySvgWidget : public QSvgWidget
{
  ...
  void useCache(const QString& path, SvgCache& cache)
  {
    cachedSvg_ = cache.getChachedContents(path);
  }

  void paintEvent(QPaintEvent *event) override
  {
    if(cachedSvg_)
    {
      QPainter p(this);
      cachedSvg_->render(&p);
    }
  ...
```

Here, we only read and parse an SVG file once and then reuse its contents for all icons. Note that we need the renderer instance as we cannot simply copy an SVG widget in Qt. You can find a full example program in this book's resources (`https://github.com/PacktPublishing/Hands-On-High-performance-with-QT/tree/master/Chapter%206`).

Conclusion

We have seen that the solution isn't optimal, but it can be used quite seamlessly with the existing code as it removed the biggest performance hit, that is, reading and parsing the SVG file. Another insight here is that sometimes the overly generic requirements cannot be simply removed at a later stage in the project and that some creative workarounds are needed.

Quadratic algorithm trap

This one isn't a problem I encountered myself – instead, I read about it in a recent blog post. However, I liked it so much that I have to retell it here!

Context

When investigating heap corruption on Windows, you can turn on pageheap so that the Windows heap puts each allocation on a separate page so that use-after-free and buffer overruns become instant crashes instead of unfathomable corruptions. This can be enabled using the standard Microsoft Application Verifier tool (for details consult `https://docs.microsoft.com/en-us/windows-hardware/drivers/debugger/appl ication-verifier`), which was done to investigate heap corruption for a Chrome build with unexpected effects!

Problem

A build run of Chrome is pretty big, and sometimes requires starting the compiler about 30,000 times! But after the page heap had enabled the build time, which normally takes 5 to 10 minutes, the build time suddenly increased to an incredible 10 hours!

It turns out that Application Verifier will create a log file for each run it does. Each log file needs to have a unique name. This was implemented by scanning all of the existing log files and finding the next free number. However, this means that at each start of the compiler, on average *30,000 * 30,000 / 2, 450* million file existence checks have to be performed! This does indeed scale rather badly!

Solution

Instead of just numbering the files consecutively, a simple timestamp would also be acceptable. Another solution would be a file containing the current log counter. This is nothing exciting, but it works.

Conclusion

Sometimes, the totally obvious and innocuous choice will be the wrong one! Try to think about algorithmic complexity and avoid $O(n^2)$ and maybe even $O(n)$ solutions.

This is another example of choosing a nonoptimal algorithm, but this time it is presenting itself in a nonobvious setting. The special twist to it is that, in real life, this solution is acceptable, but not very common – I think I implemented a similar log file numbering scheme in the past! It seems that you never know at which point you'll need to scale.

Stalls when displaying widget with QML contents

This problem was already solved when I joined the project at hand, but it is a rather typical scenario, so we will have a look at it here.

Context

In one Qt 5 project, we had a rather complicated GUI displaying an image in several different processing stages. As is often the case in image-processing applications, the user could define a **region of interest** (**ROI**) – typically a circle or a rectangle – to restrict an image operation to some part of the image. The ROI was displayed over the image and could be interactively moved and resized.

The ROI was implemented in QML because of the ease with which moving and resizing could be programmed. It was embedded into the standard `QtWidget` interface using the `QQuickWidget` class, which read and rendered the top level `RoiRootWindow.qml` file. In fact, both the current image and the existing ROI were displayed using QML, with the image as a background and ROI as a QML item.

Problem

The **Open Graphics Library** (**OpenGL**, `https://www.opengl.org/`) is a standard API for hardware-accelerated graphics (we will look at it in more detail in Chapter 8, *Optimizing Graphical Performance*). In Qt 5, QML content is rendered with an OpenGL-based scene graph. Unfortunately, some of the supported graphic cards that were opening an OpenGL context on Windows meant it was a very slow operation—it could take up to 1 second! Context-switching times were also slow.

Now, we can see the problem—since we had a `QQuickWidget` displaying QML for each stage of the processing pipeline, for any new stage the user was adding, a new OpenGL context had to be opened, slowing down the whole operation. The startup times when loading longer image processing pipelines weren't very good either. This is because each `QQuickWidget` manages its own OpenGL context.

Solution

In the early days of Qt 5, QML could be only rendered using OpenGL, so switching to the raster paint engine unfortunately wasn't an option. Thus, an easy solution wasn't possible. I suppose that on Qt 4 that solution worked because QML wasn't rendered with OpenGL and only when porting the application to a newer Qt version did the problem surface.

This was a typical case of a costly operation avoidance strategy. It was decided to have only one `QQuickWidget` displaying QML, thus opening only a single context, and using this widget only to display the contents of the processing stage that currently had the focus. All other stages would use a second implementation for displaying ROIs in a static way.

Of course, this complicated the implementation considerably as the ROI display widgets had to be switched and the QML data had to be forwarded to the static widget when the user focused on another processing stage in the GUI, but the performance problem was resolved with it.

Conclusion

Sometimes, you cannot afford to use as many resources as you can – sometimes, you have to do a complicated dance and make do with that what you have. In this case, we must share the pool of resources we can afford between many users. An analogous situation can be seen in SQL programming where we'd like to reuse the pool of a database connection because opening a connection is also a costly operation.

Secondly, the upgrade to a newer Qt version normally sped up QML rendering but, alas, not for that application. From this, we have learned that we cannot foresee the performance impacts of such upgrades, particularly when it comes to them interacting with older hardware.

Too many items in view

This was, again, a not-so-advanced problem, but it appeared quite unexpectedly and actually shouldn't even be possible!

Context

A couple of years ago, I was working on a system for measuring mobile radio transmission parameters. It was originally written in Microsoft's **Microsoft Foundation Class** (**MFC**) framework and we were porting it to Qt and adding some new capabilities along the way. As the system was quite complicated, the UI was rather advanced too, but was working quite decently.

Problem

The only problem that manifested itself from time to time was an extremely long switching time for a certain (not very complicated) measurement's tab. At first, I ignored it and blamed the MFC code that was apparently blocking Windows message pump, but after this error started showing up more regularly, I decided to investigate it properly.

As it turned out, this special measurement displayed a list of possible frequencies to be chosen from as a `QTableView`. When I programmed it, it didn't look very grave – how many frequencies could there be for a measurement? However, when I was testing, it turned out that these frequencies were set in another, seemingly unrelated measurement tab. Did I mention that the application was rather complicated? The user would define a measurement range, but the default step was 0.1 Hz. Thus, for some greater measurement ranges, this amounted to literally thousands of frequencies to be shown! Even if that wouldn't make sense for a measurement, this was a legitimate choice and should be displayed in another tab!

Solution

We will look at problems with scaling the model-view classes in one of the following chapters when discussing graphical performance, namely in Chapter 8, *Optimizing Graphical Performance,* but we can already say at this point that they scale to hundreds – but certainly not thousands—of items! This means that we clearly had too many items being displayed.

There are techniques to mitigate such situations, and we will learn about them in due course, but in that particular system, such big numbers of frequencies simply didn't make any sense. So, the solution could also be viewed as a mere hack—we just limited the number of frequencies to about 100, and then displayed a warning if there was more than that. Call it a hack or call it pragmatic problem solving—it works.

Conclusion

Sometimes, you just cannot anticipate how many items will end up being displayed in your view! Here, we can once again see that programmers are notoriously bad at estimating the bottlenecks of their systems! Thus, testing your application and measuring its performance is of paramount importance.

Two program startup stories

These are two small stories that don't deserve a section of their own, so just like in a best performance optimization manner, they will be batched together (pun intended!).

Time system calls

This one happened a long time ago when computers didn't have much CPU power at their disposal. I was only told about this after I joined a project as part of the project's history. At that time, we were developing a Windows GUI application with MFC for the management of **Asymmetric Digital Subscriber Line** (**ADSL**) endpoints.

To cut a long story short, our program suffered from long startup times in the past. The reason turned out to be quite simple, if not to say dumb. The trace subsystem needed a timestamp for each line and issued a system call to get it each time. Or was it a timeout control that was done by reading the time in some tight loop? I can't recall the exact usage pattern anymore (sorry!), but the reason was clear – there were too many system calls to get the current time! After removing them, the performance problems vanished.

Font cache

This problem appeared in a very recent embedded Linux Qt project. This time, it wasn't a problem in any tight loop – instead, it was occurring in the startup time of the Qt application. As it turned out, our embedded Linux image had a couple of thousands fonts installed by default, and upon startup, listing them and creating a cache took a long time.

The funny thing was that we only used our own special font in the application! The solution we chose was to create a font cache on the first startup of the new application's binary instead of just reusing it. However, we could also turn off the usage of the Linux font cache and switch to custom rendered Qt fonts. Due to this being more work for us, we chose not to do it.

Conclusion

These two problems illustrate that system calls can sometimes have a very high cost. Be wary of them!

Hardware shutting down after an error message

This isn't as much a performance fail as a lowly bug, but it illustrates an important principle in an unexpected way.

Context

There was an embedded Qt project I was working on that didn't have any error propagation and display facilities. At some point, we were forced to add it to the system, and I had to write it. It wasn't very difficult, as it required reading and showing the error message in a modal error dialog.

Problem

After the **Continuous Integration** (**CI**) build's new release and the testers had installed it onto their test devices, a stupid problem became apparent. If a message from the hardware came up, the system would go into emergency mode and shut down! What? The system would become practically inoperable!

It turned out that the heartbeat function that reported to the hardware that the UI was well and alive was being run in the main GUI thread. When that thread was blocked, the hardware wouldn't get its heartbeat messages and would shut the system down, as it was specified to do.

Solution

So, it was the known dictum: *Never block the GUI thread*, only backwards—*Never expect that the GUI thread won't be blocked*! The solution was, of course, running the hardware heartbeat function in a separate thread.

If you are dealing with hardware, don't be afraid of threads! This can serve as a good example of the generic software principle, that is, "separation of concerns" – your UI thread is supposed to be super-responsive so that the user doesn't get the impression that your application is slow. So, anything that has a different purpose, such as communication with the hardware, has to be put in a separate thread by default!

I learned that the team tried to do this in the past, but had been bitten by some signal and slots problem, so they simply reverted the changes. A stupid mistake or a symptom of a good enough software? It's up to you to decide.

Conclusion

We have already learned that the basic *never block the GUI tread* guideline always has to be followed – well, except when you are required to block it. In that case, the event loop stalls, so don't forget that! Secondly, apparently not every programmer can use the somehow idiosyncratic `QThread` mechanisms, but if you are still reading this book, you can probably do this now!

Overly generic design

Remember when I said that I'd retell the recent performance fail cases? Well, I lied a little. This one is really old and uses a technology you have probably never heard of, but it's instructive anyway. Bear with me.

Context

This problem occurred ages ago, in the time when the **Common Object Request Broker Architecture** (**CORBA**) was still fashionable. What is CORBA, you ask? Back then, it was a distributed object communication protocol – this was quite a nice idea, as you'd not only be able to compose your program out of some objects living locally on your computer but also on other computers somewhere in the network. I was working on a project at a big telecommunications company then, on a big network management system that had adopted CORBA as its communication layer.

Problem

The system had been designed along the lines of object-oriented design, and so the objects had exposed their methods to the remote objects in a well-crafted manner. If only there weren't any nasty performance problems! In a word, the system ended up being so slow that it was practically unusable!

The overhead that was incurred by communication proved to be detrimental, as the exported object interfaces were far too fine-grained to be used in a sensible way from remote machines.

Solution

The solution was a kind of overreaction – although the CORBA protocol didn't get dropped, the nice object-oriented mindset was gone. A single interface for each remote machine was designed to hide all of the previously exposed objects. You can name it the "facade pattern" if you want, but it also totally defeated the purpose of CORBA. It was somehow embarrassing, but it at least saved the project from becoming a shipwreck!

Conclusion

This is more an example of an architectural level mistake, but also a warning that you should not get enamored with some shiny new technology. Investigate, measure, and design – do not follow current industry fads just because they look so elegant and easy!

Other examples

Maybe they didn't catch your eye, but in the preceding chapters we have already seen some examples of performance improvements that can be achieved in real life systems, such as the following:

- Decreasing locking granularity in Windows' kernel scheduler in Chapter 5, *An In-depth Guide to Concurrency and Multithreading*
- Replacing a game engine's data structures with more efficient and cache-friendly ones in Chapter 4, *Using Data Structures and Algorithms Efficiently*
- Using **Data-Oriented Design** (**DOD**) to reimplement a CSS animation system in Chapter 4, *Using Data Structures and Algorithms Efficiently*

- Flattening data structures in a game, also in `Chapter 4`, *Using Data Structures and Algorithms Efficiently*

We won't go over them again here – just turn back a couple of pages and reread the appropriate subsections.

As we move on in this book, we will also see some more examples of performance improvements in fields we haven't discussed yet, but I think that this chapter, in the middle of our journey, was a suitable place to discuss real-life applications of essential performance techniques.

Summary

In this chapter, we looked at some real cases that the author encountered in his work. Was it only a mere listing of some unrelated cases or did we learn something from them?

For me, the recurrent theme in each of these cases was how unexpected these problems were. Some quite reasonable assumptions were made, the software was written, but then it turned out that, despite the whole reasoning there were performance problems showing up! So, one of the lessons from these problem cases is that you'll never be sure until you've comprehensively tested your system.

The other surprise is how often the underlying reason is very simple, but not exactly trivial. This includes situations where you have a poorly scaling data structure, a linear or a quadratic algorithm, or a bad locking strategy. However, this is also encouraging – once we are able to determine the problem, the solution is not very complicated.

The third problem that stands out is that we often underestimate the cost of heavy operations, like system calls or network communication. But did you notice that the problem of excessive memory allocations never showed up? The programmers just tried to do a good job, and got their basics covered.

Having finished the more generic part of this book, in the next chapter, we will start to investigate the performance of specific Qt modules. We will start with something simple – reading, writing, and parsing files and data in general.

Questions

As always, here are some questions so that you can test your understanding of the topics in this chapter:

1. When would you deem a simple linear search to be a justifiable choice?
2. How many items do you think can be shown without problems in a standard Qt's model-view setup?
3. What could be meant with the **Tower of Babel** performance anti-pattern?
4. Your program is suffering from a performance problem. How would you try to solve it?
5. You have far too many items in a view—what can you do about this?
6. How is it possible to avoid performance fails in your project?
7. What seems to be the number one reason for performance fails?
8. What about the **do it later** performance culture and performance fails?

Further reading

Interestingly, there has been a certain some amount of research done in the field of automatically detecting performance anti-patterns and correcting them! Before you get too excited, such methods can be applied to formal models of software, which was the case with deadlock detection tools. However, recently, some work has been done to apply this technique to production Java code, so if you are interested enough, have a look at *Performance Anti-patterns: Detection and Evaluation of Their Effects in the Cloud* (2014), which is available at https://ieeexplore.ieee.org/document/6930605. Who knows – maybe you'll write such a tool for C++ and Qt?

The already mentioned book *The Performance of Open Source Applications* edited by *Travish Armstrong* (2013), available at http://aosabook.org, contains a selection of performance optimization stories akin to the contents of this chapter.

If you want to read some Windows-specific performance stories and how to solve them using the **Event Tracing for Windows** (**ETW**) tool we introduced in Chapter 2, *Profiling to Find Bottlenecks*, go to the ETW Central page at https://randomascii.wordpress.com/2015/09/24/etw-central/ and scroll to the *ETW investigation write-ups* section.

7
Understanding I/O Performance and Overcoming Related Problems

As we already know, Qt is much more than a GUI framework. It also contains platform-independent APIs for all the tasks you will probably meet when writing an application. We could paraphrase and assert that Qt truly comes as C++ with batteries included: We get a GUI, graphics, multithreading, networking, string processing, file operations, XML and JSON, and even database connectivity. We already discussed Qt's multithreading and string processing when we introduced general-performance principles. In this chapter, we will turn our attention to more specific topics and explore a mixture of various topics that are loosely related to the I/O problematic, namely the following:

- Reading and writing files in Qt
- Parsing XML and JSON at the speed of light
- Connecting databases
- More about operating system interactions

We will see that, by looking at the first innocuously-looking file, I/O isn't as simple and boring as we'd like to think. Actually, it's quite the opposite—it will take us into the depths of operating systems. Don't be afraid – everything will be explained, we will stay on Windows, and only occasionally mention Linux-specific behavior, just to point out some differences between the two.

Reading and writing files in Qt

We will start this chapter with a quick review of some file processing basics in C++ so that we can build a basic understanding of what the foundations that Qt classes are building upon look like.

Basics of file I/O performance

Files can be stored on rotational (hard drive) or **solid state disks** (**SSDs**). In the case of hard disks, there are considerable mechanical overheads involved, caused by the need to position the read-write head over the correct disk sector. However, once the correct position is reached, the reading of contiguous data is relatively fast.

Reading and storing files is one of the archetypal tasks of operating systems. It is located in the kernel and is already optimized on that level – the reads and writes from several processes will be merged together and scheduled for optimal performance.

The C and C++ standard libraries provide two types of file access: unbuffered when using the `open()` system call and buffered on the library level with `fopen()`. The buffering of file operations is an example of the *avoiding big overhead* optimization technique, as writing to a file will cost us a system call and maybe a read-write head positioning. Due to this, we will batch re-read and write requests and only send them to disk when there is enough data to warrant that expense.

A useful analogy is memory access optimizations – file read/write buffering corresponds to processor caches and file reading is read ahead to memory prefetching.

Buffering and flushing

We have seen that there are two buffering levels: file stream buffering and kernel buffering. This means that when we are writing to a file, the data first ends up in the library level buffer. Sometimes, though, you'd like to send the data immediately to the disk, for example, if you are debugging your program and you'd like your trace to be saved to disk before the program crashes.

For that reason, the C and C++ standard libraries define the `fflush()` function, which will flush the buffer associated with the file. The data will thus land in the kernel's buffer and will be physically written to disk at a later date.

This means that if the computer crashes instantly and we are unlucky, the data still might not be physically written to the disk! It could simply be caught lying around in internal kernel buffers at the time of the crash. On Windows, there is a proprietary extension to `fopen()` opening modes—"C" (for commit), which will result in writing the data physically to the disk on `fflush()` by bypassing kernel buffers.

Needless to say, file flushing is quite a heavy operation performance-wise, because we will at least invoke a system call (remember the costs of a kernel trip we discussed in Chapter 5, *An In-Depth Guide to Concurrency and Multithreading*) and potentially a physical write. If we care about performance, we have to watch out for flushes, so let's look at some *gotchas*.

In the standard `iostream` library, the `std::endl` operator—besides outputting a newline character – will flush the stream. This is a rather heavy way of starting a new line, so be sure that flushing is what you really want:

```
std::cout << "Hi y'all, whassup?" << std::endl; // flush and new line
std::cout << "Hi y'all, whassup << "\n";         // only start a new line
```

If you are using the low-level `fopen()` file operations, you can use the `setvbuf()` function to change the buffer size and set buffering mode to none, line buffering, or full buffering. However, on Windows, line buffering isn't supported and will result in full buffering.

In the `iostream` library, we have to replace the attached `streambuf` to change the buffering mode, as the default `filebuf` is fully buffered. Alternatively, we can set a `unitbuf` flag, which will have the stream flushed at the end of each << operator. The `std::cerr` stream has this flag set by default. We can also manipulate the size of the buffer by calling `stream.rdbuf()->pubsetbuf(buffer, size)`.

Tied and synchronized streams

If C++ specifies some dependencies between the standard streams, we say that one stream is tied to another. For example, the standard input `std::cin` is tied to the standard output `std::cout`, which means that a requested read from `std::cin` will first flush `std::cout`. In C++11, `std::cerr` is also tied to `std::cout`, and library implementations may also be tied to `std::clog`.

You can untie a stream from all of its dependencies by calling `stream.tie(nullptr)`.

Another thing to know is that standard C++ streams (`std::cin`, `std::cout`, `std::cerr`, `std::clog`, and their wide variants) are synchronized with the standard C streams (`stdin`, `stdout`, and `stderr`) after each I/O operation.

 C++ streams don't use buffering when they're in synchronized mode, and each I/O operation on a C++ stream is immediately forwarded to the corresponding C stream's buffer! This is done to allow us to freely mix C and C++ standard streams in a single program.

We can break this synchronization by calling the `std::ios_base::sync_with_stdio(false)` function, which will allow C++ streams to buffer their data independently. In some cases, this may result in a considerably better performance. On Linux, for example, `stdout` is line buffered by default—that is, it will flush the buffer on each new line!

Reading and writing

The C++ standard `iostream` library earned a reputation of being rather sluggish. I won't bash `iostream` here, as it is doing much more than only reading data, namely the locale dependent conversion and formatting, but the fact is that some of its older implementations may be slow.

Should you encounter problems with performance of a standard stream such as `std::cin` or `std::cout`, try to untie and unsynchronize it. You could try to increase buffer sizes in the case of file streams. Setting the locale back its to default (that is, the **C** locale) will avoid the locale-based conversions. You could also use `std::filebuf` directly or through `std::getline()` to avoid conversions and formatting overhead. Using the C functions `fgets()`, `fgetline()`, and `fputs()` also avoids formatting and gives you just pure file read/write functionality. It will be faster than using `fprinf()`/`fscanf()` instead, because it doesn't have to interpret the format string at runtime.

As we've already said, we should read and write the files in big chunks to avoid potentially heavy operation costs when reading or writing small amounts of data.

Here's one last idea—what about compressing the file before you write it out? If the disk access time is a problem, this may be well worth the effort!

Seeking

The `fseek()` function that's called for a file or `seekp()`/`seekg()` on an `iostream` will set the current position in the stream. It can be potentially expensive, depending on the amount of buffered data. In some cases, you may end up with a kernel physically reading a file from the disk if it is doing a read-ahead. In other cases, it just changes an internal pointer in the library's implementation.

However, there is a potential additional cost that will be incurred, as `fseek()` will first flush the buffers with `fflush()` if there is any unwritten data!

 Don't use `fseek()` to compute the size of a file – use `fstat()` or `_filelength()` instead.

Caching files

Because each file-reading operation is costly, we should generally read big chunks of files and hold them in memory for further processing. However, you can have too much of a good thing, because after you have your data in memory, the operating system can page (that is, write) the data back to the disk if it feels like doing so! In that case, all of your reading will be in vain. I suppose you know what *paging* and *swapping* mean, but if you don't, we will have a short overview of them at the end of this chapter.

We could combat this by pinning the memory pages using `VirtualLock()` on Windows or `mlock()` on Linux, but this is messing with the memory manager in the kernel, and shouldn't be done lightly.

If the situation were to occur on Linux, it could get even worse, because in the case of memory shortage, the **Out Of Memory** (**OOM**) killer will be activated in the kernel – if your process is hogging most of the memory, it will be killed! This comes as a surprise to many Linux users. Fortunately, there isn't such a thing on Windows.

A simpler alternative is to use a memory-mapped file (`CreateFileMapping()` on Windows and `mmap()` on Linux). Now, the OS will take care of bringing your file into memory as you need it. The operating system will never swap the memory pages of the mapped file to disk; instead, it will just discard those pages as it sees fit. Additionally, we can add hints for the OS to indicate which parts of the mapping will be needed in the future (`PrefetchVirtualMemory()` or `madvise()`), so the OS might do some prefetching if it feels like that.

Unfortunately, mapping a file won't necessarily result in better performance, as it is better to do I/O in big chunks – virtual memory managers operate in page-sized chunks. Depending on the actual implementation, this could be batched for mapped files by OS. However, memory mapped files will be generally faster for random access, especially if your access file is in several distant locations! As always, measuring your use case will help.

Qt's I/O classes

Qt defines a QIODevice class as the base for all I/O classes. It provides a common interface for reading and writing blocks of data from a memory buffer a file, or a datastream.

QFile

For reading binary and text files (and Qt resources), QFile subclasses QIODevice. It implements a buffered I/O, but can be also opened in unbuffered mode using the QIODevice::Unbuffered mode. When it is opened in the text mode, it will translate the end-of-line terminators between the local encoding (for example: '\r\n' on Windows) to and from '\n'.

QFile provides the read() and readLine() functions for reading chunks of raw data (that is, QByteArray), but also the readAll() function for reading all of the contents of the file at once. It also provides support for the memory mapping of files that we discussed previously in this chapter through the map() and unmap() functions. Look at the following example for its usage:

```
QFile file("(./example.bin");
file.open(QFile::ReadOnly);

uchar* memory = file.map(0, file.size());
if (memory)
{
  // now we have the data ready-made in memory!
  double* data = reinterpret_cast<double*>(memory);
  double value1 = data[0];
  // etc ....

  file.unmap();
}
```

QFile may be used all by itself or, more conveniently, with the QTextStream or QDataStream classes, which we will introduce in the next section. The following example shows direct usage of the QFile class:

```
QFile file("("./example.txt");
file.open(QIODevice::ReadOnly | QIODevice::Text);

while (!file.atEnd())
{
  QByteArray line = file.readLine();
  // process read data ...
}
```

We can also read data into a buffer that's provided by the caller, as shown in the following example:

```
char buffer[1024];
qint64 size = file.readLine(buffer, sizeof(buffer));
if (size != -1) // ... line read
```

These two interfaces have different performance implications: In the version without the buffer parameter, a new internal buffer of QByteArray has to be dynamically allocated, and QByteArray itself could be copied when passing this further to the caller of the current function. This copy won't be very costly because of its COW implementation, and it could be elided depending on the C++ version you are using.

QTextStream and QDataStream

These two classes provide a more convenient interface for using the QFile in its two different modes – binary and text.

QTextStream provides a convenient interface for reading and writing text for a file. It will take care of converting the 8-bit data that's physically stored in the file into a UTF-16 Unicode QString. The assumed file encoding is the local system's default encoding (on Linux, it's UTF-8, while it's UTF-16 on Windows), but it can be changed using the setCodec() function. QTextStream will use an internal UTF-16 buffer to speed up this conversion.

Thus, if you are reading a non UTF-16 text file, there will be some cost associated with the format conversion. It is faster to perform this conversion in one go, rather than line by line.

This means that the `readAll()` method is often a good solution! For larger files, we could consider reading it in greater chunks and then perform the conversion, maybe by even starting the read process in a separate I/O thread and doing the translation and conversion in an additional worker thread.

The following code shows a basic example of reading a file by using `QTextStream`:

```
QFile file("./example.txt");
if (!file.open(QIODevice::ReadOnly))
{
  QMessageBox::information(nullptr, "ERROR", file.errorString());
}

QTextStream inputStrm(&file);
while(!inputStrm.atEnd())
{
  QString line = in.readLine();
  // .. process line
}

file.close()
```

We can just as well use `QTextStream` to read a memory-mapped file, as in the following example:

```
QFile file("("./example.txt");
file.open(QFile::ReadOnly);
uchar *memory = file.map(0, file.size());

if (memory)
{
  QDataStream::readRawData(memory, file.size());
  int size32Bit = static_cast<int>(file.size());
  // fromRawData() won't copy!
  auto bytes = QByteArray::fromRawData(
                  reinterpret_cast<const char*>(memory), size32Bit);

  QTextStream istream(bytes);
  while(!istream.atEnd())
  {
    QString line = istream.readLine();
    // ...
  }
  file.unmap(memory);
}

file.close();
```

We can see that we have to use an ugly cast on the file size value. This is because the legacy Qt interfaces didn't use the sane `size_t` type, but chose `int` to be able to signal an invalid value with `-1`. Needless to say, this is a very bad practice, but it's still in the API because of backward compatibility. Another required cast has to do with the default signedness of the `char` type in C++.

`QTextStream` also defines a convenient overload of the shift operator for writing to files:

```
QTextStream ostream(&file);
ostream << "Ceterum censeo ..." << endl;
```

As we can see, the `endl` stream operator is also defined and flushes the stream, exactly like its `std::endl` counterpart! So, be sure that this is what you want.

`QDataStream` offers a similar interface for manipulating binary files, thus overloading the shift operators both for reading and writing. It doesn't use any internal buffer though, instead relying on the buffering of the underlying `QFile` object.

Other helper I/O classes

The `QSaveFile` provides a transactional semantics when writing files – it doesn't have a `close()` method, but uses `commit()` to finally store the data. When an error occurs, no data will be stored at all. `QTemporaryFile` offers the safe creation of unique temporary files.

Finally, `QBuffer` is a helper class that allows us to access a `QByteArray` using the `QIODevice` interface. In this way, the `QByteArray`, which is used to store both raw bytes (including `'\0'`) and traditional C style `'\0'` terminated strings, can be treated in the same manner as a standard random-accessed file!

QDebug and friends

Qt provides some output streams that can be used for emitting debug, logging, and error messages, as in the following example:

```
qInfo() << "INFO: everything is ok!";
qDebug() << "Doing some work...";
qWarning() << "WARNING: didn't expect that!";
qCritical() << "ERROR: we have a problem!";
qFatal("PANIC - shutting down!"); // will shut down the application!
```

All of these streams use the standard `std::cerr` stream. Remember that this stream is unit buffered by default, so it will be flushed after each `operator << ()` call.

It might be unexpected, but `qDebug()` calls will not be complied in the release build by default and thus might cause a performance hit! We have to disable this explicitly by setting qmake's configuration:

```
CONFIG(release, debug|release):DEFINES += QT_NO_DEBUG_OUTPUT
```

Another way to somehow avoid the overhead of `qDebug()` and its friends is to install a custom message handler using the global function `qInstallMsgHandler()`. For example, we could just enable the writing of messages when this functionality is requested by a special runtime parameter, as shown in the following example:

```
#include <QtGlobal>

void ignoreAllMessages(QtMsgType type, const QMessageLogContext &context,
                       const QString &msg)
{
  Q_UNUSED(type);
  Q_UNUSED(context);
  Q_UNUSED(msg);
}

int main(int argc, char* argv[])
{
  QApplication app(argc, argv);

  if(!app.arguments().contains("--verbose"))
  {
    qInstallMessageHandler(ignoreAllMessages);
  }

  return app.exec();
}
```

Parsing XML and JSON at the speed of light

There are several classes in Qt for working with XML data. In this section, we will look at them and try to assess their respective performance.

QtXml classes

We will start out with an overview of classes that are contained in the *QtXml* module, because this is the module that was traditionally used to process XML data.

Right from the start, the Qt documentation states:

The module is not actively maintained anymore. Please use the QXmlStreamReader *and* QXmlStreamWriter *classes in Qt Core instead.*

You might think that this module is deprecated, but it isn't. It's simply been left as is and isn't changed anymore.

QDomDocument

This class loads the contents of the entire XML file in memory and holds it there as a tree of objects representing XML's structured **Data Object Model (DOM)**. This is the simplest way to read XML data:

```
QDomDocument doc;
QFile file("./example.xml");

file.open(QIODevice::ReadOnly);
doc.setContent(&file);

QDomeModeList names = doc.elementsByTagName("userName");
for(auto& node: names)
{
  QDomElement elem = node.toElement();
  if(!elem.isNull())
  {
    qDebug() << "user: " << elem.text() << "\n";
  }
}
```

As we see, we can simply walk the DOM tree and inspect the contents of its nodes.

However, because the entire file is read into memory, it has some performance problems. First, we are reading the entire contents, even if we'd only like to read some data for the beginning of the file. Second, even if we will need the whole contents of the file, the same problems we discussed in conjunction with caching files in memory will occur – a big file could be paged back to disk by the OS, or it might not even fit into the memory on a 32-bit system! Third, we are building a tree of nodes – each of them dynamically allocated at XML load time. This means bad XML parsing performance and bad memory locality of the resulting data, which ultimately means bad performance when accessing the nodes!

All in all, for small and simple files, it would be probably still the right choice. However, Qt offers an implementation of XPath in the QtXmlPatterns module, which is also rather slow but could be a more convenient choice for simple contents.

QXmlSimpleReader

This is an implementation of a Qt XML stream reader that's modeled after Java's SAX2 streaming interface. It is an event-driven interface and the user has to create a class with callback methods and give that class and the XML file to the SAX parser. Since the parser will invoke the callbacks as it detects specific elements, the application has to maintain state information to know where in the XML hierarchy the callback was invoked. This can be somehow inconvenient.

Here, we do not have to keep the entire XML file in memory, so we could process a much bigger file in a more performant manner. However, this time, we should abstain from using this class because although it is not deprecated, QXmlStreamReader is a newer class that's specifically designed for better stream-reading performance!

New stream classes in QtCore

QXmlStreamReader doesn't store the entire XML document tree in memory like a SAX parser, and that is already a performance advantage. Additionally, it uses the relatively new QStringRef class that we discussed in Chapter 4, *Using Data Structures and Algorithms Efficiently*, to avoid allocation costs and reference-counting overhead of small QString instances when returning new data to the caller.

Moreover, QXmlStreamReader is an incremental parser. It supports the case when the XML document cannot be parsed as a whole because it may only be available in chunks – either coming from different files or over the network. You just have to call the addData() method with the new chunk. With that, QXmlStreamReader supports the asynchronous parsing model – we do not have to wait for all of the data to be read to start parsing – and provides the corresponding performance advantages.

Unlike the SAX parser, it lets you to drive the computation – no callbacks and no local state required! Look at the following very basic example to get a general feel of this API:

```
QXmlStreamReader reader(&file);

if(reader.readNextStartElement())
{
  if(reader.name() == "users")
  {
    while(reader.readNextStartElement())
    {
      if(reader.name() == "name")
      {
          QString name = reader.readElementText();
          qDebug() << "user: " << name < "\n";
      }
      else
      {
          reader.skipCurrentElement();
      }
    }
  }
}
```

A more complete example can be found found in this book's resources (https://github.com/PacktPublishing/Hands-On-High-performance-with-QT/tree/master/Chapter%207).

Quick parsing of XML

So, how quick is the QXmlStreamReader? We have seen that it is much quicker than the classes from the old QtXml module, but in comparison with other libraries, it has one big drawback – it will still have to convert the Unicode data to UTF-16 (as it it used in QString), which will hurt performance if your document is accidentally in UTF-8 format.

It's still OK for most of your needs, but if you are looking for a lightning-quick XML parser, you could try rapidxml or pugixml. Both of them are in fact DOM parsers, but they get most of their speed by referring to strings in-place, a technique that QXmlStreamReader is also using. However, they do not support some of more esoteric XML features. Unfortunately, as DOM parsers, they are not suitable for parsing huge files. In that case, I'd probably stay with Qt's QXmlStreamReader.

Reading JSON

JSON is another widely used human readable data format. Qt offers the QJsonDocument class for parsing JSON data. The JSON elements are represented by the QJsonObject, QJsonArray, and QJsonValue classes. All of these classes are using implicit sharing. The following example shows the basic usage of QJsonDocument and the JSON value classes:

```
QByteArray data = file.readAll();

QJsonParseError err;
QJsonDocument doc = QJsonDocument::fromJson(data, &err);

if(err.error == QJsonParseError::NoError)
{
  QJsonObject topObject = doc.object();
  auto name = topObject["author"].toString();
  QJsonArray bookArray = topObject["books"].toArray();

  for(const auto& elem: qAsConst(bookArray))
  {
    const QJsonObject& book = elem.toObject();
    auto year  = QString::number(book["year"].toInt());
    auto title = book["title"].toString();
    // etc ...
  }
}
```

As we can see, QJsonDocument is a DOM-type parser, holding all the data in memory.

QJsonDocument's performance

Judging from several benchmarks available in the performance of QJsonDocument, it seems to lie in the middle of the range but rather on the faster side. However, when reading UTF-8 JSON documents (and this is the default encoding), they will be converted to the internal UTF-16 format and that will have performance costs. The parser also doesn't use the QStringRef class in its interface, which will result in string copies.

QJsonDocument provides an optimization opportunity by supporting the saving of JSON data in its own binary format. When binary JSON data is then read with the fromBinaryData() method, it is memory-mappable and very quick to access.

RapidJSON seems to be the fastest JSON parser at the moment. It offers both DOM-type as well as a SAX-type streaming interfaces. In DOM mode. it internally uses a pool allocator, which we discussed in Chapter 3, *Deep Dive into C++ and Performance*, which allocates but doesn't free the memory. For more heavy workloads, we should probably be probably prefer it over QJsonDocument – if not for the DOM performance, then for the stream parsing interface.

Connecting databases

Sometimes, data files aren't just stored on disk to be freely used, but are managed by a database runtime system. Fortunately, Qt provides us with the possibility to talk to SQL databases by using its QtSql module. We will take a cursory look at this, but general database performance is a big and deep field and lies outside of the scope of this book.

Basic example using SQLite

For this example, we will use the SQLite lightweight, in-memory database, because it is exceptionally simple to use.

To work with SQLite databases, you first have to install the SQLite tools, as the SQLite driver that's needed by Qt is already included in its installation. Go to https://www. sqlite.org/download.html, download sqlite-tools-win32-x86-3250300.zip or a later version, and unzip it to the C:\sqlite directory. Then, go to the directory where you want to place the database and create it, like that:

```
C:\sqlite\sqlite3.exe users.db
sqlite> CREATE TABLE users(ids integer primary key, username text);
sqlite> .quit
```

We just opened a SQLite shell and executed a simple SQL script by creating an example table named users in our example database stored in users.db. In the following code, we can see a basic example of adding and listing database data:

```
// open the database:
QSqlDatabase db;
db = QSqlDatabase::addDatabase("QSQLITE"); // driver type
db.setDatabaseName("./users.db");

// insert user data
QSqlQuery query;
QString username = "testuser";

query.prepare("INSERT INTO users (username) VALUES (:name)");
query.bindValue(":name", username);
if(!query.exec())
{
  qDebug() << "Error adding user:" << query.lastError() << endl;
}

// query existing users:
QSqlQuery query("SELECT * FROM users");
int nameIdx = query.record().indexOf("username");
while(query.next())
{
  QString name = query.value(nameIdx).toString();
  qDebug() << "users:" << name << endl;
}
```

We can see that in the case of the SQLite database driver, you just use the path to the database file in setDatabaseName(). We have seen how to create QSqlQuery instances, how to use positional parameters in queries, and how to iterate over results of a SELECT query.

Some performance considerations

The performance of the database access depends on the implementation of the used driver. For example, for SQLite, each INSERT will be executed in a transaction. Thus, if you are doing many inserts without explicitly surrounding them with BEGIN ... COMMIT, the database will create a new transaction for each insert operation, which will give you a performance hit. Consult your database and driver documentation for more performance advice. Of course, an inefficient SQL query remains the number one performance killer.

From a Qt programmer's point of view however, there is one important limitation in Qt's database classes, because the Qt documentation unambiguously states the following:

> "A connection can only be used from within the thread that created it. Moving connections between threads or creating queries from a different thread is not supported."

This means that we cannot reuse a single database connection to communicate with the database from several threads! Because opening and closing a database connection is a costly operation, the solution in such a case is a dedicated database worker thread holding a database connection and receiving database requests from other threads. We can implement such a worker in the same way we saw it being used in Chapter 5, *An In-Depth Guide to Concurrency and Multithreading*, when discussing an ActiveObject implementation for asynchronous logging.

Another possibility would be for the database worker to hold a pool of opened connections, but this would complicate the implementation as we'd now have to deal with concurrency at the database level. A single serializing database worker is a proven solution that should scale quite well for typical loads.

More about operating system interactions

We have seen that, when it comes to I/O, we must keep a close eye on what the operating system is doing under the covers. Let's close this chapter with a discussion about some relevant performance OS concepts that we haven't been able to discuss yet.

Paging, swapping, and the TLB

As we have seen in the *Caching Files* section, when we discussed caching entire files in memory, there is another leaky abstraction related to memory besides processor level caching that we haven't discussed yet, namely the virtual memory concept that's implemented by the OS.

You probably know that OS provides an illusion of having the entire address space of the computer at its disposal, though there are many other processes in the system at any given time. It is doing that by using a mechanism known as virtual memory. The operating system is working with memory pages, which are either present in memory or written to the swap file or partition on the disk.

When a program tries to access a memory location that is not physically there, the OS will have to read it from the disk first. This is called a page fault and it should remind you of a cache miss, only that it is much, much costlier! Why should a memory page not be present in memory? Because another program might have needed that place and the OS freed the memory for it, writing it out to the disk! This operation is commonly called swapping or paging. You can see that this can quickly become inefficient, as our program might reclaim that memory when it has the change to run its runtime slice again.

The degenerate situation when several programs are playing this memory page ping-pong with the operating system is called thrashing and is a big performance killer! This is another reason to be parsimonious with your program's allocated memory.

Virtual memory management has a dedicated piece of hardware to support this in the processor, that is, the so-called **Memory Management Unit** (**MMU**), which also implements memory protection schemes. A **Translation Lookaside Buffer** (**TLB**) is a part of the MMU where the mapping of memory addresses and pages is maintained. It is a hardware cache for the OS internal table page.

Note that as the TLB is an on-chip cache: We have the same problems with cache invalidation as we have with standard data and the instruction cache. On TLB, the cache will miss the data, and so it will have to be fetched from main memory first, and then the OS will have to deal with a page miss to boot.

This gives us a whole new perspective on data locality, doesn't it. Jumping around in memory will not only purge your CPU cashes but also mess with the TLB and page table!

Reading from disk

Sometimes, it's not the operating system swapping pages, but simply your program writing or reading many files from disk. In the case of an HDD, there's one problem that can kill performance: disk fragmentation. Remember the memory fragmentation problem and hot code relocation optimization we discussed in previous chapters? The same problem exists for the hard disk – if the file is split up between many sectors, there will be many reading heads needing to be repositioned as needed to read all of its data! A cure for this is, of course, defragmenting the disk. An optimal solution would be positioning of all of the files a program is reading or writing one next to another, but I'm not aware of any tools that do that.

Completion ports

One possibility to increase the speed of processing a big file I/O is to read a file in asynchronous chunks and forward the read data to the worker threads – this is a common approach that we learned about in Chapter 5, *An In-Depth Guide to Concurrency and Multithreading*. On Windows, there is support for such pattern at the OS level – the **I/O Completion Ports** (**IOCPs**). This kernel will start an asynchronous operation and then dispatch its results to a worker thread pool. Arguably, IOCP makes more sense with networking, and we will look at it in a due time, but it is applicable to any I/O operation type. Qt doesn't use IOCP on Windows at the moment.

Summary

In this chapter, we looked at the supposedly boring theme of reading, writing, and parsing data that's stored in files. Maybe you will never need to process big files in your Qt program, but at least you gained some understanding of I/O and virtual memory problems.

We started with a general discussion of disks, file I/O, and buffering, and then we learned about Qt's classes for reading and writing files. We followed this up with a discussion of XML and JSON processing as these are the most popular data formats that are currently in use. We also quickly discussed the database connectivity support that Qt provides and its multithreading usage. Finally, we had a closer look at some operating system aspects that can influence disk performance like vital memory support and disk fragmentation.

In the next chapter, we will look at the perhaps the most interesting part of our performance discussion, namely the vast theme of the graphic performance of Qt!

Questions

As you probably expected, we will now conclude this chapter with several questions to test your understanding of the material in this chapter:

1. Why will reading from std::cin flush std::cout?
2. What is the difference between a unit-buffered, a line-buffered, a fully-buffered, and an unbuffered stream?
3. Why is std::iostream slower than std::filebuf, and why is fprintf() slower than puts()?
4. Why is Linux killing processes if it feels like it?

5. What is a page fault? What are their soft and hard page faults?
6. What is thrashing?
7. You are on Windows. You are starting up a program and your disk starts spinning like crazy. How would you investigate this problem?
8. You are on a 32-bit system and have to hold several big images in memory. Then, you have to read another one from the camera, but there is not enough memory left. What do you do?

Further reading

The Performance of Open Source Applications, which was edited by Travish Armstrong (available on `http://aosabook.org`, 2013), contains a chapter on optimizations that are used in the `pugixml` library. The *Optimized C++* book by Kurt Guntheroth (2013) has a short chapter on the performance of `std::iostream`.

There are several good books on operating systems, but the most comprehensive when it comes to Windows is the book *Windows Internals, Part 1: System architecture, processes, threads, memory management, and more* by Pavel Yosifovich et al., *Microsoft Press* (seventh Edition, 2017). But be forewarned, it's quite a tome!

If you are interested in state-of-the-art algorithms and data structures that are used when reading data from disk and caching them in memory, you might read the recent paper *Algorithms Behind Modern Storage Systems – Different uses for read-optimized B-trees and write-optimized LSM-trees*, by my fellow Munich programmer Alex Petrov, acmqueue 16/2 (2018), which is available at `https://queue.acm.org/detail.cfm?id=3220266`. This paper covers techniques that database writers are using to achieve optimal performance, and you will notice that they are doing that by case specialization for reading and writing data!

Optimizing Graphical Performance

8

In this chapter, we will look at the part of the performance puzzle you will probably be most interested in, because at the end, Qt's main application area is found in building cross-platform GUIs. It is also very exciting on account of the significant advances in hardware and software that have occurred in recent years, and that are still taking place, as the example of NVIDIA's recent announcement of their new *Turing* architecture is impressively proving!

This chapter cannot necessarily provide an exhaustive treatment of graphics programming, because such a topic would fill an entire book on its own. Instead, we will try to provide an overview of the possibilities offered by the Qt framework and the performance trade-offs involved.

In this chapter, we will discuss following topics:

- Introduction to graphics performance—just to start you off generally on modern graphics and **graphical processing units (GPUs)**
- Qt's graphics architecture and its history—because we'd like to gain an overview of the APIs available
- Qt Widget's performance—because the Widget API is still important
- QML performance—because this is the main Qt API now
- Other modules—for a quick performance assessment of other graphics modules

Introduction to graphics performance

As already stated, we start with some general background on modern graphics systems before we look at the ways Qt is incorporating recent advances into its framework.

Graphics hardware's inner workings

How do graphics get rendered on your computer's screen? This is done by a special piece of hardware unsurprisingly called a graphics or video card. As input, it needs an array containing all the pixels that have to be displayed on screen. These pixels will be handed over using the so-called frame buffer. This means we will need to copy the data from memory to the frame buffer to get it displayed.

A frame buffer will be mostly mapped to the main memory space, so the CPU can place the image to be displayed using regular memory access operations. As to avoid the *tearing* effect (that is, half of the old frame is still shown, while half the new frame is already visible too) CPU will prepare the image in a separate location and then swap its contents with the frame buffer—a technique called **double buffering**.

We see that it is the CPU that is creating the image to be displayed and forwarding it to the graphics card. For simple 2D graphics like the traditional desktop widget-based UIs, this is good enough, but fluid animations, graphics effects, and real-time rendering can put an undue stress on CPU, killing the overall system's performance.

For that reason, there were always attempts to offload some of the work form the CPU to the specialized hardware on the graphics card and let the CPU to do what it is good at, namely, general computation. This special hardware is called GPU, and we will now have a closer look at it.

What is a GPU?

A GPU is a heterogeneous single-chip processor that is highly tuned for graphics. As for graphics, we have to do many simple computations for each and every pixel, and the first optimization that presents itself is to increase the parallelism.

A GPU is partitioned in **streaming multiprocessors (SMs)**, which are also called **compute units (CUs)**, and that can be seen as an equivalent of a CPU core. However, each SM comprises many more **arithmetic-logical unit (ALUs**, also known as execution unit) than a traditional CPU. For example, NVIDIA GeForce 1080Ti card comprises of 28 SMs, each of them containing 128 ALUs! Different than in a CPU, the execution units are not used to form a pipeline (and thus to optimize the latency) but are chained in parallel, typically in groups of four, to allow SIMD processing of data, and thus, optimizing instruction processing for throughput. In our example of 128 ALUs, we will have 32 threads of parallel execution (called **warp** or **wavefront** respectively by NVIDIA and AMD) working on the same instruction stream on a single SM. Each SM has a **warp scheduler** that manages the group of 32 threads and carries out the computation logic by driving the *dumb* ALUs. To be true, pipelining is also used in a GPU, but on the level of groups of ALUs, that is, between threads. In the next figure we can see GPU's architecture contrasted with a typical CPU:

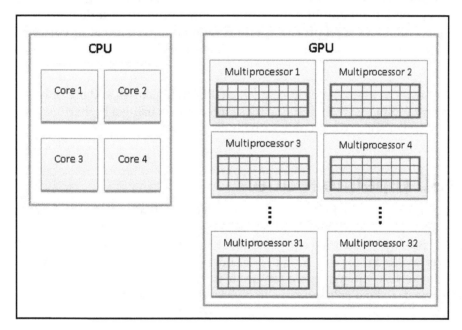

We recall from Chapter 1, *Understanding Performant Programs*, that traditional CPUs are designed to make a single thread run extremely fast—they are using big caches and latency optimized RAM. A GPU, however, is good at doing lots of the same things at once, so it doesn't invest in big caches, expanding the register space instead. Also, the cores do not need to have the complicated pipelining and out of order logic resulting in simplified design and cheaper manufacturing. Likewise, the attached RAM is not very fast, but optimized for parallel throughput instead.

This results in GPUs having much higher raw arithmetic *power* than CPUs, but higher memory latency, thus creating a bottleneck in data transfer from CPU to GPU. Note, however, that because of this sheer computational power, GPUs are also widely used to speed up deep learning algorithms and scientific computing.

The second obvious optimization for graphics is adding custom hardware capable of executing very specialized graphical operations. A modern GPU interleaves the programmable, highly parallel processing units with nonprogrammable, custom-cut graphics hardware like texture samplers, rasterizers, tessellators, pixel blenders, and mergers.

As we do not want to dive deeper into specific GPU architectures and are only striving for a general understanding, we will describe these interactions using a higher-level model, namely the so-called OpenGL graphics pipeline.

OpenGL pipeline model

OpenGL is a standardized API for interacting with GPUs. It allows the programmer to specify so-called shaders, which are mini programs written in a high-level, C-derived language (GLSL), which are then compiled to GPU instructions. We have two main types of shaders: a **vertex shader** for changing position of points and **fragment shader** for changing the colors of pixels. Additionally, we can use textures (that is, images) instead of direct colors. The objects to be displayed have to be broken in triangles.

The following diagram shows a simplified view of the OpenGL pipeline:

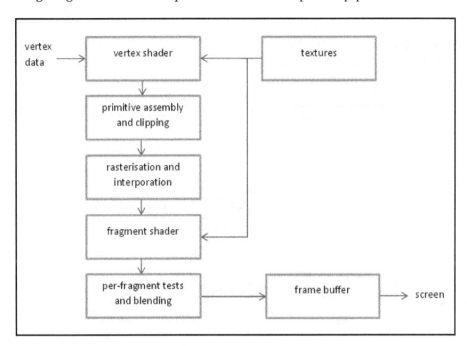

We will now provide a simplistic, short overview of OpenGL rendering stages. Keep in mind that the preceding diagram is simplified, for example, it omits optional geometry, tesselation shaders, and some fixed processing steps.

The rendering of a frame starts with an array of vertex attributes being transferred to the GPU. The attributes include the location in a 3D space and texture coordinates that map a vertex to a point in a given texture (that is, an image we already transferred to the GPU). When we start a render job, we provide the element array that determines which vertices will be sent down the pipeline for processing. The next steps are as follows:

1. **Vertex shader**: In this step, the GPU reads each selected vertex and runs it through the provided **vertex shader** program. At a minimum, the projected position of a vertex in the screen space has to be calculated.
2. **Triangle assembly**: After the positions in the screen space have been determined, GPU connects the vertices to form triangles, as they are the basic shapes used for rendering 3D graphics.

3. **Rasterization**: The rasterizer takes each triangle, clips it, and discards parts that are outside of the screen, and breaks the remaining parts into *fragments* of pixel size. The vertex shader varying outputs are also interpolated across the rasterized surface. For example, if the vertex shader assigns a color to each vertex, the rasterizer will blend those colors across the triangle, as shown in the classic **simple OpenGL** triangle as follows:

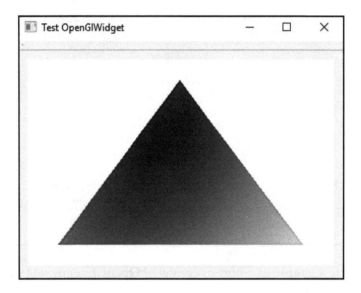

4. **Fragment shader**: The fragments generated in the previous step are then passed to the fragment shader program. Its outputs color and depth that should be written to the frame buffer, for example, implementing lighting effects or texture mapping.

5. **Testing and blending**: In the last stage, a couple of final tests will be done: the depth test to check if the given fragment lies behind already drawn ones, and the stencil test, to check if the fragment lies within the stencil provided for drawing. Fragments that survive the tests are promoted to pixels and will be written to the framebuffer. If blending is disabled, that is the end of the story. Otherwise, the new fragment has to be combined with other fragments at the same pixel position using a user-specified operation.

Now that we understand the general principle on which the pipeline operates, let's have look at the performance bottlenecks in that model.

Performance of the graphics pipeline

Graphics performance is measured in **frames per second** (**FPS**), that is, the number of frames that can be rendered in one second. FPS, in turn, depends on the time it takes to render a single frame. What are the factors that could slow the pipeline down?

Generally speaking, there can be three problems with graphics performance: either the CPU cannot provide the GPU with the data fast enough, or the GPU needs too long for rendering the data, or lastly, the communication between, CPU and GPU takes too long.

We will first have a look at internal **GPU** architecture again in order to discuss how the graphics pipeline gets influenced by the underlying hardware, which is depicted in the following diagram:

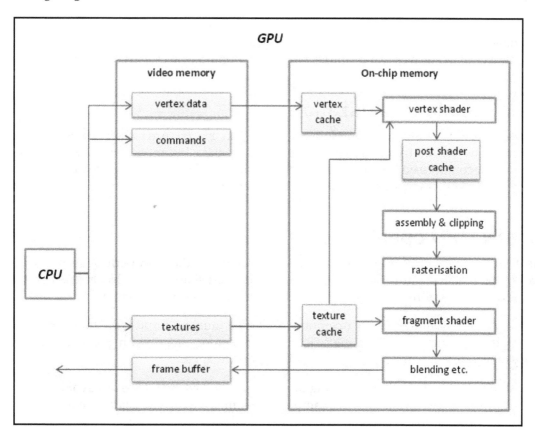

First, we can see that, similarly to CPUs, modern GPUs use two kinds of memory: the graphics card RAM memory (also known as **video memory**), holding **vertex data**, **GPU commands** and **textures**, as well as containing the **frame buffer** for the monitor. On the other hand, we have also several kinds of caches integrated for the **GPU** cores, and we know what that means—cache invalidations are bad for performance! This can be generally summed up by saying that GPU state changes are a bad thing.

CPU problems

Any time the CPU executes a synchronous operation accessing a GPU resource, it will get blocked, having to wait until the GPU pipeline returns to the idle state! So, we shouldn't access resources during rendering.

The second problem is the fixed costs of any graphics function call. We apply the fixed cost avoidance technique here and try to batch the calls as best as we can, that is, by maximizing the number of primitives (for example, triangles) submitted with each draw call.

Data transfer optimization

Vertex transfer is rarely a bottleneck in an application, but texture transfer could be. Generally, we should try to reduce the size of texture data, but modern hardware offers support for compressed texture data, which will decrease memory usage, texture bandwidth requirements, and texture cache efficiency.

Costly GPU operations

As it runs for each pixel fragment shader of the frame, it is the most performance-sensitive part of the pipeline. Thus, we should to use the simplest shader possible. One cool trick is to use textures to store lookup tables in order to replace complex functions!

Alpha blending is quite a costly operation, because it must read and write to the frame buffer, thus, potentially consuming twice as much memory bandwidth. So, we should be wary of blending if we are looking for optimal performance.

Also, the stencil and depth tests are big performance factors, and if we can avoid them, we will improve the performance. For example, sometimes we can live with a smaller 16-bit depth buffer or disable it entirely when rendering alpha-blended effects.

Newer graphics programming APIs

OpenGL is a standard, platform independent API for programming GPUs. It is constantly evolving and has already seen several versions from 1.1 up to 4.5. But this is not the only development in this field.

Recently, there has been new proposals that promise much higher performance by changing the way the graphics API operates, like Vulkan, formerly known as next-generation OpenGL. These new APIs give much more control to the programmer in contrast to the OpenGL API, which tries to hide as much as possible behind its defined abstractions. There are tests showing that Vulkan can as much as triple the performance of a game in respect to OpenGL ES 3.1.

Another example of a new approach to graphics programming is Apple's Metal API, which is also lower-level, and concentrates on simplifying the work the driver has to do internally. Apple claims that these API changes can lead to up to 10-fold increase in issued draw calls per second!

Qt graphics architecture and its history

Qt framework started its life as a GUI widget's library, much like Tk, GTK+, or Java's AWT. For a long time, it was quite sufficient, but then two things happened. First, there was the iPhone revolution, bringing fluid, hardware accelerated, swipeable GUI to the general public. On the other hand, the look and feel of the UI was radically simplified in comparison to the desktop GUI of that time marking a beginning of a new kind of approach to user interaction. Then second, less known development, was the emerging of declarative UI languages in mainstream products, such as for example, XAML in Windows.

Starting with its version four, Qt reacted to these developments by providing a wholly new way of writing GUIs, by using a declarative-style, hardware-accelerated Qt Quick module, also known for its declarative notation language as QML. This has caused a split in the Qt framework—the old widget centered APIs were not deprecated, but did receive a lot less attention than the QML ecosystem.

The Qt Quick module itself experienced some changes through its life span. It started in Qt 4 being powered by the `QGraphicsView` framework that would render its contents with a software rasterizer or an OpenGL backend. In Qt 5.0, it switched to a specially developed new QML scene graph API and required the OpenGL ES 2.0 hardware acceleration exclusively. As this proved too restrictive for many users, in a later version, the support for software rendering and OpenVG (a standard vector graphics API) was reintroduced so that QML could be used on a low-end embedded hardware as well.

But we do not want to forget that both QtWidgets and QML both implement 2D graphics, that is, just GUI elements lacking depth of real-time rendering as we know it from games. Thus, from its version 5.7, Qt includes a new module aptly called Qt3D that makes the general 3D real-time programming available to Qt programmers. As of today, it seems that in the future, in Qt version 6, the hardware accelerated 2D and 3D graphics engines will be gradually unified.

The graphics API Zoo

The development we sketched previously, and some redesign decisions we will come to speak about later, are responsible for the fact that Qt provides several graphics APIs. This makes it somehow puzzling, as many of the APIs implements the same functionality in a different way, resulting in different performance implications. So, let's have a closer look at the available possibilities, and try to somehow straighten out the confusion. The discussion of performance merits of each of those APIs, however, will be provided in a subsequent section, as we first strive to enumerate the possible choices.

Qt Widget

This is the traditional desktop application C++ API featuring the usual PC GUI controls we're all used to: buttons, menus, radio buttons, checkboxes, tabs, and combo boxes. It's been in Qt from the beginning but nowadays, it's no more considered that hot, as the main interest shifted first to QML, and lately, to Qt 3D.

Nonetheless, it's the tool of choice for the traditional desktop GUIs. It is very mature; on different platforms, it uses that platform's native styling, it can be customized with CSS-like stylesheets, and can embed native windows in the widget hierarchy, using, for example, `QAxWidget` for ActiveX on Windows. It is very efficient and implements partial-updates rendering.

A widget does its painting in the `paintEvent()` virtual function, as can be seen in the following example:

```
class TestWidget : public QWidget
{
  void QWidget::paintEvent(QPaintEvent* /*event*/)
  {
    QPainter painter(this);
    painter.setPen(Qt::blue);
    auto f = font();
    f.setPointSize(28);
    painter.setFont(f);
```

```
    painter.drawText(rect(), Qt::AlignCenter, "Test Widget!!!");
    ...
}
...
};
```

As we have seen, the painting is done using the `QPainter` class. `QPainter` can draw everything from simple lines to complex shapes, and also aligned text, and pixmaps. It can draw on widgets and other paint devices like images, pixmaps, or windows.

`QPainter` has a multi-backend architecture and supports two main paint engine implementations, namely, the software rasterizer, which does all the painting in software, and the OpenGL paint engine, designed for OpenGL ES 2.0. The OpenGL paint engine will be used when we open a `QPainter` on a `QOpenGLWindow`, a `QOpenGLWidget`, or a `QOpenGLPaintDevice`.

However, we cannot just switch the graphics backend for an existing Qt widget and paint it with OpenGL. It works the other way around—`QPainter` paints on `QPaintDevice` implementation and `QWidget` is the one using raster operations, while `QOpenGLPaintDevice` is the one using OpenGL. To do so, we had to reimplement the given widget. There was an experimental OpenGL backend for widgets in Qt 4.8, but in Qt 5 it was dropped in the course of shifting the main attention to QML.

Summing up, we can say that for their native look, optimized software rendering, excellent tooling, and easy integration of native controls, Qt Widget's are the way to go for traditional desktop applications. However, touch-aware, animated, hardware accelerated GUIs can be difficult to write using the widgets API.

QGraphicalView

When QML was introduced in Qt 4, QML applications were rendered on an underlying `QGraphicalView` class. `QGraphicalView` was a first attempt to slim down the UI classes and get rid of much of Qt Widget's baggage. It was designed as a graphics scene holding lightweight graphics elements. Additionally, it can display regular Qt Widget's using a special proxy class and offers multiple views (in separate windows) on a single scene. Just as widget classes, `QGraphicalView` provides only a C++ API. By default, it uses a software renderer, but by changing the viewport, OpenGL hardware-accelerated rendering could also be enabled. In that case, the `QPainter` would use the OpenGL engine in the background.

However, in Qt 5, QML became its own scene graph implementation, replacing Qt Quick 1 of Qt 4, and `QGraphicalView` fell in disgrace, and the current advice is that we shouldn't use it for new projects. It's even possible that it will get deprecated in Qt 6.

QOpenGLWidget

This class implements a widget for rendering OpenGL graphics. It is very simple to use as it has an interface similar to that of `QWidget`. We can choose between the familiar `QPainter` class or standard OpenGL rendering commands for drawing, as seen in the following example:

```
class TestOpenGLWidget
  : public QOpenGLWidget, protected QOpenGLFunctions
{
public:
  TestOpenGLWidget(QWidget* parent = nullptr);

  void initializeGL() override;
  void resizeGL(int w, int h) override;
  void paintGL() override;
  {
    // use OpenGL 1.0 functions to draw a triangle:
    //  - doesn't use GLSL shaders!
    glClear(GL_COLOR_BUFFER_BIT | GL_DEPTH_BUFFER_BIT);
    glBegin(GL_TRIANGLES);
    glColor3f(1.0, 0.0, 0.0);
    glVertex3f(-0.5, -0.5, 0);
    ...
  }
  ...
};
```

We implement our painting in the `paintGL()` method using OpenGL functions that are available through the `QOpenGLFunctions` class we inherited from. However, as it can be seen in our example, this is rather error prone, because we can erroneously reference global functions instead of the `QOpenGLFunctions` as we did in the preceding example—`QOpenGLFunctions` doesn't support OpenGL 1.1, but OpenGL ES 2.0! In that way, we are able to use the old style, deprecated API.

The OpenGL 2.0 version would, for example, require usage of shaders, that is small programs written in a high-level GLSL language, which operate on vertexes and pixels. Just like the Compiler Explorer for C++, there is also the Shader Playground site (`http://shader-playground.timjones.io/`) where you can play with GLSL and its DirectX equivalent, HLSL.

As this isn't a graphics programming tutorial, we will only mention that a modern OpenGL API will require usage of classes such as `QOpenGLBuffer`, `QOpenGLVertexArrayObject`, and `QOpenGLShaderProgram` to specify the vertex array with its color parameters and the both shaders, to bind them to the context, and to draw them using the `glDrawArrays(GL_TRIANGLES, ...)` function. An example for the basic triangle included in `QQuickFrameBufferObject` is in the book's resources (`https://github.com/PacktPublishing/Hands-On-High-performance-with-QT/tree/master/Chapter%208`).

Furthermore, examples for the basic triangle rendered in the old and modern way are included in the book's resources.

`QOpenGLWidget` replaced the previously used `QGLWidget` from the deprecated Qt OpenGL module. As `QOpenGLWidget` renders into an off-screen framebuffer object, it doesn't require a native window like `QGLWidget`. This, however, can be a problem with embedded Linux drivers where only one window is possible. There were many other improvements we won't describe here, so please, just don't use the legacy `QGLWidget` class!

As an alternative for OpenGL painting there is also a `QOpenGLWindow` convenience class which has no dependency on the widgets module and thus offers better performance. Like `QOpenGLWidget` it allows either usage of `QOpenGLFunctions` or `QPainter` APIs.

QVulkanWindow

We already mentioned the modern graphics API named Vulkan. In Qt 5.10 support for Vulkan rendering was added to the Qt framework. We need two classes for rendering our graphics through Vulkan: a global `QVulkanInstance` object to provide the rendering context, and a `QVulkanWindow` to do the painting.

Conceptually, `QVulkanWindow` is the counterpart of `QOpenGLWindow` in the Vulkan world. However, there's no counterpart for the `QOpenGLWidget` class, so in order to integrate a Vulkan rendered window into a widget hierarchy, we have to use the `QWidget::createWindowContainer()` method to create an embeddable wrapper. Note also that we cannot (yet) use `QPainter` on Vulkan windows or paint devices, as there's no Vulkan backend for `QPainter` yet!

Qt Quick

Qt Quick, also called QML for its GUI specification language, was designed to be touch friendly and to take advantage of mobile and embedded, hardware accelerated graphics.

The QML language, an acronym for Qt Meta Language, has a JSON-ish syntax, which is used for description of GUI's hierarchical setup, and also lets us add behavior by writing JavaScript code. Look at the following example:

```
Window {
    visible: true
    width: 640
    height: 480
    id: root

    Text {
        id: textItem
        text: "Hello QML!"
    }

    Button {
        text: "click me!"
        anchors.top: textItem.bottom
        onClicked: textItem.text = "clicked..."
    }
}
```

You see we do not program, do not create widgets, do not wire them together, but only describe how the UI has to look. We can position the widgets relatively one to another using the anchors property and to add behavior with JavaScript code for predefined events, for example `onClicked`.

As we already mentioned, in Qt 5 the Qt Quick module was first designed to run exclusively on OpenGL ES 2.0 hardware. Later, the support for software rendering and OpenVG (a standard vector graphics API) was (re)introduced so that QML could be used on a low-end embedded hardware as well. Additionally, in Qt 5.12, experimental support for Direct3D 12 was added; however, there is still no support for newer graphics APIs such as Vulkan or Metal. Given that Apple recently deprecated QpenGL support for some configurations, clearly something has to be done in future QML versions!

QtQuick Controls 1 and 2

In the preceding example, we have seen the usage of the button QML items, which required us to import the QtQuick Controls module. As with Qt Quick, there are two versions of QtQuick Controls; version 1 was introduced with the original Qt 4 QML and tried to reproduce the native look and feel of the buttons, checkboxes, and menus on the given architecture. In Qt 5, this version was deprecated and QtQuick Controls 2 was introduced, which instead provide a platform-independent, mobile-oriented, unified look and feel to the controls. As they do not try to imitate the native looks, the performance of QtQuick Controls 2 is much better that of their predecessor.

Extending QML

There are several possibilities to write custom QML object, resulting in several more APIs to learn about. Let's start with the simplest alternative.

Canvas 2D

Canvas 2D is a JavaScript API modeled after the 2D context for HTML. A basic usage is shown in the following example:

```
Canvas {
  id: triangle
  property real triangleWidth: width * 0.8;
  property real triangleHeight: height * 0.8

  onPaint: {
    var ctx = getContext("2d");
    ctx.lineWidth = 4
    ctx.strokeStyle = "blue"
    ctx.beginPath();
    ctx.moveTo(0, 0);
    ctx.lineTo(triangleWidth, 0);
    ...
```

```
        ctx.stroke()
    }
  }
```

As you see, we will do our painting in the `onPaint` event handler using JavaScript. This API is only useful for non-complex items, because, well, it's a JavaScript API, and thus, not very fast. It might, however, be useful for quick prototyping as you can pull in existing JavaScript visualization libraries.

There is also the Canvas 3D interface, which is essentially a WebGL's equivalent in QML, that is, a low-level OpenGL API in JavaScript. As already the case with Canvas 2D, it is compatible with HTML5 JavaScript frameworks (`three.js` is already bundled with Canvas 3D) and can be very useful for quick prototyping—but do not expect high performance. However, for desktop applications where we have tons of power, JavaScript could deliver an agreeable speed.

QQuickPaintedItem

This is a convenience class using the `QPainter` interface internally. It can be used much in the style of a standard widget class, as can be seen in the following example:

```
class PaintedItemTriangle : public QQuickPaintedItem
{
public:
  void paint(QPainter* painter)
  {
    const QPolygonF polygon({ ... });

    QBrush brush(Qt::yellow);
    painter->setBrush(brush);
    painter->drawPolygon(polygon);
  }
};
```

This is very familiar and convenient, but it results in somehow not-so-amazing performance, as we will discuss in detail later in this chapter.

QQuickItem

Here, we will subclass the `QQuickItem` class and reimplement its `updatePaintNode()` method. It is the most powerful, but also most difficult, method by which to implement a custom QML item. You are in the middle of QML scene graph's workings, as can be seen in the following example:

```
class QuickItemTriangle : public QQuickItem
{
  ...
protected:
  QSGNode* updatePaintNode(QSGNode* oldNode, UpdatePaintNodeData* data)
  {
    QSGGeometryNode* triangle = static_cast<QSGGeometryNode*>(oldNode);
    if (!triangle) ... // create new one

    QSGGeometry * geometry =
        new QSGGeometry(QSGGeometry::defaultAttributes_Point2D(), 3);
    QSGGeometry::Point2D* points = geometry->vertexDataAsPoint2D();

    const QRectF rect = boundingRect();
    points[0].x = rect.left();
     ... // and so on...

    triangle->setGeometry(geometry);
    QSGFlatColorMaterial* material = new QSGFlatColorMaterial;
    material->setColor(Qt::blue);
    triangle->setMaterial(material);

    return triangle;
  }
};
```

We see, we are working with QML scene graph classes, which can be recognized by the `QSG` prefix, and directly changing the scene graph. We already mentioned that QML used a scene graph to do its rendering, and we will discuss its design later in this chapter, but at this point, it's enough to know that it contains a graph of nodes, most important of them being `QSGGeometryNode`, used to define custom geometries and materials (that is, the rendering state for a shader program).

While it requires learning a new API, it is the most powerful and performant method of extending QML as it integrates neatly with the existing mechanisms and optimizations for OpenGL rendering.

QQuickFrameBufferObject

The `QQuickFramebufferObject` allows us to wrap custom OpenGL code in a QML item. The rendering gets redirected off screen to an OpenGL frame buffer object and Qt creates the required scene graph object to accomplish that. The following example shows the basic usage:

```
class FrameBufferTriangle : public QQuickFramebufferObject
{
public:
   Renderer* createRenderer() const override;
   ...
};

class FrameBufferTriangleRenderer : public
QQuickFramebufferObject::Renderer
{
public:
   void synchronize(QQuickFramebufferObject *item) override;
   QOpenGLFramebufferObject *createFramebufferObject(const QSize &s)
override;
   void render() override
   {
      QOpenGLFunctions* f = QOpenGLContext::currentContext()->functions();
      // use OpenGL functions
      f->glClearColor(1,1,1,0); // white
      ....
   }
};
```

We see that we need two classes here—one to represent the QML item, and the second, to do the actual rendering. This is the result of the fact that we have to synchronize with the rendering algorithm of the QML scene graph, and it can, as we will see later have a multithreaded implementation.

As useful as it is to bring complete OpenGL scenes into a QML application, it is tricky to make sure custom OpenGL code does not interfere with Qt Quick renderer, and to avoid race conditions between FBO object and its renderer!

An example for the basic triangle item implemented in the preceding four ways is included in the book's resources (`https://github.com/PacktPublishing/Hands-On-High-performance-with-QT/tree/master/Chapter%208`).

More APIs

If that's not enough APIs, then, for the fun of it, we have even more possibilities to include custom content in a QML scene!

During QML rendering, the QQuickWindow object will emit the sceneGraphInitialized(), beforeSynchronizing(), beforeRendering(), sceneGraphInvalidated(), and other signals. We could connect to those signals and do our initializing and rendering in the corresponding slots using the currently valid OpenGL context. As you'd expect, it is somehow tricky to synchronize with Qt Quick renderer, however, not overly so. In this way, we are bypassing the creation of the scene graph nodes we had in the preceding case of QQuickFrameBufferObject.

If you want even more control, you can use the QtQuickRendererControl class to manually drive the QML rendering. This can be beneficial when integrating with third-party OpenGL renderers, but also if you'd like to decide when and how to redraw QML contents.

And what about the direct usage of the ShaderEffect QML item? You can insert the shader code directly as attribute values, as you can see in the next example:

```
Image {
  id: img;
  source: "qt-logo.png"
}

ShaderEffect {
  property variant src: img

  vertexShader: "
    attribute highp vec2 qt_MultiTexCoord0;
    ... "
  fragmentShader: "
    varying highp vec2 coord;
    ... "
}
```

Wow, there are quite some QML APIs out there! We can do even more—we can embed a QML scene in a widget hierarchy with QQuickWidget, as in the following example:

```
auto qmlWraper = new QQuickWidget(this);
qmlWraper->setSource(QUrl::fromLocalFile("TestItem.qml"));
qmlWraper->show();
```

Qt 3D

Qt 3D is a different take on OpenGL rendering—another one! It offers both QML and C++ APIs, and provides a high-level OpenGL API, but it uses a frame graph instead of QML's scene graph for rendering.

The difference is that in QML, there is a hard-coded renderer for the scene graph, which renders the scene in a predefined way, optimized for 2D rendering and using rather standard rendering methods. However, there is a steady stream of innovations and new approaches in 3D rendering, and Qt 3D trying to design a framework that is both more flexible and more extensible.

As a result, the frame graph doesn't specify what objects are to be rendered as the QML scene graph does. Rather, the position of a node in the frame graph tree will determine when and where the subtree contained in that node will be the active configuration in the rendering pipeline. This allows you, for example, to specify the normal forward rendering scheme or a deferred rendering (that is, using shaders as a post-processing step) by building different frame graphs.

The following QML example shows a doubly-rotating sphere using the classic Phong lighting:

```
Entity {
    id: sceneRoot

    Camera {
        id: camera
        projectionType: CameraLens.PerspectiveProjection
        aspectRatio: 16/9
        position: Qt.vector3d( 0.0, 0.0, -40.0 )
        ...
    }
    components: [
        RenderSettings {
            activeFrameGraph: ForwardRenderer {
                clearColor: Qt.rgba(1, 1, 1, 1)
                camera: camera
            }
        }
    ]
    PhongMaterial {
        id: material
    }
    SphereMesh {
        id: mesh
        radius: 10
```

```
    }
    Transform {
        id: transform
        property real userAngle: 0.0
        matrix: {
            var m = Qt.matrix4x4();
            m.rotate(userAngle, Qt.vector3d(0, 1, 0));
            m.translate(Qt.vector3d(10, 0, 0));
            return m;
        }
    }
    NumberAnimation {
        target: transform
        property: "userAngle"
        ... // standard animation
    }
    Entity {
        id: sphere
        components: [ mesh, material, transform ]
    }
}
```

We see that the framework lets us specify the rendering type for the activeFrameGraph (here the traditional forward rendering), various OpenGL 3D parameters (Camera, Transform), and offers implementation of some nontrivial features (PhongMaterial, SphereMesh). Another effect we'd be able to implement using Qt 3D is displaying the same content from a different point of view in separate windows, just like the deprecated QGraphicView was able to do. Thus, the design goals of being reconfigurable and extendable seem to be met.

In a more realistic application, you would probably create your meshes using a 3D modelling software and load it from file using the Mesh item. So, if you are implementing your own 3D content, you might consider using the Qt 3D module, but be aware that you'll have to learn a new framework and won't be quite able to leverage your knowledge of the OpenGL API. On the other hand, given that the new 3D graphics APIs that emerged recently can be integrated in that model, the Qt 3D module will probably gain more prominence in future Qt versions!

OpenGL drivers and Qt

As we have chosen Windows to be our platform for this book, let's quickly outline the state of OpenGL driver support on Windows and how Qt is handling the driver configuration theme.

The truth is OpenGL isn't a first-class citizen on Windows. The reason for this is that Microsoft has, for a long time, tried to position its own DirectX API as a competitor for the title of industry standard. Therefore, there is no OpenGL 2 driver on Windows and we have to install manufacturers' drivers, which unfortunately, can often be buggy. More correctly, if there's no **installable client driver** (**ICD**) implementing OpenGL 2, Windows will fall back to the outdated OpenGL 1.1 software layer.

To amend this situation a little, Google has implemented the **Almost Native Graphics Layer Engine** (**ANGLE**) driver that emulates OpenGL API on top of several versions of DirectX. The ANGLE driver is included in the Qt distribution and will be used if there's no OpenGL (two or higher) driver on your machine. However, if your graphics card is blacklisted or fails to initialize properly, ANGLE can switch its backend from DirectX to a software rasterizer (WARP or Mesa llvmpipe).

Graphic drivers and performance

Performance-wise, the best option is using the proper OpenGL driver, then the ANGLE driver, which has to pay the overhead of the emulation layer, then the software rasterizer fallback, which will give you the worst performance.

This is general advice and there are some special cases—for example, a good software rasterizer can sometimes outperform a native OpenGL driver for a low-cost integrated GPU. However, even a low-end dedicated graphics card will always be several times faster than software rendering.

So how can we learn which driver Qt is using on our Windows installation? If we set the QSG_INFO environment variable to 1, then on startup, any QML application will output the used driver configuration, as can be seen on the following screenshot:

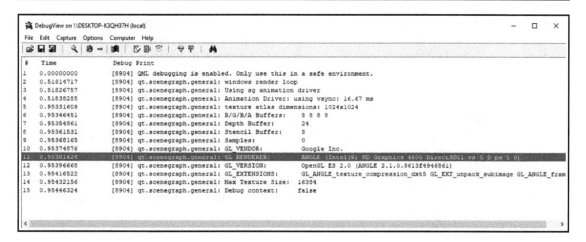

You can see on my laptop, by default, the ANGLE driver is used over Intel's DirectX DLL for the integrated Intel GPU. Here, we see the output captured in Sysinternal's tool **DebugView**, but it will also be visible in Qt Creator's **Application Output** window.

 In order to set an environment variable in Qt Creator, you go to **Projects** | **Run** | **Run Environment** | **Details**, click on the **Add** button on the right, and insert a new environment variable to be used when starting the program. An example of setting **QSG_INFO to 1** is shown on the following screenshot:

However, as we have seen, the ANGLE library contained in the Qt distribution that we've have been using provides only OpenGL ES 2.0, a slimmed-down version for embedded devices, despite the fact that the installed Intel driver supports OpenGL 3.3. Qt Creator has chosen ANGLE as the underlying driver by default when creating the project.

If Qt is using ANGLE and tries to render over DirectX, you might need to install the optional Graphic Tools Windows 10 package if the DirectX drivers are not present on your system. Go to **Settings** | **Apps** | **Manage optional features** | **Add a feature** and choose **Graphic Tools**.

Now we have two problems: first, we are compromising performance by the intermediate ANGLE layer, and second, all the cool OpenGL 3.3 features you'd like to use in your shaders won't compile. What can we do?

Setting the OpenGL implementation for QML

We can change the graphics driver to be used without the Qt application by seating the environment variable QT_OPENGL to desktop for the native OpenGL driver, ANGLE for OpenGL emulation on DirectX, or software for the Mesa software rasterizer.

The ANGLE driver will automatically choose the underlying DirectX driver, but we can force a given version by setting the environment variable QT_ANGLE_PLATFORM to d3d9, d3d11 for the corresponding DirectX version, or WARP, for the built-in DirectX software rasterizer.

If you'd like to know why your chosen graphics driver wasn't used by Qt, you can enable the logging category qt.qpa.gl by setting QT_LOGGING_RULES=qt.qpa.gl=true to see why the specific OpenGL implementation was chosen. The typical reasons are a missing OpenGL 2.0 driver, blacklisted driver, or having the environment variable QT_OPENGL set.

So, if your complicated QML application runs sluggishly in the fullscreen mode, make sure you didn't end up with software rendering due to some driver misconfiguration! Also, if the installed driver cannot provide the level of OpenGL support Qt requires, you can experiment with changing the underlying renderer to software or DirectX's WARP.

Qt Widget's performance

When speaking of Qt Widget's performance, we mean the performance; either the graphics performance of their respective software or OpenGL backends, or the performance of often used model/view model. We will start this discussion with performance.

QPainter

The software rasterizer will be used when painting the regular widgets through the QPainter class. However, QPainter class will never paint directly to the window, but rather uses a QBackingStore object, which will contain a buffered representation of the window contents. This enables Qt to implement partial updates by using QPainter only to update a subregion of the window. QBackingStore contents will be finally flushed, that is, written to the underlying OS's window by using a subclass of a QPlatformBackingStore class. On Windows, this will result in calling UpdateLayeredWindowIndirect or BitBlt system calls for respectively for translucent and opaque contents. In fact, you could also use QBackingStore and QPainter all alone, without the widget framework, to implement a lightweight raster painted window. There is even a convenience class, QRasterWindow, that does just that.

The other backend QPainter supports is painting to QWindow with a OpenGLSurface type, such as QOpenGLWidget or QOpenGLWindow. In this case, we will use the OpenGL 2.0 backend.

The default behavior of QOpenGLWidget and QOpenGLWindow (since Qt 5.5) is not to preserve the rendered contents between paint calls, because, according to Qt documentation, it provides performance benefits on some mobile and embedded hardware architectures if a framebuffer object is used as the rendering target. However, when using QPainter to render incrementally, it could be beneficial to sacrifice some performance at this point and not have to redraw the entire window on each paintGL() call. This behavior can be changed by calling QOpenGLWidget::setUpdateBehavior() with PartialUpdate.

Images

When rendering images, use the QPixmap class. In contrast, the QImage class is optimized for I/O and direct pixel manipulations.

The raster engine internally does all rendering in `Format_ARGB32_Premultiplied`, as it has the benefit that the the the alpha channel multiplication will be spared. The `Format_RGB32` is a binary equivalent of `Format_ARGB32_Premultiplied` with the alpha channel set to `0xff`, but other formats will first have to be converted to the internal representation, making the drawing much slower! Another format for which drawing will be optimized in most contexts is `Format_RGB16`, but any other format has significantly worse performance.

In general, we should also avoid the alpha channel in images if we want to improve performance.

Optimized calls

`QPainter` supports different backends, implements a great variety of graphical operations, and works on different hardware. Because one cannot optimize for every combination of these factors, Qt decided to select a subset of the `QPainter` API and to guarantee its performance will be as good as one can reasonably get. The following operations are part of this optimized subset:

- `QPainter`'s compositions using `Source` and `SourceOver` are special cased for most operations.
- Simple and common transformations are always optimized, namely translation, scaling, and `0-90-180-270` degree rotations.
- Rectangle fills are very common, thus, they are optimized for solid color, two-color linear gradients, and simple transformations. Also rounded rectangle fills are optimized, but not with transformations.
- The `drawPixmap()`, without translucency and smoothing transformations, also in combination with simple transforms. Furthermore, `qDrawBorderPixmap()` is optimized too.
- Rectangular clipping is also special cased, even with simple transformations.

As laying out text can be costly, there is a `QStaticText` class, which provides caching of layout data for a block of text, so that it can be drawn more efficiently. You have to use `QPainter::drawStaticText()` to use this class' cached layout, `drawText()` will trigger a new calculation.

Software rasterizer implements antialiasing, but be aware that this will have significant costs!

In some settings, other operations can be fast too, but it is not guaranteed. Remember that you can always boost your performance using caching—store the result of a slow operation in QPixmap, reuse it later! Qt already provides a ready to use implementation of pixmap caching in the QPixmapCache class, so don't hesitate to use it.

OpenGL rendering with QOpenGLWidget

Why don't we make OpenGL the default rendering mode for widgets? The problem is the integration with native theming—you cannot simply forward your OpenGL context to the OS calls painting the GUI elements. Even if you could, this would result in many OpenGL calls for drawing small elements with many state changes making it rather inefficient. This makes OpenGL optimal for graphics contents embedded in some widget hierarchy, as with the QOpenGLWidget.

For rendering the general QpenGL, the following guidelines apply:

- Minimize state changes such as brush, color, texture. If you are using QPainter for drawing, do not switch between two painter instances!
- Render batches of primitives of the same type together, bunch up lots of small pictures into a single big one (sprite).
- Minimize usage of translucent pixels and blending.

Images

Images will be rendered as OpenGL textures. Depending on the OpenGL versions supporting Frame Buffer Objects extension, the image will be rendered to the internal user-defined frame buffer on the GPU.

Typically, the OpenGL ES 2.0 drivers do not have this extension available, so in this case, we will first render into QImage, and then upload it to the GPU to be used as a new texture!

Threading and context sharing

Offscreen rendering in a worker thread, for example, in order to generate textures that are later used in the GUI thread in paintGL(), is possible by sharing QOpenGLWidget's OpenGL context with the worker thread.

We can also render directly to the QOpenGLWidget framebuffer from the worker thread by reimplementing paintEvent() to do nothing and moving the QOpenGLWidget's QOpenGLContext to the worker thread with QObject::moveToThread(). After we've rendered the contents in the worker, we move the OpenGL context back to the GUI thread, and call update() to trigger further processing.

Usage of QPainter

When using QPainter with an OpenGL surface, the same performance is guaranteed that we have seen in the previous sections.

However, the rendering result will be sent to the GPU as a texture with caveats we discussed previously. If the QOpenGLWidget will be redrawn with QPainter each time, we will force a texture transfer to the GPU with each frame! Performance-wise, this technique lends itself best to rendering of static contents, such as logos or backgrounds.

QGraphicsView

We already said that you shouldn't use this framework in modern Qt applications, but what if you have to support it in some legacy systems?

One of the USPs of QGraphicsView was that it supported multiple views of the same scene. However, it didn't really strike a chord with the users and resulted in a complicated code base, which proved not to be suitable for optimizations! If you care for performance, you could consider migrating to QML, as even with OpenGL backend, the performance of QGraphicsView is expected to be worse than those of QML.

If you are nonetheless determined to stay with QGraphicsView, be aware that the convenient QGraphicsProxyWidget class, which can embed a straight Widget instance in the graphics view, is a performance killer.

Model/view framework

When we are displaying a collection of objects, we have to set of classes: the convenience classes of QListWidget, QTableWidget, and QTreeWidget; and the model/view based classes of QListView, QTableView, and QTreeView.

`QTableWidget` and so on are convenience classes; if we need fast updates, it is better to use a `QTableView`, and its cousins, `QListView`, and `QTreeView`. In this case, you will have to write a model class containing data to be shown in the corresponding view class. However, there are limits to model/view classes as well. As a rule of thumb, we could use the following gradation:

- **Under hundred items**: `QTableWidget` and so on
- **Hundreds to (maybe) few thousand items**: `QTableView` and so on
- **More than that**: We'll need some optimization

What optimization techniques are possible? What we want to do is to decrease the number of view updates during model population. Some possibilities to achieve that are the following:

- Using the `QContiguousCache` class to manage the model's data, instead of populating the model in one go. This class is already optimized for the specific task of caching data that are displayed in a user interface view.
- Using the `canFetchMore()` and `fetchMore()` functions to populate the model gradually, and not in one go. For example, we could dynamically populate a tree model so that `fetchMore()` is called when a branch in the tree model is expanded.
- Writing a custom model instead of using `QStandardItemModel`, so you can control the granularity of view updates when inserting objects. This would allow you building models by inserting data in bigger chunks than single items.

QML performance

The first and most important performance QML improvement technique is the *use newest Qt version* trick, as in each new release, QML performance gets steadily improved. So, let's start this section with a look at the performance improvements achieved in the current LTS version of the framework.

Improvements in 5.9 and beyond

For the Qt 5.9 LTS version we are using in this book, one of the most important objectives was to significantly improve the QML performance compared to the previous LTS version, that is, Qt 5.6.

This objective was met quite impressively, as in some areas the performance could be improved even up to 130%, the average over all modules being 14%. More specifically, the following improvements were implemented:

- **QML application startup time**: Qt 5.8 already introduced QML caching and Qt 5.9 added a possibility to pre-populate it, so that already the first start will be fast
- **Qt Quick Controls 2 were fully supported as replacement for Qt Quick Controls 1**: Their performance was hugely improved (by up to 140% in some cases)
- **Shader cache**: If your Qt application is using OpenGL shaders, the newly introduced shader cache will improve startup times

Other improvements that were introduced include: improved binary size, reduction when using Qt Lite configuration system, rewritten QML garbage collection, and improved JavaScript performance.

In the next versions, that is, Qt 5.10, Qt 5.11, and the planned Qt 5.12 LTS version, further performance improvements will be introduced, such as a completely new JavaScript and QML compiler architecture, support for compressed OpenGL textures, inclusion of the Qt Quick compiler in the open source version, improved `TableView` performance, and a tool for pre-generation of GPU font rendering information (distance fields).

Measuring QML performance

How can we see what FPS we are achieving in our QML application? There are two ways to accomplish that. The first one is kind of a poor man's solution, but can be quite effective nonetheless. We can use the QML Profiler we introduced in `Chapter 2`, *Profiling to Find Bottlenecks*. We can record a trace, and then switch to the timeline, select the **Scene Graph,** and then the **Select Range** tool button on the left. This will allow you to select the **Start** and **End** time of frame rendering and QML Profiler will display the elapsed time, as is shown in the following screenshot:

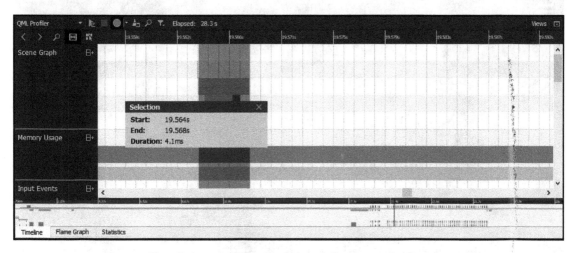

Now you know how long it takes to render a frame, you just have to invert it and you will obtain the FPS, for example, render time of 16 millisecond results in 1000/16 = 62.5 FPS. Thus, to obtain the smooth-looking 60 FPS, your render time cannot be greater than 16 millisecond.

If you look closely at the scene graph's time bar in the preceding screenshot, you'll see that it consists of three parts corresponding to the rendering phases: scene synchronization, rendering, and FBO buffer swap. We will explain these phases later in this chapter.

The second method is to programmatically record the FPS rate and display it in a custom QML control. Technically, this can be achieved by connecting to the signals emitted by the rendering thread of the QML scene graph we already introduced in this chapter, for example, `QQuickItem::afterRendering()`, and measure the number of frames that were rendered in a second. One of the examples bundled with the Qt installation uses this technique to monitor the FPS rate for various shader effects, as can be seen in the lower right side of the following screenshot:

An example implementation of a counter similar to one shown in the preceding screenshot is included in this book's resources (`https://github.com/PacktPublishing/Hands-On-High-performance-with-QT/tree/master/Chapter%208`).

Another way to investigate QML's performance issues is to use graphical performance tools we learned about in `Chapter 2`, *Profiling to Find Bottlenecks*. For example, *apitrace* and its companion viewer, *qapitrace*, can be used to show all OpenGL calls executed and the thumbnail view of the respective contents of the frame buffer for each call! That can be a great help. The GPU View tool we have also seen in `Chapter 2`, *Profiling to Find Bottlenecks*, can show you whether the bottlenecks lie in the CPU, GPU, or the driver.

Startup of a QML application

In the startup phase QML files have to be loaded, compiled, the bindings will be assigned, images loaded, text items layouted, and view delegates instantiated.

We can optimize the startup time by doing less in each of these phases, namely, the following:

- **Compilation**: This is rarely the problem, as experience tells us, but the first method here is to have less items to compile. We can also use the Qt Quick compiler (free since Qt 5.11), which can reduce the duration of this phase up to 50%. If your version doesn't have free Qt Quick compiler support yet, the alternative method is to pre-populate the QML cache (which is possible since Qt 5.9), so that already, the first start of the application will be fast. It is reported that both approaches offer comparable performance.
- **Bindings**: As before, using less and less complex bindings help. Also, moving your bindings to C++ will speed things up, as JavaScript execution is slower. Unexpectedly at this point, the Qt Quick compiler could also help. It compiles QML to C++ code, which is later passed to the C++ compiler, and the GNU C++ compiler can do a much better job at optimizing code than JavaScript's V8 **just in time (JIT)** compiler!
- **Creation of items**: You knew it was coming, but just create less items! One well-known technique is to use a Loader element to asynchronously load things after the startup phase at the point when they are needed. This can be done by simply setting the `asynchronous` Loader's property. A different scenario is shown in the following example, namely the on signals `needToLoadPage2` or `page2Exit`, the QML file `Page2.qml` will get loaded or unloaded:

```
Item {
  id: startPage

  Loader {
    id: pageLoader
    source: "Welcome.qml"
  }
  Connections {
    target: pageLoader.item
    onNeedToLoadPage2: pageLoader.source = "Page2.qml" // load & replace
    onPage2Exit: pageLoader.source = "Welcome.qml"     // unload
  }
  ...
}
```

As we have heard that most QML developers miss that technique, we will reiterate: don't forget about Loaders! They are a great way to speed up the startup times too—we show a minimal fist page, maybe even a splash screen, and then we show the first real content using a Loader. However, don't forget that Loaders have a price too, so do not use it to load small items!

To speed up the rendering of fonts on the GPU, QML will preprocess the used fonts to create a so-called distance-field. This happens the first time a glyph is displayed.

If we want to additionally optimize startup performance, it is possible to pre-generate this font data, using the Distance Field Generator tool (since Qt 5.12) for all glyphs in the fonts, or just for those that are known to be displayed during a critical startup phase. However, for most cases, the default behavior of Qt is expected to be good enough, so don't jump to this technique if it isn't an identified bottleneck.

QML rendering

To understand the performance of QML rendering we have to understand the OpenGL pipeline, which we already discussed, and additionally, the architecture of the underlying QML scene graph. So let's start with exactly that.

Scene graph optimizations

Qt Quick 2 makes use of a scene graph instead of a traditional imperative painting API as it is, for example, provided in the `QPainter` class. Instead of issuing a number of drawing commands, the QML application builds up a tree of `QSGNode` instances (the already mentioned scene graph) to be rendered by the GPU. Then a separate renderer module will say **have a look** at the scene graph, and decide how it will render it on the GPU.

A performance advantage inherent to such an approach is that the renderer sees the entire contents to be painted from the start, and that opens up opportunities for a number of optimizations! This situation is analogous to the whole program optimization advantages for the compiler we discussed in `Chapter 1`, *Understanding Performant Programs*.

As we already learned, GPU works best when the number of draw calls is low, and the state changes are very infrequent. In order to achieve it, the renderer will try to merge the graphics element in *batches*, which can be rendered using a a single OpenGL call. In this manner, we try to minimize the number of draw calls and state changes.

Qt documentation is quite explicit on that subject: *uploads should happen only when really needed, batches should be fewer than 10 and at least 3-4 of them should be opaque*. We can examine how our program is rendered by enabling the scene graph renderer's trace. This is done by setting the environment variable QSG_RENDERER_DEBUG=render. In the following screenshot, we can see that the rendering trace contains detailed information about used batches:

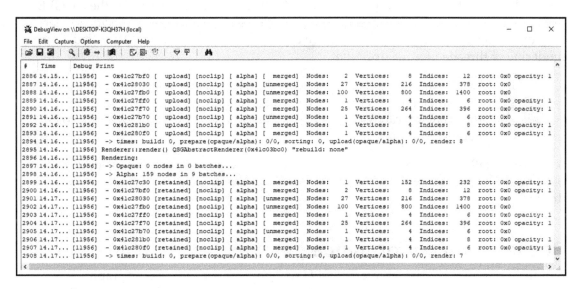

The second optimization used by the renderer is discovering the parts of the tree that have not changed since the last frame and recusing the geometry already stored on the GPU for the non-changed parts.

Moreover, the Qt Quick scene graph uses a form of batching of the textures, namely, it allows for multiple QSGTexture objects to be allocated as sub-regions of a larger texture. This technique is called **texture atlas** and will minimize the state changes on the GPU as several QSGTexture instances will be placed in a single GPU texture buffer.

Scene graph and threading

To improve rendering performance, a multithreaded approach is used in QML. When the UI thread requests an update, the renderer thread will get the current scene graph status from the QML objects by calling the `QQuickItem::updatePaintNode()` function on all items that have changed since the previous frame. This phase is called synchronization and the GUI thread is blocked until it is finished. After this phase the GUI thread is free to advance animations and do the event processing, while the rendering thread will interact with GPU, issue rendering calls and at the end set the new frame buffer contents.

But there is some bad news also—for some OpenGL driver the multithreaded rendering is disabled and QML will do everything in the GUI thread! This is the case for the ANGLE driver on Windows and Mesa drivers on Linux. We can force usage of a specific render loop by setting `QSG_RENDER_LOOP` variable to Windows or basic for non-threaded rendering or threaded for the opposite.

 The *windows* render loop should be used on Windows; *basic* on other platforms. If the OpenGL driver can provide so called *v-sync based throttling*, we can use *threaded* or *windows* loops, otherwise, we have to fall back to *basic*.

So, if we are falling back to ANGLE, or even worse, to Mesa, we will pay an additional performance overhead by disabling multithreaded rendering. So, watch out for your drivers!

Scene graph performance gotchas

Building on our knowledge of internal GPU working and the QML scene graph optimizations, we will now formulate a couple of guidelines for achieving good QML performance.

Batching

First and foremost, we should strive to preserve good batching. Unfortunately, there are some operations that will do that. Thus, we should avoid the following:

- Item clipping—instead of clipping text, use eliding; instead of clipping an image, use one that is already cropped
- Overlapping compound items as they cannot be batched
- Using 32-bit indices in custom geometry and some material flags, such as `RequiresFullMatrix`, as they prevent batching

Surprisingly, breaking the batching can sometimes get you out of trouble! For example, if you have a UI containing 1,000 static labels and decide that one of them should blink, this changing one label can cause a redraw of the complete batch of labels! In the future Qt versions, this optimization could be done in the scene graph, but for now, the workaround is to break the batch setting clip property for the blinking item! This will let the big batch go unchanged and update only the changed item.

> You can use the QSG_VISUALIZE environment variable to debug batching, by setting its value to **batches**. This will result in displaying items belonging to merged batches drawn with a solid color, and those of unmerged batches drawn with a diagonal line pattern. Other possible values are **clip**, **changes**, and **overdraw**, for visualizing, clipping, changed items, and overdraws, respectively.

Texture atlas

Make sure the texture atlas is used for Image and BorderImage QML items, this will be enabled by default, for textures created in C++, you have to set an appropriate flag. Setting the **QSG_ATLAS_OVERLAY** environment variables will show you all used texture atlases in a nice visualization.

Occlusion, blending, and other costly operations

If an item shouldn't be visible, set its visible attribute to false, this will spare the GPU some work. In the same vein, use opaque primitives and images where possible to spare GPU from alpha blending work.

You should also avoid costly operations like scaling or smooth transformation, and make animated area as small as possible to avoid updates of big portions of the screen.

Antialiasing

There are two forms of antialiasing in QML: vertex antialiasing and multisample antialiasing. Multisample antialiasing is a hardware feature, and thus, won't cost you very much. It can be set by the QSurfaceFormat::samples() method. However, this is an extension of the OpenGL and isn't present on all chips, especially in embedded domain. The vertex aliasing is set by the Item::antialiasing property, will be done in software, and provide better quality, but it will require blending; slow down the batching algorithm and it may also result in less batching.

Use caching

Caching is a basic performance improvement technique, and we can also put it to good use in QML by doing the following:

- Using caching of whole QML items by setting `layer.enabled: true`
- Using a cache buffer for the `ListView` element—it is enabled by setting the `cacheBuffer` attribute to a nonzero value

Which QML custom item should you choose?

We already introduced the four possibilities to write custom QML elements, so let's sum up their respective performance.

As we said QML Canvas item is slow. We can use it for non-complex items or prototyping.

`QQuickPaintedItem` uses the `QPainter` for drawing and then creates a texture to be used by the GPU, thus making it a two-step operation and inducing the costs of GPU state change. Make sure you don't redraw such items too often, this will slow down the GPU with texture changes! Additionally, it only implements `QPainter`-based antialiasing. All this makes `QQuickPaintedItem` convenient, but slow.

When using `QQuickFramebufferObject`, its contents will also be displayed in the scene graph as a texture, so the same caveats as previously stated still apply. This class is best used for rendering underlays or overlays for the entire windows. On the more advanced side, it is also possible to combine multiple rendering contexts and multiple threads using this API.

The best choice thus is to reimplement `QQuickItem`'s `updatePaintNode()` method as it will optimally insert itself into the QML scene graph mechanics!

JavaScript usage

Generally, we shouldn't use JavaScript for implementation of application's logic, but instead implement the UI with QML and the functionality with C++. The reason for that general guideline is that execution of JavaScript code will be much costlier than those of C++. While this may be okay on beefy desktop machines, embedded or mobile environments may be less forgiving in that respect.

It can be especially detrimental in animations, thus also in scrolling of lists, because JavaScript code then gets evaluated in every frame as many times at there are instantiated delegates!

We should also avoid the following:

- Javascript calculations in bindings; remove them to C++ code instead
- Conversions of property types, for example, by using *string* instead of the URL property for an image's source
- Resolving properties in tight loops (as we should avoid JavaScript code anyway)
- Changing sequence properties in tight loops—you can fill a locally created sequence and swap it with the property to increase the performance somehow (but we should avoid JavaScript code anyway!)

Moreover, we can optimize memory usage of a QML application by destroying unneeded elements, either by calling `destroy()` on them, or, when they were created using a `Loader`, by resting the `source` property of the `Loader`.

Qt Quick Controls

We already mentioned that there are two versions of the Qt Quick Controls module—Quick Controls 1, which were designed for the traditional desktop environments, have a very broad scope and provide a flexible styling system.

The second version, Quick Controls 2, are specifically designed for embedded systems where the hardware has limited resources, have an optimized implementation (for example, the internal event handling was rewritten in C++), and no longer support pre-built native styles. This all results in better performance compared to Quick Controls 1.

We already mentioned that with each new Qt release, the QML performance gets better. One of the biggest improvements in this field that came with Qt 5.12 was the introduction of the `TableView` item in Quick Controls 2, sporting a much better performance compared to the old `TableView` in Qt Quick Controls 1! The reason for the improvement is that the old `TableView` was implemented on top of `ListView`, which is optimized for displaying only a single column. Because of that, the old `TableView` couldn't achieve optimal performance. The new `TableView` was reimplemented in C++ on top of the `Flickable` item and seems to scale up to models with thousands of elements without performance problems.

Other modules

In this section, we will briefly have a look at the performance of other graphical Qt modules; however, we will not be discussing them in detail.

Qt 3D performance

In the recent Qt releases, especially Qt 5.11 and Qt 5.12, there was a constant stream of performance improvements for Qt 3D, be it in CPU memory usage or improved SIMD support. Thus, this module seems to be under very active development.

One interesting feature is that, internally, Qt 3D uses the task-based approach to parallelism we have already spoken about in `Chapter 5`, *An In-Depth Guide to Concurrency and Multithreading*; that is, it dispatches tasks to the worker threads, each running on a single core. This approach will naturally scale when more cores are available in the system. This also makes it possible to automatically generate multiple render commands and render views in parallel.

This looks very promising, and it will be interesting to watch the evolution of Qt 3D in future Qt versions!

The commercially available Qt 3D Studio 2.0 sports the Debugging and Profiling UIs, which display basic information about rendering performance and structure of the 3D scene. It is implemented in a game-like manner as an immediate overlay GUI (they even used the well-known *Dear ImGUI* to implement it!). Unfortunately, there isn't such a tool in the open source version.

This leaves us with general-purpose tools, such as *apitrace*, profilers, ETW, and GPU View. Let's hope that in future releases, the Profiling UI will also be available in the open source version.

Hybrid web applications

Qt also offers a possibility to integrate an actual browser in your application to display graphics contents. As browsers are running JavaScript engines for custom code, the performance will not be as good as those of native C++ based Qt modules.

There are there Qt modules that support this functionality: Qt Webkit, Qt WebEngine, and Qt WebView. Out of the three, Qt Webkit is based on the *Webkit* open source browser engine. Currently it is deprecated, and it is recommended to use Qt WebEngine instead.

The Qt WebEngine module uses the open source *Chromium* web engine and offers both QML and C++ APIs. However, it will embed the complete web browser stack in your application. A much lighter alternative is offered by the Qt WebView module, which will invoke the native browser for a given platform, that is, Edge, Chrome, or Safari.

Summary

In this chapter, we looked at the vast theme of graphics performance. It's a very deep topic given the recent advances in graphics hardware and APIs. Additionally, there is an almost infinite number of Qt APIs for drawing and painting as a consequence of its long history.

Nonetheless, we started by learning about modern graphics hardware, the OpenGL pipeline as its abstract programming model, and its possible bottlenecks. Then we moved to an overview of the Qt's graphics APIs and learned which ones should still be used and which should be avoided. Next, we had a closer look at the two most important parts of Qt: the Qt Widget's and Qt Quick modules. We learned about their internal mechanisms and techniques to improve their performance. We also had a quick look at the relatively new and very promising Qt 3D module.

With this amount of information, you are now in position to doing your own graphics performance optimizations of Qt programs! We will thus move on and, in the next chapter, we will look at the Qt way of doing network communication.

Questions

Now, there's time for some more questions testing your understanding of the topics we learned in this chapter:

1. Which OpenGL version will be used if your application uses the ANGLE driver? And what is an ICD?
2. Which draw calls of `QPainter` are safe to use in the critical path?
3. You see the following OpenGL code we used in one of the examples:

   ```
   glBegin(GL_TRIANGLES);
   glColor3f(1.0, 0.0, 0.0);
   glVertex3f(-0.5, -0.5, 0);
   ...
   ```

   What is your reaction?
4. What is a stencil and when will it be applied in the graphics pipeline?
5. What optimizations are performed by the default QML scene graph?
6. You are a platform vendor and you'd like to take advantage of non-standard hardware features with your QML applications. What can you do?
7. Why would you consider using `QGraphicView` in a new project?
8. What kinds of shaders are possible with OpenGL?

Further reading

Real-Time Rendering, 4th Edition by *T. Akenine-Möller et al. CRC Press (2018)* is a very comprehensive, 1,000 page long treatment of the subject of 3D graphics and rendering. It starts with the basics and discusses every facet of graphics programming, ending with a discussion of graphics hardware. It also boasts quite an extensive list of online resources including additional downloadable chapters.

Game Engine Architecture, 3rd Edition by *J. Gregory, CRC Press (2018),* has a chapter on rendering that includes a discussion of the rendering pipeline, so to say condensing the 1,000 pages of the previous book to about 100. It is also a classic introduction to game programming in general.

There's also NVIDIA's book series: *GPU Gems 1, GPU Gems 2,* and *GPU Gems 3* that are laudably and freely accessible online at `https://developer.nvidia.com/gpugems/GPUGems`. The books cover different aspects of 3D graphics, and also computational usage of GPUs, and are also available in print from *Addison-Wesley*.

Optimizing Network Performance

9

We cannot imagine the world of today without ubiquitous wireless communication and instantaneous network access. Since Qt is not just a GUI toolkit but rather a general application framework, it has to support networking if it wants to stay relevant in the modern programming world. In this chapter, we will look at the performance of network protocols, the networking support to be found in the Qt framework, as well as its performance characteristics and optimization options.

In this chapter, we will discuss the following topics:

- **Introduction to networking:** To get you started on data communication
- **Qt networking classes:** An overview of what Qt Network has to offer
- **Improving network performance:** To show you some useful techniques
- **Advanced networking themes:** To give you more perspective

You do not need any previous networking knowledge to read this chapter, as we will introduce the basic networking notions and then build on that knowledge.

Introduction to networking

We don't want to explain the entirety of networking here as it is another vast, traditionally acronym-riddled theme with its own long history, but we will try to give a simple introduction to the most popular protocols. What is a protocol, you may ask? Let's say that it is a predefined, already implemented solution for sending data between computers. This implementation is located in the OS kernel and the programmer can use it out-of-the-box.

When communicating between two computers over a network, we can use two types of protocol: the so-called **Transport Protocols**, whose only purpose is to send opaque data from endpoints A to B, and the so-called **Application Protocols**, which will implement some logic using a transport protocol to send data.

Protocols are layered, that is, they are placed on top of each other, as any protocol higher up in the stack will use the lower protocol and enhance it. The protocol logic we mentioned previously denotes the kind of conversation the two endpoints can engage in; for example, in **HTTP (HyperText Transfer Protocol)** they can say *GET me a list of users* and receive *OK, here are the users* in response. Potential conversations are determined by the definition of the protocol and are carried out by sending and receiving data packets (also called **Protocol Data Units (PDUs)**) as follows:

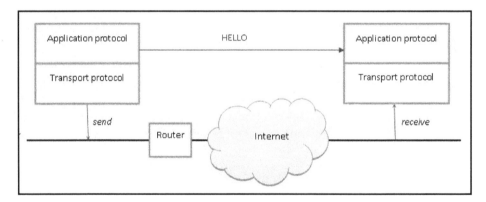

There are many protocol layers that are needed for our mobile networks to function, but as this isn't an academic treatise, we won't discuss them all here. Instead, we will limit ourselves to two already-introduced broad classes: transport and application layer protocols.

Transport layer

On the transport layer, we have two choices: either send the data out and hope it will arrive at the destination, or be mistrustful and require that the remote endpoint should send an acknowledgement when the data really arrives there.

Why should the data get lost in transit? Aren't we being overcautious? Well, there are several reasons that cannot be discounted—overflowing a network router's buffers, cosmic rays flipping bits in the message, or a crashed server or router. Thus, if we want to make sure that our data will arrive at its destination, we need some double-checking to be put in place.

User Datagram Protocol (UDP)

The protocol that implements the simple fire-and-forget strategy is the **User Datagram Protocol** (**UDP**) (datagram being another word for data packet). We only have to specify what the IP address of the other machine is and then send the data forward. That's all – sweet and simple.

Transmission Control Protocol (TCP)

If we are looking for a more reliable data transfer, we will have to employ the **Transmission Control Protocol** (**TCP**) protocol. It is also known as TCP/IP due to its usage of IP addresses and the eponymous underlying lower-level protocol.

TCP uses a networking concept known as **connection**, meaning a contract between two endpoints in which that data will be sent between them using some contextual data describing the current state of the connection. This is put to use in TCP to maintain counters for the sent and received packets on both ends of the connection. There are several aspects to the TCP protocol, such as the following:

- **Connection setup:** If we want to communicate with TCP, we must first establish a connection between both endpoints. The mechanism that's used is called a **three-way handshake** – first, a connection request (called **SYN**) is sent, then the counterpart responds with **SYN-ACK**, signalling the intention of participating the connection, and lastly the initiator sends it off with ACK. This sequence is illustrated by the following diagram:

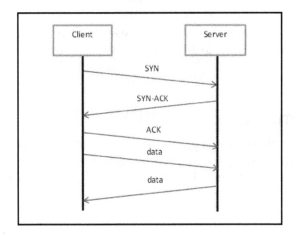

- **Data transmission:** After that, exchange data can be sent between both endpoints over the connection. Each sent packet will need to be acknowledged by the receiving side (that is, ACK) for the next packet to be sent. If we don't receive the ACK in some fixed interval but we are willing to wait for it, we declare the packet as lost and send it again—a procedure known as **retransmission**. Of course, if we re-transmit too soon, the remote node gets two copies of the data and has to cope with that by discarding one of them.
- **Flow and congestion control:** The TCP protocol also contains mechanisms to avoid overflowing the receiver with data faster than it can process it, as well as preventing the entire network from overloading.

This describes the basic mechanism of TCP, however the real implementation contains many more features and optimizations. We will describe them shortly when we discuss TCP's performance later in this chapter.

A better TCP?

Generally speaking, we can see that there is quite some overhead in TCP over and above the simple fire-and-forget approach, especially in the connection setup phase. Flow and congestion control also take their toll on performance.This raises the question: why don't we just take UDP, re-implement the re-transmission counters, and discard all the fancy TCP stuff? If you think that way, you are not alone – such implementations are attempted all the time. In this case, don't write your own – use one of the already existing implementations such as **UDP-based Data Transfer (UDT)**, ENet, or RakNet. Back in the day, the **Stream Control Transmission (SCTP)** protocol was considered to be TCP's successor, but as of today, the most promising candidate seems to be another UDT, namely Google's Quick **UDP Internet Connections (QUIC)**.

If you wonder why TCP has all of these fat features, just keep in mind that it wasn't optimized for general-case end-to-end delivery and latency, but rather for reliable file transfer and throughput.

Application layer

Let's be frank, the most important application layer protocol today is HTTP. It powers everything on the internet that we come to rely on in our daily life. The other application level protocol that used to be supported in Qt was **File Transfer Protocol (FTP)**, but support for it was removed as of Qt 5.0 and was replaced with HTTP access to `ftp://` addresses. Thus, we will only discuss HTTP and its related protocols.

Domain Name Service (DNS)

As you already know from your daily experience in HTTP, we don't use IP addresses directly, but rather **Unified Resource Locations (URLs)** such as `www.google.com/index.html`. The first thing we have to do before we can even access HTTP is to translate the first part of this character string into a corresponding network address. We do this by using the **Domain Name Service (DNS)** protocol, which can query a hierarchical collection of servers on the internet holding address data for given domain names. DNS uses the (unreliable) UDP protocol for its transport layer.

HyperText Transfer Protocol (HTTP)

HTTP is a relatively simple protocol that follows the request-response pattern. Its most popular version is HTTP/1.1. The protocol is text-based, and so it's human readable and easily debuggable. It uses TCP as its transport and thus doesn't have to be concerned about lost packets and re-transmissions. An HTTP request consists of the command, which in this example is GET, and several headers that act as lines of the general name : value form:

```
GET /path/file.html HTTP/1.1
Connection: close
Host: www.somedomain.com
```

With this simple command, we have requested the contents of a HTML file to be sent back in response. The response, in turn, could look like this:

```
HTTP/1.1 200 OK
Date: Fri, 7 Dec 2018 23:59:59 GMT
Content-Type: text/plain
Content-Length: 44

abcdefghijklmnopqrstuvwxyz1234567890abcdefgh
```

We can see that we have received the OK return code and several headers containing the date of the file's last modification, the file's encoding type, and the length of the file's data. After the blank line, the actual file's contents follow. Other basic HTTP request types are POST and PUT for creating and changing remote data and DELETE for deleting them. Indeed, by using these high-level commands and an appropriate naming scheme in the URLs, we can build entire APIs (so-called **REST (Representational State Transfer) APIs**), which can then be accessed remotely with the HTTP protocol. In this non-passive usage, HTTP is the crucial part of the interactive, distributed web 2.0 world we are living in today.

The protocol itself already contains some mechanisms to allow for optimization, such as the following:

- **Chunked responses:** If we use chunked replays, we don't have to specify the length of all data – only for the current chunk we send. In that manner, we don't have all of the data present before sending it back and responding.
- **Conditional requests:** Because a server cannot send us a notification when a resource changes, the client has to repeatedly poll the resource to detect changes. To avoid always sending the entire resource back, we can use an If-Modified-Since header, as shown in the following example:

  ```
  GET /path/file.html HTTP/1.1
  If-Modified-Since: Fri, 7 Dec 2018 23:59:59 GMT
  Host: www.somedomain.com
  ```

Only if something has changed will the whole resource be sent back. Normally, the server will reply only with the `304 Not-Modified` return code. However, as the timestamp we rely on is rather crude (seconds only), for high frequency changes, we should use the `ETag` header, which contains a hash of the entire resource's contents, and the `If-None-Match` header in the request.

- **Compression of contents:** A client can request compressed contents using the `Accept-Encoding` header with the `gzip` and `deflate` values. This can considerably reduce network traffic. However, this only applies to resource contents, as the headers will be always sent in plain text!
- **Caching:** HTTP design introduces the notion of caching as a basic performance optimization mechanism. Caching can be done everywhere in the network and is controlled by two headers: `Expires` and `Cache-Control`. By using these two headers, a sever can announce how long a given page can be cached and when it has to be refreshed.

There are many more headers and options that we cannot discuss here due to a lack of space. Consult the books that are mentioned in the *Further reading* section of this chapter for additional information.

Secure data transfer

The **Secure Socket Layer (SSL)** and its successor, the **Transport Layer Security (TLS)**, is the protocol that provides end-to-end encryption of the data to be sent over a TCP connection. There is also a variant that uses UDP as the transport mechanism called **Datagram Transport Layer Security (DTLS)**.

TLS employs a complicated handshake to set up the encryption, and involves **Client Hello**, **Server Hello**, **Client Finish**, and **Server Finish** messages, thus requiring two round-trips before the encoded data can be sent. Besides data encoding, TLS will use certificates to confirm the identity of the server and optionally the clients. It relies on a public/private key pair cryptographic mechanism in the connection setup phase. Later, a fast block cipher is used to secure the data.

SSL and TLS are placed below HTTP in the protocol stack so that HTTP can use an encrypted end-to-end transport stream for its data. In this case, HTTP is known as **HTTPS (Hyper Text Transfer Protocol - Secure)**.

Now we have learned about all of the commonly used modern protocols. The following diagram visualizes their interdependencies:

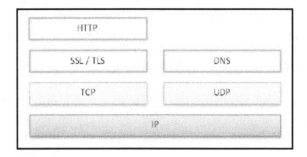

Can you decipher all of the acronyms?

A better HTTP?

As we have already seen, HTTP builds on TCP, which already has its own set of performance problems and adds a couple of its own, such as plain text context encoding, SSL negotiation overhead, resending the headers, and relying on cyclic polling. Because of that, considerable work has been done on defining improved protocols such as WebSockets and Google's SPDY, which has then served as a base for the recent HTTP/2 standard. The very fresh HTTP/3 standard even includes the **Quick UDP Internet Connections** (**QUIC**) protocol that we mentioned previously as a possible transport layer! We will discuss these innovations in more detail later in this chapter when we discuss HTTP performance optimizations.

Qt networking classes

We will now introduce Qt networking classes and look at their basic usage patterns. During this discussion, we will introduce even more networking terms and concepts.

TCP and UDP networking classes

Lower level transport protocols are implemented by the `QUdpSocket` class for the UDP protocol, as well as `QTcpSocket` and `QTcpServer` for the TCP protocol.

We identify the remote communication endpoint by using the IP address of the remote machine and a port that identifies the program on the remote machine we want to talk to. Ports are identified by their port numbers, and some of these numbers (called **well-known ports**) are reserved for servers implementing higher-level protocols such as 80 for HTTP or 443 for HTTPS.

> Note that there are two types of IP address: IPv.4 and IPv.6 addresses. The latter was introduced after the former, since it was on the verge of exhaustion. When QTcpServer and QUdpSocket are bound to QHostAddress::Any, they will be able to receive both IPv4 and IPv6 connections. In this book's examples, we are using the older IPv.4 addresses.

QTcpServer and QTcpSocket

The TCP defines two roles for communication – the server that waits for a client to initiate the connection, and the client that will then send and receive data. The following code example shows the basic usage of a QTcpServer class:

```
server = new QTcpServer(this);
server ->listen(QHostAddress::any, 8044);
connect(server, &QTcpServer::newConnection,
        this, &MyClass::acceptClntConn);
```

We are starting a server and listening on the local port 8044, willing to accept incoming IP v.4 and v.6 connections. The second thing we notice is that QTcpSocket works asynchronously and emits signals to report status changes. Internally, the QTcpSocket will use asynchronous native operating system interfaces such as the MsgWaitForMultipleObjectsEx() system call on Windows and ppoll() on Linux, to wait for events on the underlying socket file description. Due to this, we have to connect to QTcpSocket signals and react to them asynchronously in callbacks.

Some example callbacks for handling new incoming connections and receiving client data are as follows:

```
void MyClass::acceptClientConn()
{
  QTcpSocket* conn = server->nextPendingConnection();
  connect(conn , &QTcpSocket::readyRead, this, MyClass::readClientData);
}

void MyClass::readClientData()
{
```

```
QTcpSocket* conn = dynamic_cast<QTcpSocket *>(sender());

if (!conn->canReadLine())
    return;

char buf[1024];
conn->readLine(buf, sizeof(buf));
... // process data
}
```

Here, we used the convenience method readLine(), but we could also use the read() or readAll() methods. We are reading the data from the internal QTcpSocket read buffer, so if we don't read all the data at once, it will still be available later. The incoming data will be appended to that internal buffer, whose size can be changed by calling setReadBufferSize(). By default, the size is 0, meaning unlimited data buffering.

On the client side, we first have to connect to the server port and also to the signals that QTcpSocket emits, as is the case with QTcpServer. Take a look at the following code:

```
QTcpSocket* client = new QTcpSocket(this);

QHostAddress remoteAddr(...);
client.connectToHost(remoteAddr, 8044);

connect(client, &QTcpSocket::connected, this, &MyClass::connectionOpened);
connect(client, &QTcpSocket::readyRead, this, &MyClass::readServerResponse);

// sending data:
QByteArray data("Hello from client!");
client->write(bytes);
```

In this book's resources (https://github.com/PacktPublishing/Hands-On-High-performance-with-QT/tree/master/Chapter%209), there is an example program that implements bidirectional client-server communication over TCP.

QUdpSocket

We can use a QUdpSocket along the same lines as QTcpSocket, but the difference is that there is no connection setup between the client and server, and so there's no specific UDP server socket class.

If we want to listen for incoming data, we must use the `bind()` method, as shown in the following example:

```
socket = new QUdpSocket(this);
socket->bind(QHostAddress::Any, 8044);
connect(socket, &QUdpSocket::readyRead, this, &MyClass::readIncomingData);
```

The callback for incoming UDP data can be written as follows:

```
void MyClass::readIncomingData()
{
    QByteArray buffer; // how much data?
    buffer.resize(socket->pendingDatagramSize());

    QHostAddress sender; // from what client?
    quint16 senderPort;

    socket->readDatagram(buffer.data(), buffer.size(), &sender, &senderPort);
    ... // process the data
}
```

As we already know, the client doesn't need to open a connection first, so it can just send data at any IP address, as in the following example:

```
QByteArray data;
data.append("Hello from the other side!");

QHostAddress remoteAddr(...);
clientSocket->writeDatagram(data, remoteAddr, 8044);
```

We can use `writeDatagram()` to send raw data, or send an instance of the `QNetworkDatagram` class, which gives you access to all of UDP's features, including methods such as `setHopLimit()` and `setInterfaceIndex()`.

`QUdpSocket` also supports UDP's multicast feature, that is, sending the same data packet to several receivers. However, be aware that UDP's multicast feature will work fine in the local network but will probably be blocked by internet routers!

QAbstractSocket

Although the TCP and UDP protocols use two pretty different approaches, Qt implements both the `QTcpSocket` and `QUdpSocket` classes using a common `QAbstractSocket` superclass. This class glosses over the differences between the protocols by implementing a virtual connection that can also be used in the UDP case!

In this context, one peculiarity of the QUdpSocket class can be explained, namely that we can use QTcpSocket's convenience methods read(), write(), readLine(), and readAll() after the socket is directly connected to a peer, by calling connectToHost(). In this case, the data will be sent over UDP to the remote address we passed to the connectToHost() method.

QAbstractSocket and the QTcpSocket and QUdpSocket classes offer an additional blocking socket API containing methods such as waitForReadyRead(), waitForBytesWritten(), waitForConnected(), and so on. Be aware that these methods will block the Qt event loop, so do not use them in the GUI thread!

Another interesting feature of the QAbstractSocket is that we can instantiate it and then call setSocketDescriptor() to wrap an already existing native socket. We can then use the native socket in an unified manner through the QAbstractSocket interface!

One possible application of this feature is a technique that allows us to implement threaded UDP or TCP servers when used in conjunction with QTcpServer's incomingConnection() method. The following code explains this idea:

```cpp
class ThreadedServer: public QTcpServer
{
  ...

  ThreadedServer(QObject *parent) : QTcpServer(parent)
  {
    pool = new QThreadPool(this);
    listen(QHostAddress::Any, 8044);
  }

  void incomingConnection(qintptr socketDescriptor) override
  {
    TcpRunnable* task = new TcpRunnable(socketDescriptor);
    task->setAutoDelete(true);
    pool->start(task);
  }

private:
  QThreadPool *pool;
};
```

The `incomingConnection()` method can be used to customize the handling of new TCP connections in `QTcpServer`. In our case, we just wrap the native socket descriptor in a `TcpRunnable` instance and forward it to the thread pool for execution. Now, the runnable task will pick up the socket and communicate with the client in an own thread (one of the threads in the thread pool), as shown in the following code:

```
void TcpRunnable::run()
{
  if(!socketDescriptor_) return;

  QTcpSocket socket;
  socket.setSocketDescriptor(socketDescriptor_);

  socket.write("Hello from your humble server!");
  ...
}
```

QSslSocket

`QSslSocket` is a subclass of `QTcpSocket` and provides SSL and TLS encryption for both clients and servers. Internally, it uses the well-known open source library OpenSSL and supports SSL 3 and TLS 1.2. Thus, the newest TLS 1.3 version is currently not available.

In the simplest case, we just connect to a SSL server using the `connectToHostEncrypted()` method, as shown in the following example:

```
QSslSocket client(this);
connect(&client, &QSslSocket::encrypted, this, &MyClass::socketEncrypted);

client.connectToHostEncrypted("imaps.somehost.com", 993);
```

We can see that, in this case, we need the DNS name of the host, which can then be used to check its certificate. Data can be sent to the remote host using standard `write()` methods.

On the server side of the connection, we should call QSslSocket's `startServerEncryption()` method upon receiving the incoming connection through a `QTcpServer`. For this purpose, we subclass `QTcpServer` and reimplement the `incomingConnection()` method, as we did in the previous example in the *QAbstractSocket* section, except that the native socket descriptor is given by `setSocketDescriptor()` to a new instance of `QSslSocket`.

Once the encryption has been established, `QSslSocket` can be used like a regular `QTcpSocket`.

For some legal and licence reasons, the officially available Qt distributions do not contain OpenSSL binaries! We have to install them by ourselves or else the SSL operation will fail with warnings such as `qt.network.ssl:` `QSslSocket: cannot call unresolved function` `SSLv23_client_method`.

Other socket types

In Qt 5.12, the `QDlts` class was added. This implements the aforementioned DTLS protocol, which basically constitutes a TLS-encrypted UDP communication. No new socket class for this protocol was introduced; instead, an additional class was added to be used in conjunction with `QUdpSocket`, as shown in the following code:

```
QUdpSocket udpSocket;
QDtls dtlsConn;

QHostAddress address(...)
dtlsConn.setPeer(address, 8044, "udp.somehost.com");
dtlsConn.doHandshake(&udpSocket);
```

For more information on a complete handshake sequence, please consult the excellent Qt documentation (`http://doc.qt.io/qt-5/qdtls.html#details`).

Qt also provides an implementation of the SCTP protocol via the `QSctpServer` and `QSctpSocket` classes. As this protocol isn't very popular at the moment, we won't discuss the details of these classes.

HTTP networking using Qt classes

Several Qt classes are involved when it comes to HTTP communication. First and foremost, we have to translate the URL to the network address using the DNS protocol.

DNS queries

There are two ways we can look up a host address using DNS. The older one is provided by `QHostInfo` in the form of the static blocking function `fromName()` and an synchronous one called `lookupHost()`. The newer class, `QDnsLookup`, offers an asynchronous interface and allows us to issue any type of DNS query – not just the IP address, as is the case with `QHostInfo`.

The following example shows the basic usage of `QDnsLookup`:

```
dns = new QDnsLookup(this);
connect(dns, QDnsLookup::finished, this, MyClass::dnsQueryResolved);

dns->setType(QDnsLookup::A); // IP v.4 address
dns->setName("www.qt.com");
dns->lookup();
```

We can see that we have to invoke the `lookup()` method and will be notified with `finished()` when the lookup has completed. We will than have to check for errors using `QDnsLookup::error()` and if there aren't any, we can access the DNS records through the `QDnsLookup::serviceRecords()` method. Using `QHostInfo` will simplify this for the common IP address case.

When invoked asynchronously, the DNS lockups will be executed concurrently in a separate DNS worker thread. In older Qt versions, five DNS queries were allowed to run concurrently, but in newer versions, this number was increased to 20. A synchronous DNS lookup is not recommended due to the unpredictable nature of network traffic. In any case, do not start it in a GUI thread!

The DNS lookup will be invoked internally (and cached) by Qt when a HTTP request is issued. Its direct usage will be only needed if we are using transport level protocols like TCP or UDP.

Basic HTTP

For high-level network access, Qt provides the `QNetworkAccessManager` class. This class abstracts the request-response interaction pattern and uses the `QNetworkRequest` and `QNetworkReply` classes to encapsulate exact HTTP requests and responses. Look at the following example:

```
QNetworkAccessManager netAccessMgr;
QUrl url = getUrlToDownload();
QNetworkReply* reply = netAccessMgr.get(QNetworkRequest(url));

connect(reply, &QNetworkReply::finished, this, &MyClass::httpFinished);
connect(reply, &QNetworkReply::readyRead, this, &MyClass::httpReadyRead);
```

We can see that `QNetworkAccessManager` uses a `QUrl` class for the address of a HTTP resource, wraps it in a `QNetworkRequest`, and then invokes the GET method through its `get` method.

We could also invoke the PUT method, as shown in the following example:

```
auto putReply = netAccessMgr->post(netReq, contents.toAscii());
connect(putReply, &QNetworkReply::finished, this,
&MyClass::httpPutFinished);
```

The next thing we notice is that QNetworkAccessManager works asynchronously, just like the Qt socket classes do. Therefore, we connect to emitted signals such as readyRead() or finished() and read the data in callbacks. In this book's resources (https://github.com/PacktPublishing/Hands-On-High-performance-with-QT/tree/master/Chapter%209), you will find an example implementation of a HTTP file download client.

Note that there isn't a HTTP server class in Qt 5. Previously, there were classes available in Qt 4 such as QHttpRequestHeader and QHttpResponseHeader, which made such an implementation possible. In Qt 5, they were removed. At the time of writing, the Qt Company is working on a HTTP server class which will be included in some future Qt version.

The implementation of QNetworkAccessManager differs from that of QTcpSocket and QUdpSocket in that it uses a dedicated worker thread for each instance. This thread provides a working context for HTTP network connection implementation classes. HTTP/1.1 allows up to six parallel TCP or SSL connections to a single host, so upto six QTcpSocket or QSslSocket instances can be active for one host. If HTTP pipelining is activated (we will discuss this later in this chapter), there can be even more data in flight. The existing connections aren't immediately closed, but are kept open to be reused for later requests.

There's also support for HTTP caching; however, it is not enabled by default. We will discuss this later in this chapter.

HTTPS and other extensions

Qt supports HTTPS, that is, the HTTP protocol over the encrypted SSL/TLS connection. We can connect to a HTTPS endpoint using the URL scheme https:// instead of http://.

We can also use newer protocols such as Google's SPDY (since Qt 5.3) and the new HTTP/2 protocol version (since Qt 5.8). We can enable SPDY by setting setAllowedNextProtocols() in QSslConfiguration with NextProtocolSpdy3_0 and then passing QSslConfiguration to the connectToHostEncrypted() method of the QNetworkAccessManager. This is explained by the fact that the SPDY protocol only runs over an SSL connection.

Another way to control the usage of HTTP successor protocols is to set
`HTTP2AllowedAttribute` and `SpdyAllowedAttribute` in the `QNetworkRequest` so that
they're sent. We can set those attributes to true or false, thus enabling or disabling these
protocols in the protocol negotiation, which will take place between the client and server.
Setting `Http2DirectAttribute` (since Qt 5.11) will even exclusively require the HTTP/2
attribute to be used!

Qt WebSocket classes

`QWebSocket` implements a TCP socket that understands the WebSocket protocol. As we
already know, **WebSocket** is a binary protocol that can be switched to from a regular HTTP
connection using the `Upgrade: websocket` header. Once we have switched from HTTP to
WebSocket it's upto us to determine the format of the binary data to be exchanged between
endpoints.

The `QWebSocket` class can be used both on the client and server side of the connection. It
doesn't subclass `QTcpSocket`, but its interface was modeled after the `QAbstractSocket`
class. As with other socket types, the API is asynchronous, as shown in the following code
snippet:

```
QWebSocket ws;
QUrl url(...);

connect(&ws, &QWebSocket::connected, this, &MyClass::wsConnected);
connect(&ws, &QWebSocket::disconnected, this, &MyClass::wsClosed);
ws.open();
```

Once the connection has been established, both parties can send and receive data without
conforming to the strict request-response schema. The following code example shows the
client sending text data from its connection-completed callback:

```
void MyClass::wsConnected()
{
  // prepare for messages from server
  connect(&ws, &QWebSocket::textMessageReceived, this,
&MyClass::textRecvd);

  ws.sendTextMessage(QStringLiteral("Hello WebSockets over there!"));
}
```

Currently, all major browsers support the WebSocket protocol, so a web application can
switch from text-based HTTP to a binary WebSocket format to improve performance. Using
the `QWebSocket` class, we can also communicate with the server backends of such
applications!

Miscallaneous classes

There are more Qt classes involved in networking, but we cannot discuss all of them, as this would fill a sizable book of it own. Instead, we just give a short list of classes for readers to look up if they wish to:

- The `QNetworkSession` and Bearer Management support classes are used mainly for connection management in mobile setups when the network connection can be lost
- `QNetworkCookie` and `QNetworkCokieJar` are for you guessed it—HTTP cookies
- Classes that support SOCK5 network proxies
- Classes for HTTP multipart messages, which are used for data uploading
- `QHstsPolicy` supporting **HTTP's Strict Transport Security (HSTS)**

Other higher-level communication classes

There are some more network communication solutions apart from the ubiquitous HTTP protocol. Let's talk about those that I've heard about.

Qt WebChannel

Do you remember that we stated that implementing a HTTP server in Qt is not currently possible? However, we can use another technology, namely Qt's `WebChannel` module.

This module consists of two parts – a JavaScript library and the `QWebChannel` C++ class, or the `WebChannel` QML item, to expose Qt objects to the web. Communication between these two parts can be done using the proprietary `QWebChannelAbstractTransport` object or by using the standard WebSocket protocol.

In this way, a Qt C++ or **Qt Modeling Language (QML)** application will be able to interact with any modern HTML browser or standalone JavaScript runtime, such as `node.js`. This means that we can have our HTTP server in the end – well, sort of.

Qt WebGL streaming

This is another cool technology (since Qt 5.10) where we can open a WebSocket server on a device, run the `OpenGL` rendering code there, and forward the encoded `OpenGL` commands to the WebSocket server.

A JavaScript client application can connect to the WebSocket server, read the encoded OpenGL calls, and render them in the browser using HTML5's WebGL calls. In this way, remote devices can stream their graphics contents when requested!

Qt remote objects

This module allows us to expose Qt objects to remote clients, but it does it more along the lines of the legacy **Common Object Request Broker Architecture** (**CORBA**) framework, complete with the generation of client and server stubs. However, the difference is that we extend the signal-slot mechanism beyond the process boundaries, thus allowing notifications to be sent spontaneously.

I'm quite curious as to how this mechanism will perform in the real world, given that CORBA wasn't really an overarching success in its day.

Improving network performance

Now that we have learned a lot about networking and classes that Qt has implemented to support it, we can start to discuss network programming performance challenges. Let's start with the basics.

General network performance techniques

These are just applications of the basic techniques that we learned about in Chapter 1, *Understanding Performant Programs*, namely the following:

- **Cache the contents:** This one is simple – if we have already fetched some content, we do not have to fetch it again! QNetworkAccessManager supports caching, but it has to be explicitly enabled.
- **Don't send unnecessary bytes:** Another no-brainer. What we don't send we don't have to pay for.
- **Parallelize communication:** Do not block when waiting for data to arrive – do something different. Maybe you can process the previous response in parallel? Or even request some other data in parallel?

- **Avoid fixed overhead:** This is a problem with connection-oriented protocols – an extra setup step is necessary before we can start transmitting data. And if we heap a connection-oriented protocol on another, it gets worse! The classic measure here is to say that a *cache* is an already opened connection, that is, we're keeping it open a little longer and reusing it for further communication. However, even in connectionless protocols, we have some overheads, namely the costs of a system call and the transmission costs. We can avoid that cost by using the batching technique – not sending every single byte separately but gathering them first before we send them over the network.
- **Use a better implementation:** Not all communication protocols were created equal. Some were created for ease of use (HTTP), while others were created for speed (WebSockets). Choose your poison.
- **Avoid copying data:** Data copies are a bad thing to have. Due to its importance, we will discuss it in more detail in a subsequent subsection.

Receiving buffers and copying

One important aspect of networking code performance is that we want to avoid copying data around. On a socket, **read()** call data will be copied out of the operating system's internal buffer and ideally it should end up at its final destination, not in an intermediate buffer that will be copied out by the ultimate consumer of the data.

Likewise, a dynamic reallocation of the receiving buffer is a bad thing! So the very convenient code that we saw in the previous UDP example, where we call `buffer.resize(socket->pendingDatagramSize())` for new incoming data, is a performance sin. We use static receive buffers if we care about performance.

In this context, `QAbstractSocket` doesn't score particularly well as it uses an internal read buffer, which provides convenience at the cost of performance. The Qt documentation states the following:

> *TCP sockets cannot be opened in* `QIODevice::Unbuffered` *mode.*

We cannot disable this buffer. Thus, with Qt, we have chosen convenience and pay for that with data copies. Note that `QUdpSocket` doesn't use buffering apart from OS buffers.

TCP performance

First, we will say a little bit more about the possible performance problems that can occur when using the TCP protocol. The classic TCP problems are as follows:

- **Connection setup:** We have already seen that it takes at least one network round-trip. The final client ACK reply can be used to send some data along (piggy-backing).

- **Head-of-line (HOL) blocking:** This term describes a situation where one lost or corrupted packet will block consecutive packets. Even if we physically received all packets after the lost/corrupted one, we cannot access their data for as long as the lost packet hasn't been re-transmitted!

- **Slow start and exponential backoff:** Because we do not want to overload the network, a TCP connection will start with a small so-called congestion window. This window determines how many packets can be sent before the sender is forced to wait for the first ACK. This window will then grow if the communication works well, but will be also reset in an exponential manner if there are some problems in the network! This is not so good if we want to achieve maximal throughput.

- **Nagle's algorithm:** By default, TCP data won't be physically sent out; instead, it will first be buffered in the TCP stack to avoid sending many small TCP packets. This sound sensible, but what if you want to send some urgent data and they aren't that long? You might get stuck with this data, and thus have to wait until the internal OS buffer gets filled. That's a killer when latency (that is, fast reaction times) is your objective, and typically we'd like to disable that.

The question is: Are these problems or are these features? We know the answer: TCP was designed for throughput and not as a have-it-all, general interactive network protocol. However, there are also TCP extensions that optimize some of these aspects, such as **TCP Fast Open (TFO)**, which sends the data with the SYN request (piggy-backing again) or the delayed ACK option, which will wait until enough payload data is present before sending an ACK with that data piggy-backed on it.

Some TCP stack behavior can only be changed on the OS level (setting the congestion window size, disabling a slow-start after idle, or enabling TFO, or updating the kernel to the newest version). Qt socket classes provide a few cross-platform settings through QAbstractSocket's options, such as the following:

- `LowDelayOption`: This can disable Nagle's algorithm if we need maximum responsiveness.
- `KeepAliveOption`: This option enables TCP's built-in keep-alive mechanism. When using TCP, we generally cannot know if the other end of the connection is still alive and/or reachable. We will only find this out when we try to send some data, and that could be too late. TCP keep-alive will monitor the connection state for us, but Qt doesn't offer an API for setting the frequency of the keep-alive messages. This must be done with a native OS API, that is, on Windows by setting the `SIO_KEEPALIVE_VALS` socket option.
- `ReceiveBufferSizeSocketOption` and `SendBufferSizeSocketOption`: As the TCP protocol works, if the local OS receive socket buffer is full, the remote sender will be forced to wait until there a is place in the buffer for the data. Conversely, if the local send buffer is full, the `send()` system call will also block or return an error. If the OS buffers are too small for our use cases, this will slow down communication.

HTTP and HTTPS performance

The biggest performance problem with HTTP is the overhead of the connection setup. In order to fetch any web content we have to do the following:

- **DNS query:** 1 round-trip (can be omitted if it's already been cached at the OS level)
- **TCP handshake:** 1 TCP round-trip
- **SSL handshake:** 2 TCP round-trips
- **HTTP request and reply:** 1 TCP round-trip

The following diagram visualizes this mechanism:

We can see that, in the worst case, we will need up to five network round-trips! Taking 200 ms as a typical WiFi round-trip time could in at as high as 1 second! Therefore, the biggest performance win will be, in the case of TCP, reusing HTTP connections!

Connection reuse

`QNetworkAccessManager` will automatically try to reuse opened HTTP connections. This is also the reason why we should use only one `QNetworkAccessManager` instance—two separate instances cannot coordinate reusing of their connections, which results in unnecessary network traffic!

HTTP/1.1 defines a connection being `keep-alive` by default. However, the HTTP server will usually terminate a connection after some predefined time (typically 1 second). Here, we can see the tension between clients and the infrastructure that we have already observing in the case of Nagle's algorithm – the server's interest is in decreasing resource usage and being responsive to the new clients, while the client's interest is in keeping the connection open for as long as possible.

We can fool the server into not closing the connection by sending some dummy keep-alive requests to the server. This will reset the server-side timeout and give us another grace period.

Resuming SSL connections

There's a feature in the TLS protocol that allows for a secure session to be preserved between a TCP connection, thus eliminating the initial TSL handshake and sparing one round-trip delay for a given connection! Many servers such as Google, Facebook, Twitter, and so on support this feature.

In Qt, we can achieve this by storing and resuming so-called TLS session tickets, as shown in the following example:

```
// reply received:
QNetworkReply* reply = ...;
QByteArray tlsSessionData = reply->sslConfiguration().session();

// resume
QSslConfiguration sslConfig;
sslConfig.setSslOption(QSsl::SslOptionDisableSessionPersistence, false)
sslConfig.setSession(tlsSessionData );

QNetworkRequest req(url);
```

```
req.setSslConfiguration(sslConfig);

networkAccessManager->get(request);
```

Note that session ticket support has to be turned on explicitly! We can see that we can save TLS session data to a `QByteArray` (in ASN.1, an older data encoding format), then save it to disk, read it again later, and reuse it to resume the old TLS session. However, a session may expire, so check it through its `sessionTicketLifeTimeHint()` method.

Another TLS protocol extension(the so-called *false start* that will allow for a client to piggy-back data that's already on its second message, **Client Finish**, instead of waiting for the final response of the server) is not supported by Qt as the underlying `OpenSSL` library currently doesn't seem to implement it. If implemented, this would have the same net effect as session ticket resumption.

Preconnecting

Since Qt 5.2, we can preconnect to the HTTP server on the TCP or SSL level, without making any HTTP request at first. Why should this be used to improve performance?

The answer is that we can increase parallelism when fetching several files from a server. Let's assume that we just received a file with hyperlinks pointing to another 4 files. If we now start 3 additional connections to the server, we have to wait until the whole handshake dance is done and then receive the data. However, if we have those 3 connections already preconnected, we can start with concurrent data transfer right away!

Qt has supported preconnecting since Qt 5.2 through the `connectToHostEncrypted()` and `connectToHost()` methods of `QNetworkAccessManager`, which implement SSL and TCP preconnections, respectively.

Currently, HTTP/1.1 allows 6 parallel connections to a given port at the server. So, if we know that we will communicate with a server very intensively, we could consider preconnecting!

Pipelining

This is a HTTP feature that allows the client to request several pieces of content in a row over a TCP connection in a row and then receive several responses in a row instead of going through the request-response cycle for each piece of content. This technique is especially effective for connections with high latencies.

The following diagram visualizes this concept:

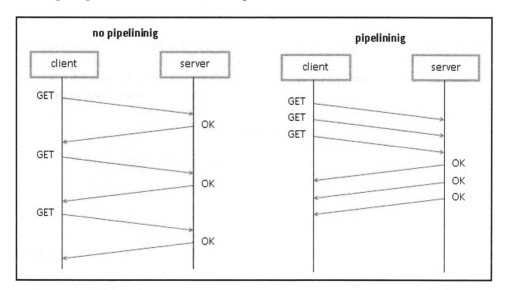

However, pipelining isn't enabled by default by major browsers because of several issues including buggy proxy servers and the possible head of line blocking of the entire pipeline. On the other hand, there are some measurements that document noticeable gains when many requests to a single server are made.

In Qt, we can enable pipelining by setting the `HttpPipeliningAllowedAttribute` in `QNetworkRequest` to sent.

Lately, pipelining as a technique has been superseded by multiplexing data streams over a single connection in the HTTP/2 protocol.

Caching and compression

These classic networking optimizations can be also used with the `QNetworkAccessManager` class. If the HTTP server is sending data in a compressed form, then `QNetworkAccessManager` will automatically uncompress it.

Caching HTTP data is also available, but it has to be enabled manually first. You need to instantiate the `QNetworkDiskCache` class and then set it on your `QNetworkAccessManager` instance by calling `setCache()`.

Now, `QNetworkAccessManager` will load resources from the cache (that is, from disk) if the resource is still **fresh** and fetch it over network if it's not. We can fine-tune cache handling by setting `CacheLoadControlAttribute` in `QNetworkRequest` to `AlwaysNetwork`, `PreferNetwork`, `PreferCache`, or `AlwaysCache`. Please consult the Qt documentation (`http://doc.qt.io/qt-5.9/qnetworkrequest.html#CacheLoadControl-enum`) for a detailed description of these options.

You can also implement your own HTTP cache if you are not happy with Qt's implementation, simply by subclassing the `QAbstractNetworkCache` base class.

Using HTTP/2 and WebSocket

We already mentioned the newer HTTP/2 version and the WebSocket protocol. They both improve protocol performance as they use the binary data format. However, they introduce one more step into the connection setup, namely the protocol switch phase. This will increase the connection's setup latency, but at least in HTTP/2 (and also SPDY) we have the option to merge this step with the **Client Hallo** SSL message. This is done with the **Application-Layer Protocol Negotiation** (**ALPN**) or **Next Protocol Negotiation** (**NPN**) extension, as can be seen in the following diagram:

```
root@server:~#
root@server:~# nghttp -nvv https://nghttp2.org
[  0.348] Connected
[  0.765][NPN] server offers:
          * h2
          * h2-16
          * h2-14
          * spdy/3.1
          * http/1.1
The negotiated protocol: h2
[  1.290] recv SETTINGS frame <length=12, flags=0x00, stream_id=0>
          (niv=2)
          [SETTINGS_MAX_CONCURRENT_STREAMS(0x03):100]
          [SETTINGS_INITIAL_WINDOW_SIZE(0x04):65535]
[  1.293] send SETTINGS frame <length=12, flags=0x00, stream_id=0>
          (niv=2)
          [SETTINGS_MAX_CONCURRENT_STREAMS(0x03):100]
          [SETTINGS_INITIAL_WINDOW_SIZE(0x04):65535]
[  1.293] send SETTINGS frame <length=0, flags=0x01, stream_id=0>
```

Here, we are using the `nghttp` tool from `https://nghttp2.org` and can see that the server offers some preliminary versions of HTTP/2: the current version (h2), SPDY, and HTTP/1.1. In Qt, we can skip the negotiation phase by requesting HTTP/2 right away by specifying `Http2DirectAttribute` in `QNetworkRequest`.

 Note that this server doesn't support HTTP/2 over naked TCP (protocol code `h2c`), but only over SSL (protocol code `h2`). The original SPDY protocol also only supported SSL as a transport layer. Qt supports both versions on all platforms, at least as of Qt 5.12.

HTTP/2 also adds multiplexing of data over single connection, prioritizing of streams, compressing headers, and server push. The last term denotes the possibility of sending data from the server without it being requested by client – for example, the server could push CSS files that are used in the site it hosts directly after TCP connection setup! Server push replaces the old HTTP/1.1 technique, that is, the so-called *long polling*, and can be used to emulate spontaneous server event notifications by sending an asynchronous request to the server and waiting for the response. After the response arrives, we issue the next request if we want to wait for the next server event.

 Please note that even HTTP/2 isn't immune from head of line blocking! This problem can be avoided by using the QUIC protocol instead of TCP as HTTP's transport layer.

The WebSocket protocol has essentially the same features as HTTP/2, but it lacks connection multiplexing. These two protocols are incompatible and seem to be in direct competition. While the older WebSocket protocol is more popular at the moment, HTTP/2 is probably more future-proof.

Advanced networking themes

In this chapter, we will try to provide a few glimpses into high-performance networking themes that lie somehow lie outside standard Qt use cases.

The classic (and perennial) network programming problem is writing high-performance networked servers. Since Qt isn't very well-suited for that task—I, for example, used the C++ RestSdk library to write a HTTP server—we will only gloss over some problem areas to give you a little more of an overview:

- **User-space networking stacks:** Normally, network protocol handling is implemented in the OS kernel. But for the highest performance, there are user space implementations that reduce the syscall overhead and give the user total control over buffer handling!

- **Threading considerations:** We have already mentioned in `Chapter 5`, *An In-Depth Guide to Concurrency and Multithreading*, that, for optimal threading, we use a preallocated thread pool and task-based parallelism, that is, we split the interactions with the client into smaller chunks, which will then be scheduled on the thread pool.

- **Careful memory management:** As always, memory management is crucial for achieving high performance. Lately, concepts such as **sharding** (that is, allocating a fixed memory pool to be exclusively used by a given core) or **staged event-driven architectures** (that is, **SEDA**—carefully partitioning the logic in a set of stages along with batching the processing at each stage) had proven to be instrumental in achieving high performance. Of course, different variations on the caching theme are also very central to high server performance.

- **Using the latest OS features:** If we do not want to go the way of total control and use user space network stacks, we should have a look at the newest OS developments. For example, on Windows, the I/O completion ports offer new possibilities for optimization. Qt, however, doesn't use completion ports, which is another reason why we rather would use Qt on the client side.

Summary

In this chapter, we looked at network communication and the support provided by the Qt Network module. We first learned about commonly used modern network protocols and their interdependencies. Then, we gained some insight into existing Qt networking classes and their implementation. The next thing we discussed was performance problems with TCP and HTTP, ways to work around them, and some recent advances in communication protocol design. Finally, we learned about some Qt features that can be used to optimize the performance of networking code.

Maybe you are not a network programming expert right now, but you have gained some solid insight if you would like to start down that path!

In the next chapter, we will apply our hard-won performance knowledge to one of the most exciting fields where Qt is currently expanding: the world of mobile and embedded devices.

Questions

This time you can test your understanding of networking questions discussed in this chapter by answering the following questions:

1. If, in the UDP protocol, there is no guarantee that the packet will arrive at the destination, why do we bother with it at all?
2. How can we enable a network cache in Qt? What will get cached there?
3. What is the IP protocol?
4. Is there a Qt cache for DNS? How can we use it?
5. Why would you consider using HTTP/2?
6. What HTTP-like protocols are supported by Qt? Is REST supported?
7. What are some examples of well-known ports? What are they, anyway?
8. Ever heard of OSI's 7-layers protocol stack model?
9. What are the performance gains from reusing a TCP connection?
10. What is the TLS protocol? Isn't it the same as SSL?

Further reading

High Performance Browser Networking by I. Grigorik, O'Reilly (2013) – although aimed more at the performance of browser-based JavaScript applications, this book gives you quite a broad background of the standard UDP, TCP, and HTTP protocols, as well as wireless networking development and standards. Strongly recommended!

The Performance of Open Source Applications, edited by Travish Armstrong (available at http://aosabook.org, 2013) contains case studies on networking performance optimizations in the Chrome browser, Warp server implementation, and mobile networking techniques.

The series of three *TCP/IP Illustrated* books by W.R. Stevens, Addison–Wesley (2011), is a classic, very thorough, albeit a little dated description of the IP protocol family up to HTTP. It also includes a discussion of the IP protocol stack in 4.4 BSD Linux. For a similar introduction in a Windows context, try *Microsoft Windows Networking Essentials* by D. Gibson, Sybex (2011).

And, as always, read the Qt source code! For the network module, you can browse it online at `https://code.woboq.org/qt5/qtbase/src/network/`.

Qt Performance on Embedded and Mobile Platforms

10

This chapter will go over specific performance considerations pertinent to two relatively new platforms that Qt is expanding to from its originally desktop-centric focus, namely the embedded and mobile platforms. Using our hard-won knowledge from the previous chapters, we will look at networking challenges on mobile devices and problems with resource and graphic constraints on embedded ones.

You do not have to know a lot about embedded and mobile development, as we will first introduce both subject areas.

However, we won't provide a detailed introduction to mobile and embedded development, as we would probably need an entire book on its own for that. Our goal here is rather to provide a basic overview of both fields and then discuss the performance-relevant themes that can be encountered there.

In this chapter, we will cover the following topics:

- **Challenges in embedded and mobile development**: To introduce the topic
- **Qt usage in embedded and mobile worlds**: To describe how Qt supports embedded and mobile
- **Embedded Linux and Qt performance**: To discuss embedded optimization themes
- **Mobile-specific performance concerns**: To look at how mobile is similar and, at the same time, different to embedded

So, are you ready to have a look at some new environments?

Challenges in embedded and mobile development

Embedded and mobile devices are just computers, only with less memory, less CPU/GPU power, and, in the case of mobile devices, finite power supply, and sometimes problematic network performance. As on a desktop computer, we usually don't have to think about such constraints in embedded development; they are a part of the game.

Specifically, power constraints give rise to the usage of CPUs that are different than those found in desktops. Currently, the most commonly used CPUs come from the ARM's Cortex line, which follows the **reduced instruction set** (**RISC**) processor architecture design, resulting in simple instructions, less transistors, and lower power usage.

Besides power constraints, embedded and mobile devices come with size and price limitations, resulting in less-performant hardware. The hardware is customarily bundled as a **system-on-chip** (**SoC**), which contains a complete computer as a single chip, composed of a CPU, GPU, cellular radio unit (on mobile), WiFi controller, and other periphery controllers.

Basic performance themes

Due to inherent hardware constraints, the following problems have to be tackled on embedded and mobile devices:

- **Executable size**: We have to watch the size of our program, because we do not have that much RAM and persistent memory on embedded devices. Additionally, there are application size limits on mobile platforms.
- **Startup time**: Despite slower hardware, users aren't willing to wait for an embedded device's seconds-long startup.
- **Application responsiveness**: This is even more important here than for desktop applications, because on an embedded device it will be often a single, full-screen application running. On mobile, we do not want to block the UI waiting for an unreliable network transmission either.
- **UI fluidity**: The user still expects fluid and state-of-the art GUIs even on low-end mobile and embedded devices.
- **Algorithmic improvements**: As many low-end embedded devices don't even have a **floating point** (**FP**) unit, often, we have to resort to low-precision computations and approximate mathematical methods.

All these problems can appear in the traditional desktop environment, but are much more prominent in embedded and mobile environments, as they will be amplified by slower hardware. The problem we do not have elsewhere, and which is of the highest importance for embedded and mobile devices, is power management. We will discuss that in the next subsection.

Run to idle

Modern embedded and mobile devices are trying to save battery life in many different ways. One technique we know from laptop computers is the dynamic down-clocking of CPUs to match the current performance requirements. Another technique is the so-called **big.LITTLE** architecture of ARM, where we pair a powerful but power-hungry processor with a smaller but a more power-friendly one, ensuring cache coherence between them and switching to one or the another, depending on the amount of work to be done.

The OS will control the dynamic CPU frequency, in the case of embedded Linux through the frequency driver, as well as switching between the small and big cores in the big.LITTLE architecture. On a mobile OS such as Android, the kernel will additionally try to put the entire system into sleep mode as soon as possible. Modern peripherals also support various power level states, and their drivers take part in Kernel's power management mechanisms.

Some hardware data

Let's have a closer look at some embedded and mobile hardware to illustrate the hardware constraints we have to deal with.

The popular **Raspberry Pi 3 B** single-board, credit card-sized computer comes with a Broadcom SoC containing a quad-core (x4) ARM Cortext A53 64-bit processor clocked at 1.2 GHz, a Broadcom Video Core IV GPU, and 1 GB of dynamic RAM. The RAM has to be shared between the CPU and the GPU, but the memory split can be adjusted.

You can have a look at the Raspberry Pi 3 B board and the peripheral devices it contains in the figure below:

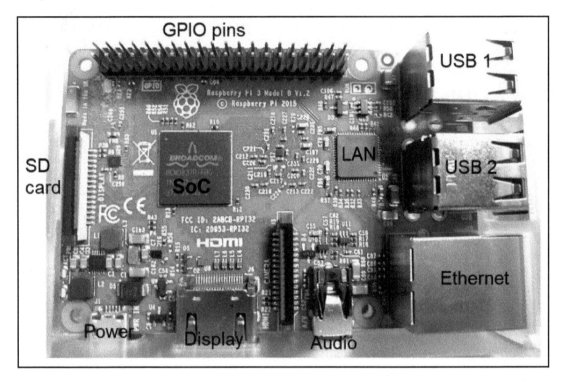

Broadcom's Video Core IV GPU contains 24 ALUs running at 400 MHz and delivering 38 **giga floating-point operations** (**GFLOPs**) computing power. That isn't really a mouthful, as the Intel HD Graphics 4,600 integrated GPU found in my somewhat older laptop can deliver 432 GFLOPs. The first Pi generation's processor was a 700 MHz ARM11 32-bit processor that was ten times slower than the current one, and the GPU achieved only 24 GFLOPs.

Author's mid-range mobile phone comes with 3 GB dynamic RAM, a Qualcomm Snapdragon 450 SoC containing LTE unit, camera, WiFi controller, and so on. The SoC has an octa-core (x8) ARM Cortext A53 processor clocked at 1.8 GHz and a Quallcom Adreno 506 GPU consisting of 96 ALUs running at 650 MHz and delivering 130 GFLOPs of performance. We see that is much better than what we have on the Raspberry board.

However, Raspberry Pi has comparatively good hardware when we take embedded **microcontrollers** (**MCUs**) into account. The relatively high-performance **STM32 F469NI** board contains an ARM Cortex M4 CPU running at 180 MHz, provides 2 MB of persistent flash memory, 324 KB of dynamic RAM, and no GPU at all.

Embedded hardware and performance

Speaking of performance on embedded platforms, the first reason for performance problems is choosing underpowered hardware for your project. Yes, it's as simple as that—you have seen previously that there are big differences in embedded hardware, from a relatively well-equipped mobile phone, through Raspberry Pi, down to a microcontroller. It is self-evident that a 38 GFLOP GPU cannot manage the same workload as a 130 GFLOP one, to say nothing of systems without a GPU.

The usual solution for that problem is to prototype and run the application on the target device early. Another possibility is to run a hardware benchmark as to measure what is possible on a given device. There are some commercial benchmarks, but on the open source side, we could use the qmlbench tool available at `https://github.com/qt-labs/qmlbench`. The tool will benchmark Qt Core, QML, and Qt Quick as a whole stack rather than in isolation, so it should give you some rough performance estimates for your device. However, it was designed as a QML performance regression-testing tool, so it doesn't include Qt 3D tests.

 If you are interested, you can see the current results of Qt and QML regression tests visualized with **Grafana** at `https://testresults.qt.io/grafana/`.

Unfortunately, it is not an unusual situation when a project is trying to take an old hardware platform that has limited memory, slow CPU, and no OpenGL support and refurbish it with a new QML-based application. Of course, it is possible, but it will cost you a significant amount of time, and the UI will never be fully satisfactory. So, measure GPU limitations, and take them into account when designing the UI.

Qt usage in embedded and mobile worlds

As we were discussing graphical performance in `Chapter 8`, *Optimizing Graphical Performance*, we already mentioned that QML was introduced as to allow for the easy development of Qt application for hardware-accelerated UIs on mobile devices. On the other side, some embedded devices use the more traditional widget bases, UIs, especially as initially Qt Quick 2 required the hardware to support OpenGL in Qt 5.

Qt for embedded

Traditionally, Qt in the embedded world was used in the embedded Linux context, as Qt already supports Linux as a platform. Moreover, the Qt company ported the framework to other embedded environments such as QNX Neutrino RTOS, Windows CE, Windows Embedded, Integrity RTOS, and VxWorks. Additionally, the Android, iOS, and WinRT mobile platforms are supported as well.

However, QNX, Integrity, and VxWorks are contained in the commercial Qt license, and Windows CE/Embedded was last officially supported as of Qt 5.6, and seems to be dropped in the newer versions. So, in the open source version, we are left with embedded Linux as the only platform.

Qt usage on embedded Linux

The simplest possibility to get Qt running on an embedded system is to download the source code and compile it on the target device. As compiling a project as big as Qt on a small embedded device is tricky, a better option is to cross-compile it (that is, let the compiler on one platform emit code destined for another) on your development host.

Another possibility on embedded Linux is to install the Qt as a ready-made package, if available. For example, if we are using Raspberry Pi with the default Raspbian Linux distribution, we could do it with the following commands:

```
sudo apt-get install qt5-default
sudo apt-get install qtcreator
```

After that, we had both the Qt distribution and the Qt Creator development environment on the embedded device and could work there directly. However, an embedded device as a development environment isn't a very convenient solution, because of the slow processor and limited screen resolution.

A more convenient way to develop for an embedded Linux device is to use the development environment on your usual developer machine, and then cross-compile it for the target device, bundle it with a custom-made Linux kernel, make a bootable image, and install it on to the target device. In the case of the Raspberry Pi board, it would be done by writing the image to the SD card, inserting it into the board, and rebooting it. On a board such as Raspberry Pi, we don't have to do it every time, as we can send the new executable over FTP, but on boards without network access, there is no other way.

As this can be understandably quite cumbersome, we can also use an emulator such as QEMU to emulate Raspberry Pi on Windows or Linux desktop as an intermediate solution.

As we see, there's quite a big amount of tooling required in the general case: cross-compiling, Linux kernel generation (there are tools such as **Buildroot** or **Yocto**), creation of a bootable image, and writing it to the SD card. We won't discuss it in more detail in this book, because it would go well beyond the scope of this book. Qt, unfortunately, doesn't provide such tooling in the open source variant, but it offers it in the commercial distribution.

Qt's embedded tooling

Qt offers in its commercial version the much-needed tooling for embedded development in an offering called **Qt for Device Creation**.

First, it provides reference images of Linux for several officially supported devices and ported Qt sources for other supported RTOSes to be built by the user. An image for our example Raspberry Pi 3 board is supported since Qt 5.7. The images for embedded Linux are based on the so-called Boot-to-Qt software stack, which is a lightweight, Qt-optimized, full software stack for embedded Linux systems that is built using Yocto. The Yocto tool also allows us to customize the used Linux kernel to our specific needs.

Moreover, Qt for Device Creation also provides emulators for the supported devices, deploying, and starting applications on an embedded device out of Qt Creator and remote debugging and profiling on the target. We can also use a Windows machine as a Boot-to-Qt development host using a **VirtualBox** virtual machine. With the additional Qt Device Utilities module, an easy access to various embedded device settings is possible through simple QML and C++ APIs.

As executable size matters very much in embedded development, Qt provides, in the commercial version, a configuration tool named Qt Lite that allows us to minimize executable sizes by excluding unneeded Qt functionality. Qt reports that using Qt Lite could decrease the size of a non-trivial QML application by 60%.

Qt also offers Qt Automotive Suite, which is built on top of Qt for Device Creation and offers extra tools and software components for car infotainment systems.

Supported hardware

Qt doesn't go for totally low-end hardware, as the currently officially supported devices are all of ARM Cortex-A level, with minimal hardware requirements of approximately the following:

- 256 MB of dynamic RAM
- 500 MHz CPU (1 GHz preferred)

Previously, there was also requirement for GPU supporting OpenGL ES 2.0, but it was dropped, and now also hardware without graphic accelerations and with OpenVG cards is supported. Additionally, for systems where a fixed amount of memory is reserved for the GPU, at least 128 MB of GPU memory is advisable.

There are some attempts by the Qt company to port Qt to MCUs of ARM Cortex-M level, but they remain experimental, although the results seem to be encouraging. However, Qt Lite had to be used, and a C++11 compiler and a POSIX conformant RTOS for the platform were required.

Support for different embedded Linux hardware is encapsulated by the so-called Qt Platform Abstraction and implemented by platform plugins. For hardware with OpenGL ES 2.0 support, the EGLFS plugin is used; if OpenGL is not available, the LinuxFB plugin uses the Linux frame buffer directly. Two other plugins, namely DirectFB and Wayland, use the hardware through the two like-named drivers. To request a specific plugin on the target device, the `QT_QPA_PLATFORM` environment variable or the `-platform` command-line parameter can be used.

Example usage with Raspberry Pi

We have seen that Qt offers the needed tooling only in the commercial version, but with a board such as Raspberry Pi, it is possible to work without it. Possibly the simplest variant would be to set up your Raspberry Pi with a VGA screen, keyboard, mouse, and WiFi network in a standard way, as described in `https://projects.raspberrypi.org/en/projects/raspberry-pi-setting-up`. Next, we could install Qt and Qt Creator packages on the device using the `apt-get` commands we already know:

```
sudo apt-get install qt5-default
sudo apt-get install qtcreator
```

After that, we'd develop our OpenGL-accelerated QML application on the usual Windows machine and then send the sources with FTP to the board only for compilation and target tests. Note that after the application is compiled and started, it will fill the whole screen because the default EGLFS plugin doesn't offer any window management (we'd need the Wayland plugin for that).

 The standard EGLF and LinuxFB plugins will show the main window using the complete screen and without any window decorations in Qt 5. Qt 4 has had its own windowing system that was used on embedded devices, but it was dropped in Qt 5.

We won't describe the complete process in detail; instead, we leave it as an exercise for you. Try it out; it's fun!

 With a little more effort, we could use Qt Creator's built-in support for generic remote communication with Linux devices over SSH connection to deploy and start our application on Raspberry Pi. The relevant Qt Creator documentation is to be found at `https://doc.qt.io/qtcreator/ creator-developing-generic-linux.html` and `https://doc.qt.io/ qtcreator/creator-deployment-embedded-linux.html`.

Qt for mobile

As we said, Qt supports the Android, iOS, and WinRT mobile platforms. In the case of mobile development, the situation is simpler than in the embedded field, as Qt Creator offers a built-in support for mobile development in the open source version. On Windows, we can target Android devices, while for iOS development, we'd need an XCode development environment and a Mac computer. Because of that, next, we will discuss Qt's mobile usage using Android as an example platform.

Android support in Qt Creator

To use Qt Creator's embedded support, we have first to install several software packages, namely these:

- Java SE Development Kit—for the Java language
- Android SDK Tools—Android development toolkit
- Android NDK—support for native C development
- Android SDK Platform Tools—contains **Android Debug Bridge** (**adb**) for remote debugging on a device

After that, you have to create a so-called device definition for Android in Qt Creator by selecting **Tools** | **Options** | **Devices** | **Android**. There, you will have to insert the Java JDK, Android NDK, and SDK paths and choose your deployment and remote debugging options.

When you now connect an Android device to the development PC with a USB cable, create a new project using the created Android Device definition, and try to deploy it, you will be presented with a dialog when you can choose your connected device for deployment.

Detailed Qt Creator documentation can be found at `https://doc.qt.io/qt-5/android-getting-started.html` and `http://doc.qt.io/qtcreator/creator-developing-android.html`.

Profiling Android applications

We remember from `Chapter 2`, *Profiling to Find Bottlenecks*, that on desktop we could use the QML Profiler, a general CPU profiler, and a memory-leak detector to profile our application. The good news is that QML Profiler will work with applications launched on an Android device. Remote debugging also works out of the box. In the commercial version, Qt Performance Analyzer will use Linux **perf** tools to sample the started application and display data in Qt Creator. Usage of **valgrind** to profile remote Android applications seems not to be supported.

There are no Qt tools to profile battery or network usage on a mobile device. In the case of Android, we have to use the built-in profilers in Android Studio. Alternatively, we can use AT&T's free Video Optimizer tool (`https://developer.att.com/video-optimizer/`), which, besides evaluating an application's video streaming performance, can also profile its battery and network usage and even recommend fixes for the most common problems.

Mobile APIs in Qt

The Qt framework provides several modules to support cross-platform mobile development, such as the following:

- Qt Positioning—provides geographic position by satellite, WiFi, or other sources
- Qt Sensors—provides generic-mode access to hardware sensors, plus the motion gesture recognition API
- Qt Location—provides interface to maps and route queries

- Qt Bluetooth—encapsulates Bluetooth communication
- Qt Purchasing—supports purchases in the App Store on iOS and Google Play on Android

However, for more OS-related APIs, we have to resort to Android Java classes, which can be accessed from C++ through Java's **Java Native Interface (JNI)**. The Qt Android Extras module encapsulates generic JNI access and a couple of other Android APIs, such as access to Android Services. We will have to use JNI for the following:

- **Android OS notifications**: SD card notifications, network state notifications, battery-level notifications, and so on
- **Android OS features**: Telephony, contacts, speech API, USB, system preferences, and so on

The `QNetworkSession` and `QNetworkConfiguration` classes from the Qt Network module will give us access to mobile roaming and access point change notifications, but also can provide information on the network type the session is running on(2G, 3G, 4G, Bluetooth, or WiFi), as in the following example:

```
QNetworkAccessManager netwAccessMgr;
...
QNetworkConfiguration config = netwAccessMgr.activeConfiguration();
if(config.bearerType() == QNetworkConfiguration::BearerLTE) ...
```

Embedded Linux and Qt performance

Let's recount the classic embedded system optimizations. These are as follows:

- Minimizing executable size
- Minimizing memory usage, removing dynamic allocations
- **Optimizing your math**: Looking for fast and slow instructions, using fake or low-precision floating-point calculations, modifying algorithms
- **Lowering power consumption**: Turning off unused hardware, slowing down to save battery, putting the processor to sleep

Although the hardware where Qt is running doesn't require drastic optimizations, many of the classic techniques are still used. Let's look at some examples to illustrate that fact.

Executable size

As embedded devices as a rule do not have much memory to offer for persistent storage and dynamic RAM memory, we might come to a point when the size of our Qt executable starts to be a problem. Generally speaking, Qt and QML applications are generally rather memory-hungry—make a minimal Qt 5.9 QML application on Windows and you'll see that it uses 12.7 MB of RAM when running in **Release** mode, and it isn't even doing anything yet.

How can we minimize that size? One option is to turn to your old and trusty compiler for help. First, you can use compiler switches to enable optimizing the generated code for size. Second, you could link your application statically, as the linker will then only include those functions from Qt libraries that are also actually used by your program.

If you are using commercial Qt version, you could additionally customize your Qt libraries using the Qt Lite configuration system. The Qt Company reports that it was able to reduce the size of a non-trivial QML application from 25.5 MB with dynamic linking, respectively 13.8 MB with static linking, to 5.4 MB using Qt Lite. So, the gains here are very real!

Another option we could use is the link time optimization (LTO, LTCG) technique we discussed in Chapter 3, *Deep Dive into C++ and Performance*. Unfortunately, to use this technique with Qt, you have to build Qt from source and add -ltcg to the command-line options in the configure step. The Qt Company reported a size reduction of 15% for an example QML application, when compared to the regular, statically linked executable.

Minimizing assets

As on embedded and mobile devices there isn't much space for static storage, the graphic resources we use could also be a problem analogous to the executable size. As we already mentioned in Chapter 8, *Optimizing Graphic Performance,* GPUs support compression of texture data (that is, images). This will speed up the transfer of texture data from CPU to GPU but also the loading times when our application starts. Qt 3D includes support for compressed textures from the beginning, and starting with Qt 5.11, the QML Image element also supports the loading of compressed texture data.

Apart from that, a further optimization that can be applied is the minimization of the contained 2D images. There are some commercial tools that will minimize `.jpg` and `.png` images while preserving their visible quality at the same time, but you can also shrink your images online using, for example, the `Kraken.io` (`https://kraken.io/`) service. Saving rates of up to 50-60% possible.

In the same vein, we could also use Qt Quick Compiler to precompile our QML code. Since Qt 5.11 Qt Quick Compiler is for the first time available in the open source Qt version.

Power consumption

On embedded and mobile platforms, power consumption is always a problem. However, when using embedded Linux, we do not have to do it all manually, as the kernel will already do most of the work for us by scaling down unused cores and putting system and periphery devices to sleep. However, the configuration of some drivers can sometimes be optimized. In such cases, we can use the Powertop Linux tool to diagnose issues with power consumption and power management and obtain suggestions on most common problems.

However, our application should try to conserve energy too. Some hints for that include the following:

- Prefer dark colors and avoid large areas with light colors, as the display will probably consume most of the energy.
- Devise your own screensaver, and minimize activities when screen backlight is off.
- Avoid unnecessary wake-ups of periphery devices by continuous polling of some resources.
- Minimize disk and network I/O.

Start-up time

As we already said, smaller images and texture data can be loaded faster and will reduce start-up time. But also a smaller executable will load faster, and if it is also statically linked, the OS doesn't have to waste time dynamically resolving the dependencies. Thus, a lean, statically linked executable and optimized images already give us an advantage regarding start-up time. Next, other techniques will be briefly discussed.

Using the current Qt version

We shouldn't forget about one most important start-up optimization technique, namely using the latest Qt version! We've already discussed how several new features were added to recent Qt versions, such as Shader and QML cache (Qt 5.9), QML Compiler (Qt 5.11), distance fields (Qt 5.12), and compressed textures (Qt 5.11), can speed up your application's startup.

In Qt 5.12, we have additionally seen considerable performance improvements, especially for ARM processors on embedded platforms. For example, the Qt Company recently reported a reduction of start-up time on embedded Linux and i.MX6 Quad processor (4x Cortex A9 core) between a Qt 5.9 application using shader cache and compiled QML and a Qt 5.12 application, using the same techniques, from 4,853 milliseconds to 2,034 milliseconds. When distance fields and compressed textures were used, the start-up time could be further reduced to 1,258 milliseconds.

Using loaders

The general setup of a fast-loading QML application should comprise an initial frame to be seen first by the user, followed by asynchronously-loaded heavier contents. In that way, we are cutting the time the user has to wait for before they have an impression that the application has already started.

For example, if we had an automotive instrument cluster to be displayed, we would first load only the image containing instrument frames, followed by the actual gauges, and maybe even a 3D model of the car. In a more traditional application, we could first show a welcome page or splash screen and then load the first real page asynchronously, as we have already explained in Chapter 8, *Optimizing Graphic Performance*.

3D asset conditioning

We already mentioned in Chapter 8, *Optimizing Graphic Performance*, that a Qt 3D application can load ready-made 3D assets (that is, ready-made 3D graphic scenes) produced by third-party design tools. However, the default formats used by those tools are designed for ease of use and can come across as rather bloated, and may take a long time to be loaded.

To solve this problem, a special new format for 3D assets, optimized for efficient transmission and loading of 3D scenes and models, was proposed, namely glTF. The Qt tool **qgltf** is bundled with the Qt 3D module and will convert any 3D asset format to glTF and make additional optimizations to the usage of binary JSON in glTF.

The 3D contents can be also directly optimized for size by reducing the number of vertices and removing parts that are not visible. This can be done in the 3D design tool, but there is also an open source C++ library called **Meshoptimizer** (`https://github.com/zeux/meshoptimizer`), implementing many 3D content optimization algorithms we could use.

Linux start-up optimizations

The uncustomized embedded Linux kernel can be rather sluggish to start up, so it's better to optimize it. The usual Linux start-up optimizations are as follows:

- Kernel customization—As there are many unneeded packages in a full Linux distribution, you certainly don't need them all. Use a tool such as Yocto to customize your Linux installation.
- Kernel decompression—If you can't switch it off, at least try some alternative compression methods; it may be worth it.
- Bootloader (*uboot*) customization—To optimize the boot phase and remove drivers.

We won't discuss them in more detail, as they are outside the scope of this book. If you are using the commercial Boot2Qt toolset, the Linux installation is already quite lightweight. In principle, it should be possible to push the Linux start-up time to under two seconds.

Hardware matters

An embedded hardware obviously matters, even when it comes to startup, some boards will power off faster and activate their flash memory sooner. Also, fast memory chips and good memory bandwidth will make a difference.

Graphical performance

Generally speaking, a QML application should run reasonably well on supported GPU-accelerated hardware. However, there's no such thing as a program that's too fast, so we will repeat some of the most important guidelines for good graphical performance:

- Do not use `opacity`—As we know, GPUs do not like transparency and stencils very much! Beware the situation where your designer has done the 2D UI design in Photoshop using several transparent layers out of convenience.

- Do not use `clip`—Clipping prevents scene graph's batching.
- Do not use Qt Quick Controls 1 on embedded—The performance is too bad, and in Qt 5.12, they even became deprecated. Use Qt Quick Controls 2.

On low-performance hardware without GPU acceleration, we could encounter some UI performance problems. In that case, we should strive for changing smaller parts of the screen, instead of updating it at once.

One problem that was reported with animations using software rasterizer on embedded was that the animation could run smoothly but would consume 100% of CPU time! In Qt 5, the problem seems to be that the internal animation timer runs at a rather high rate but will be scaled down using **vsync** throttling (explained in `Chapter 8`, *Optimizing Graphical Performance*) when using OpenGL ES. The proposed solution was to re-implement the animation manually using a much lower timer frequency, as there is seemingly no way to adjust it through the Qt API.

Time series chart display

One common problem on embedded devices is the need to display many thousands of measurement points as a time series chart. If there are that many points, then of course we could have a performance problem showing them. Next, we will discuss two possible optimizations.

Qt Charts and OpenGL acceleration

Since Qt 5.9, the Qt Charts module is included in the open source version, so it will be our prime choice for displaying diagrams and charts. *Qt Charts* are based on `QGraphicsView`, which isn't super performant in itself. As we have already learned, we can enable QpenGL rendering for `QGraphicsView` by calling `setViewport(new QGLWidget)` on it.

However, for a time series, there is an extra optimization provided. By setting `setUseOpenGL(true)` on `QLineSeries` or `QScatterSeries`, the chart will instantiate a transparent `QOpenGLWidget` to draw the accelerated series on top of the chart as an OpenGL overlay. The following example shows the intended usage:

```
auto chart = new QtCharts::QChart;
auto chartView = new QtCharts::QChartView(chart);

QList<QPointF> pointsToPlot = { ... };

auto curve = new QtCharts::QLineSeries;
```

```
curve->setUseOpenGL(true); // accelerate!
curve->append(pointsToPlot);

chart->addSeries(curve);
chart->createDefaultAxes();
```

We see that we have to enable the OpenGL overlay for each displayed time series. In this book's resources (`https://github.com/PacktPublishing/Hands-On-High-performance-with-QT/tree/master/Chapter%2010`), there is a complete example plotting two curves with 100,000 points each, as shown in the following diagram:

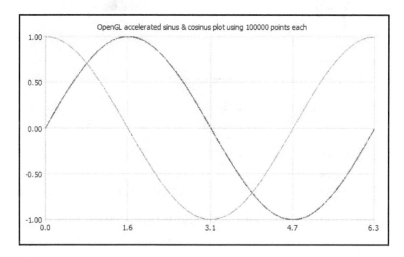

If you feel like it, you might try to deploy it to your Android device or Raspberry Pi board and play with it by varying the number of points to be displayed.

The open source `QCustomPlot` library (available at `https://www.qcustomplot.com/`) also provides comparable OpenGL accelerations.

Polyline simplifications

This technique is a nice example of an algorithmic improvement applied to a graphic. The idea is to simplify the displayed diagram by omitting some points and lines, while maintaining a good approximation of the general shape of the curve. Such techniques are known as **polyline simplification**, and there are a couple of algorithms implementing this idea, such as Douglas–Peucker or Visvalingam's algorithm.

One often-employed simplification method that is, for example, used by the popular LabView scientific software, is the so-called max-min **decimation**. Its main idea is illustrated here:

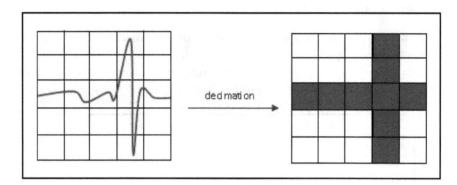

As we can see, the curve segments are replaced by bars, whose height is determined by the minimal and maximal value of the curve in a given interval preserving its rough outline. If we don't want to implement this algorithm by ourselves, the popular **Qt Widgets for Technical Applications** (**QWT**) library (`http://qwt.sourceforge.net/`) will use a similar technique for `QwtPlotCurve::Lines`, when the `QwtPlotCurve::FilterPointsAggressive` flag is set for plotting (since Qwt 6.2).

 The official QWT site only provides the 6.1 version of the library, and this version only supports `QwtPlotCurve::FilterPoints`! The unofficial 6.2 version seems to be the current SVN trunk code base. Fortunately, there are some GitHub repositories providing the SVN trunk code, such as this one: `https://github.com/svn2github/Qwt_trunk`.

Floating-point considerations

Qt defines the `qreal()` macro, which is float-on embedded and double on a desktop, so that we can use `100/qreal(4.54)` instead of `100/4.54` and gain performance.

Why's that? Well, some microcontrollers (for example, Cortex-M series) do not have a **floating-point unit** (**FPU**), or their FPU supports single-precision operations. In both cases, we will fall back to software emulation, and that can be super costly. But as Qt for embedded Linux as a rule doesn't run on such small systems, we shouldn't be bothered with it for normal floating-point usage.

In speed terms, there's no difference between float and double on more modern embedded and mobile hardware, but floating-point will be still about two-times slower than integer operations. Moreover, on some processors, even integer division and modulo operations can be much slower than multiplication and addition. So, when doing lots of math, you might consider checking relative costs of processor instructions.

Mobile-specific performance concerns

First, we want to state that all the embedded systems optimizations apply in equal measure to mobile devices. Moreover, as they are normally equipped with OpenGL hardware (that is, GPU), the techniques we learned in Chapter 8, *Optimizing Graphical Performance*, will also apply. In this section, we will thus only point to mobile-specific applications.

Executable size

Typically, mobile devices of today will have around 16-32 GB of persistent memory and 1-2 GB of dynamic RAM, so the memory resources are not even close to the resources we have on a desktop system. Additionally, there are limits on the maximum size of the applications on Android and iOS platforms. Just as on an embedded device, we could get into a situation where there's a need to minimize an executable's size.

The techniques that can be used are basically much the same as the ones we have on embedded platforms: static compilation, usage of Qt Lite, 3D asset, and image minimization. For really big applications, you can split them into several parts (slicing) by mobile platform-specific means.

Power usage

On a mobile device, there are basically the same power-saving mechanisms as on an embedded one, such as avoiding waking up peripheral devices and sensors (such as GPS), minimizing of network transfers and disk I/O, and reducing activity when an application is not visible.

One difference from embedded devices is that the Android OS adds its own power management extension, built on top of Linux power management, which will try to put the system, and thus the CPU, into sleep mode as soon as possible. An application can request and also call `WakeLock` from `PowerManager` to prevent the system from going into sleep mode. We can do this from Qt through the `QAndroidJniObject` class, but normally it's not recommended, as it will increase battery usage.

Another difference is the presence of a radio unit to run cellular radio protocols and IP networking. Besides the LCD display, the wireless radio unit is the one piece of hardware that consumes the most energy on a mobile device. When transmitting at full power, the radio unit could drain the battery in a matter of hours.

In an attempt to optimize its power usage, the radio unit will move to a lower energy state if the network is idle for a given amount of time, as depicted in the following diagram:

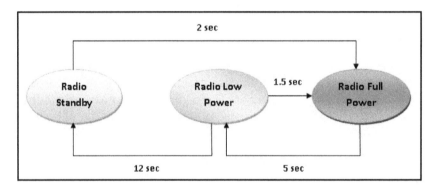

The previous diagram shows the state transitions of a typical 3G wireless radio unit. It will fall back from full transmission power to 50% after the radio unit is idle for more than **5 sec**, and to inactive state after a further **12 sec**. It returns from low power to full power in **1.5 sec**, and from standby to full power in **2 sec** (or more). For other radio technologies (2G, 4G/LTE), idle times and power resumption delays will vary, with newer technologies achieving resumption times of 100 milliseconds and fewer, but the general principles are applicable to all wireless radio implementations.

These state transitions are, however, controlled by the mobile network operator and not the mobile device itself. This enables the radio module to recover from the standby state if there is incoming data of phone calls to be received.

We can see that starting a data transmission for a duration of one second will cost us 18 seconds of power usage. This is a clear example of the **big fixed costs** problem, similar to the kernel trip costs in system calls, and we already know from `Chapter 1`, *Understanding Performant Programs,* that the solution for that will be the batching of send requests and prefetching of remote data. We will discuss this in more detail in a subsequent section.

Mobile networking

When using network communication on a mobile device, the general networking optimization techniques we discussed in `Chapter 9`, *Optimizing Network Performance,* were TCP and SSL connection reuse, SSL session resumption, HTTP content caching, and content compression. The last technique especially could be quite effective as the power consumption of the radio unit is much higher than that of the CPU.

However, there are some mobile-specific complications, namely the following:

- **Shaky connectivity**: A mobile device can fall back to an older and slower mobile protocol, so you'd better assume that the network access will be slow. This is exacerbated by the wake-up latency of the radio unit. The device can lose network connectivity altogether, so the application should be able to work in offline mode. For example, instead of requesting some state change on a server and waiting for a response, we should change the state locally and then align the server state when we are online again.
- **Radio device energy state transitions**: We explained in the *Power usage* section that, basically, waking up the radio unit is a **bad thing**. We will have to resort to batching and prefetching.
- **Different types of connectivity**: Besides the different types of mobile network connections (2G, 3G, 4G/LTE), the device can use WiFi and Bluetooth for networking. Each of the technologies has different performance and power characteristics, and an application should be able to adapt its behavior according to that.

Next, let's discuss some techniques to mitigate these problems.

Batch and piggyback

Because each network transmission incurs an energy tail, sending short data packets intermittently is a mobile networking anti-pattern. What we should strive to achieve instead is to send a maximal amount of data in one chunk and then let the radio return to the idle state. Ideally, we'd even like to start the transmission when the radio is already powered on.

 In Android, we could use the `ConnectivityManager` Java class and its `addDefaultNetworkActiveListener()` method to be notified when the system default network has gone into a high-power state. We could access this method from Qt through `QAndroidJniObject`, but we have additionally to define a Java callback class calling a `native` C++ method. Qt doesn't seem to provide such a notification.

The mechanism we can use is to batch the transfers by queuing delay-tolerant, not-time-critical transfers, and only send them when some necessary, time-critical transfers are pending. A time-critical transfer could be, for example, a user request to download a full-sized version of an image or a full article for a given headline. Delay-tolerant content could be, for example, some usage statistics or analytics data gathered by our application.

Some applications will, however, still need to periodically check for the newest server data. We know that polling on mobile network is bad, so what can we do about it? One possibility is to replace polling with server notifications, which we will discuss next. If we don't want or cannot do that, we should simply decrease polling frequency. Now, there is a trade-off to be made between the value of up-to-date information for the user and battery life.

If we go for periodic status checks, we can piggyback them on time-critical transfers, and likewise, we can use them as an opportunity to send batched delay-tolerant contents. Moreover, we use adaptive check frequency dependent on the available network type, remaining battery power, and the application running in the foreground or background.

Consider a push model

Because polling as a mechanism is rather inefficient in itself, we should use server notifications and push delivery where possible. A natural choice for that would be WebSockets, HTTP/2 protocols, or long polling (also known as Comet) techniques with classic HTTP, as we discussed in Chapter 9, *Optimizing Networking Performance*.

However, server notifications can be optimized for mobile exactly in the same way we would optimize client-side transfers, namely by batching the notifications and sending them to the client only when its radio is in the active state. On the Android platform, Google's **Firebase Cloud Messaging (FCM)** solution offers, among other things, exactly that: it can aggregate notifications and send them in one batch when the device's radio becomes active. The server could then push its updates to FCM, and FCM would determine an optimal delivery schedule. Using FCM will also automatically synchronize transfer times between different applications that use it, further reducing battery drain.

If we use a server push model, this gives us new opportunity for saving battery life. The device could use the high-power state it switched to when receiving server notifications to send the queued client-side data; that is, to piggyback them on the notifications.

Prefetch data

A classic technique to work around slow access times is to speculatively fetch more data than needed, hoping for a linear access pattern. As we already learned, the CPU is doing that when accessing memory and the OS kernel does that when reading files from disk.

On mobile, we don't only have bigger network latencies, but we must also take the radio energy tail into account, so fetching a big file in chunks is an anti-pattern. When we have to access a big file on the server, such as a music or video file, the right way to do so is to download it as a whole and let the radio return to idle.

But we don't have to stop there. For the music file example, if the user is listening to a song from some album, we could prefetch the next one, but downloading the entire album would be overkill. However, when downloading a large video file, we should probably only prefetch an amount of video data likely to be viewed in the next couple of minutes.

So, we can see that prefetching at an application level isn't that straightforward as in the case of file I/O, because a user's behavior cannot be predicted that easily. The application could use some metrics, statistical models, or heuristics to anticipate what your user might need. In any case, designing a prefetching strategy leaves ample room for creativity.

Reuse connections

Opening a new TCP connection will require the radio unit to go to the high-power state and then actually send some data to the server. By contrast, an idle connection lurking around doesn't need to use any power until some payload data has to be sent. We learned that we should reuse connections on desktop systems, but this is doubly true on mobile.

If the radio unit goes to the idle state, the TCP connection won't be terminated by the network equipment and will be still there when the radio switches to high power. However, there are some timeouts employed by network and NAT routers that will terminate idle connections. So, if we want to keep our connections alive, we should periodically send keep-alive messages. Various sources recommend times between 5 and 15 minutes for the network infrastructure, and you also have to take into account timeouts on the server.

Adapting to the current network connection type

A mobile device can be connected to different mobile network types (2G, 3G, 4G/LTE) or local networks such as WiFi or Bluetooth. These networks have different performance characteristics we must be aware of.

A WiFi connection has the biggest bandwidth and lowest battery costs of all those technologies, so we should try to use it for data transfers whenever possible, and we should decrease network activity if we switch from WiFi to the cellular network.

As 4G cellular networks can compete with WiFi on throughput and latency, they incur much higher battery costs. 3G and 2G networks offer much worse throughput and latency; however, they also require much less power. That means for us that because of greater bandwidth, we can prefetch data much more aggressively with 4G, but at the same time the tail-time battery costs are much higher. That is an incentive for keeping radio active for longer times and download even more, to reduce the frequency of updates.

Graphic hardware

Let's at last have a look at the graphic hardware typically found on embedded and mobile platforms. As embedded devices will generally support OpenGL ES 2.0 hardware (as Raspberry Pi does), mobile devices as a rule support more modern 3D APIs. For example, my midrange mobile phone's GPU supports APIs such as Vulkan, OpenGL ES 3.1 + AE (3.2), OpenCL 2.0, and Direct3D 12. Using these newer APIs, it is possible to achieve much better graphical performance through more fine-grained control of the GPU.

In contrast to the desktop GPUs we discussed in Chapter 8, *Optimizing Graphical Performance*, mobile GPUs use so-called tile-based rendering, while desktop GPUs traditionally used immediate-mode (that is, whole-frame) rendering. Tile-based rendering splits the frame into separately rendered tiles to reduce the bandwidth requirements (and thus the power costs) of accessing off-chip framebuffer memory, but it can introduce more rendering latency as a trade-off in the process.

The Vulkan API has specific features supporting optimization of tile-based rendering, such as control over whether to load or clear previous framebuffer content and others. OpenGL ES can also achieve it but only using extensions that are not universally supported.

 One point where we have to take this into account emerges in the context of the QOpenGLWidget class introduced in Chapter 8, *Optimizing Graphical Performance*. When using it on tile-based GPUs, we have to call glClear() as early as possible in the paintGL() method, so that the tile buffer won't be reloaded with the framebuffer's previous contents, which could lead to a significant performance drop.

As these details are abstracted away when we are using QML, we won't discuss them here in more detail. When using Vulcan or OpenGL calls directly, you might, however, want to further investigate this topic.

Summary

In this penultimate chapter, we had a look at a new field where the Qt framework has been increasingly employed in the last couple of years, that is, embedded and mobile. We first learned about the hardware used for embedded and mobile devices, and then we had a look at the question of hardware requirements for the usage of Qt on embedded and mobile devices and introduced Qt's tooling for development on those platforms. Finally, we turned to performance questions and learned how to minimize executable and asset sizes, how to improve application start-up times, and graphical performance and power consumption. For mobile platforms, we also looked at techniques to optimize radio network usage.

This chapter finished our discussion of performance themes in a Qt context. In the next and final chapter, we will discuss what's left, after you've finally optimized your application, namely testing and deploying it.

Questions

Here are some questions that will test your understanding of the topics discussed in this chapter:

1. On what embedded hardware could we use Qt 5.9 and higher?
2. What's the fuss about fast startup on embedded? My car's digital console starts in no time! Any explanations?
3. What is an SoC? What is an MCU?

4. Should we bother about floating-point operations on embedded platforms?
5. What does the Wayland plugin for embedded Linux do?
6. What is the worst possible polling interval for 3G mobile radio access?
7. What would a mobile device most like to do?
8. What is a tile-based architecture, and why is it widespread on mobile? Why aren't we using it on desktop?
9. The GPU performance of Raspberry Pi 3 is often (incorrectly) quoted to be 24 GFLOP. What could be the reason for that?

Further reading

If you would like to learn more about the topics discussed in this chapter, these are the resources I'd recommend.

Making Embedded Systems, by *E. White, O'Reilly* (2012), is an introduction to the field of resource-constrained devices and their programming. It only covers C programming language and techniques.

Embedded Linux Development using Yocto Projects, 2nd Edition, by *O. Salvador* and *D. Angolini*, *Packt Publishing* (2017), provides a thorough explanation of the Yocto build system for embedded Linux, and applies it to the BeagleBone, Raspberry Pi, and Wandboard boards.

The blog post *A Speed-Up for Charting on Embedded* by *Ch. Merz* (2018) is available at `https://www.kdab.com/a-speed-up-for-charting-on-embedded/` and describes the implementation of a polyline simplification technique that uses a flattened min-max tree to yield significant performance gains.

High Performance Browser Networking, by *I Grigorik, O'Reilly* (2013), discusses mobile network architecture and protocols in much detail and also gives some advice on the performance of networking on mobile devices.

If you'd like to dive deeper into networking and other mobile optimizations, have a look at Android's developer documentation, especially the networking section at `https://developer.android.com/training/efficient-downloads/` and the power management section at `https://developer.android.com/topic/performance/power/`.

11
Testing and Deploying Qt Applications

This chapter is the final chapter of this book, and, for a change, its tone is somewhat lighter. As our application is hopefully performing blazingly fast now, we will try to test it and then to deploy it when all the tests are passing. At that point, we will end this book, because maintaining and refactoring the application is a theme for a different book.

In this chapter, we will discuss following topics:

- The testing of Qt code—or how to test GUI applications.
- The deployment of Qt applications—as we want to distribute our application.
- Summary—as we have to say goodbye.

Testing of Qt code

Testing is an important part of software development. First, it helps us to compare the written software with our expectations, and, after that is done, it helps to keep the software working in the future by detecting unwanted regressions.

As you are an intermediate developer, you will probably know a lot about testing, so we won't restate the basics; we will only have a look at the available Qt tooling and GUI-specific testing techniques, as the Qt framework is prevalently used to write GUI applications.

Unit testing

So, let's start with a simple question: How do we test a GUI application? How do we test a QML application? Testing non-GUI classes is simple: We just instantiate a class, call its methods, and check the results. In the case of Qt GUIs, we can, fortunately, use a similar strategy: We can invoke slots and event-handler methods and then test the contents of a given widget's properties.

We could drive it so far that we first write tests and deliver an implementation fulfilling them only then, a practice known as **test-driven development** (**TDD**). In the context of UI development in Qt, TDD is however somehow impractical, as we have first to cater for a UI's visual appearance before we can test it.

So, let's stay with a more moderate unit-testing approach that consists of writing test cases for single classes. We can do that in two ways: either by using a unit-test framework in the tradition of the venerable *jUnit*, or by automating the creation of test cases with tools recording mouse clicks and keyboard actions.

Qt Test

Qt Test is a Qt module supporting unit testing in the standard way. Its unique strength is that it includes utility functions, allowing us to simulate GUI events, such as mouse clicks and keyboard input, and test the results. Moreover, there is also a QML interface for Qt Test with a TestCase QML type and built-in Qt Creator support.

A QTest test case is simply a QObject defining test cases as private slots, as shown in the following example:

```
class SomeWidgetTest : public QObject
{
  Q_OBJECT
public:
  SomeWidgetTest();
  ~SomeWidgetTest();
private slots:
  void initTestCase();
  void cleanupTestCase();
  void testA();
  void testB();
  ...
};
```

As we can see, there two special slots for the initialization and cleanup of the test case. In a test case, we can use several `QTest` helper methods to simulate GUI events:

```
void SomeWidgetTest::testA()
{
    auto tstLineEdit = widgetUnderTest->lineEdit;
    auto tstPushBtn = widgetUnderTest->ui->pushButton;

    // keyboard
    QTest::keyClicks(tstLineEdit, "XXXXXX");
    QCOMPARE(tstLineEdit->text(), QString("XXXXXX"));

    // mouse
    QTest::mouseClick(tstPushBtn, Qt::LeftButton);
    QCOMPARE(tstLineEdit->text(), QString("XXXXXX"));
}
```

As can be seen from the previous example, see how Qt Test defines macros to specify pass/fail criteria for tests, namely, `QCOMPARE()` and `QVERIFY()`.

Additionally, Qt Test provides a `QSignalSpy` class, which can be used to count and examine signals emitted by `QObjects`:

```
QSignalSpy spy(tstPushBtn, SIGNAL(clicked()));
QTest::mouseClick(tstPushBtn, Qt::LeftButton);
QCOMPARE(spy.count(), 1);
```

We already mentioned Qt Test's support for benchmarking, that is, the measuring of the average time needed by some operation we are interested in. The syntax to be used is shown in the following example:

```
void SomeWidgetTest::testB()
{
    auto tstLineEdit = widgetUnderTest->lineEdit;

    QBENCHMARK {
        QTest::keyClicks(tstLineEdit, "XXXXXX");
    }
}
```

Another feature Qt Test supports is so-called **data-driven testing**, that is, repetition of QCOMPARE() macro using tabular data. A data table will be first defined using QTest::addColumn() and QTest:newRow() and can be then referenced using a QFETCH() macro:

```
void SomeWidgetTest::testB()
{
  // test data created in testB_data()!
  QFETCH(QString, inputColumn);
  QFETCH(QString, resultColumn);

  QCOMPARE(myStringOperation(inputColumn), resultColumn);
}
```

In the previous example, the QCOMPARE() operation will be repeated for all rows of the predefined tabular data.

Now we can create several tests in their turn, containing several test cases, and let them run from the command line (consult the Qt documentation for more information on how to do this), or we can use Qt Creator's support for unit tests, as described in the following, *Test support in Qt Creator*, section.

Test support in Qt Creator

In Qt Creator, we can create a project of type **auto test project**. It can be either a standalone project or integrated as part of a **subdir project**, as shown in the following screenshots:

We can switch the view type from **Projects** to **Tests** to see all the tests present in the opened projects, as shown in the previous screenshots. We can also see that we can have `QTest`, `QML Test`, and `Google Test` test cases side by side in a single project.

We can choose the test we wish to run, and start it from the context menu, Run Selected Tests or Run All Tests. The test results will be then displayed in the lower pane of Qt Creator, as shown in the next screenshot:

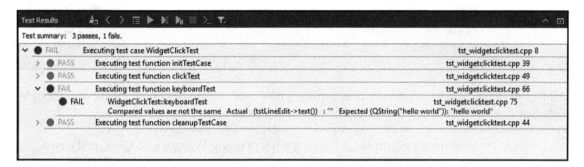

The results of QML tests will be also displayed in the **Test Result** pane as shown in the figure below. Clicking at a given row in the **Test Result** will show the corresponding test-case in Qt Creator's editor:

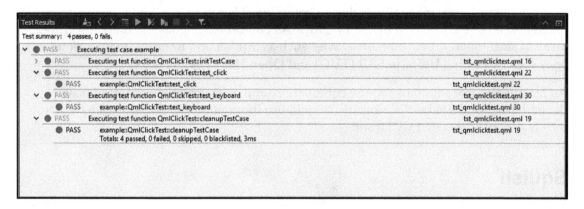

When running a benchmark, the measured average operation time will be displayed for the given test case, as shown in the following screenshot:

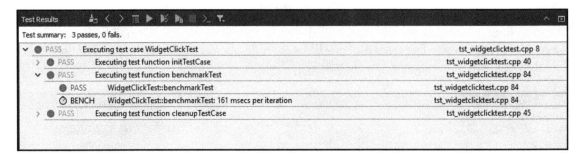

All things considered, Qt Creator offers quite a nice integration of QTest, QML, and Google Test test cases. If you want to test it, this book's resources (`https://github.com/PacktPublishing/Hands-On-High-performance-with-QT/tree/master/Chapter%2011`) contain an example Qt Creator project using Widget and QML test cases.

Automated GUI testing

With unit tests, we can conveniently test one or several classes in separation, but we have to write all the test cases manually. Is there a better way? For example, could we record our clicks instead of coding them in C++ or QML? As you probably guessed, there is a whole array of such tools—from commercial ones such as **Squish** and **Ranorex**, to open source ones such as **Testing Unitario GUI (TUG)** and **Open HMI Testing (OHT)**.

As the open source solutions require compilation, and even sometimes have a Boost dependency, for the sake of simplicity, we will use the commercial Squish tool to illustrate the concept of automated GUI testing.

Squish

We have chosen Squish because I have encountered it in a couple of real-world projects, and it seems to be rather widely-used. Although it is commercial, it is possible to request an evaluation licence (`https://www.froglogic.com/squish/free-trial/`) if you want to try it out.

That is what I did, and after I got an email with my evaluation licence key, I downloaded an installer from the home page (`https://www.froglogic.com/squish/`) and installed Squish on my machine.

The Squish version matching the Qt installation used in this book is
`squish-6.4.2.1-qt59x-win32-mingw_gcc53_posix_dwarf.exe`
Squish/Qt Evaluation (Binary for Windows 32 Bit, Qt 5.9.x, MinGW, gcc 5.3, dwarf exception handling, posix threading).

In the following *Example Squish test* section, we will see how to record and reply a GUI test for Qt Widget and QML-based applications. In this book's resources (`https://github.com/PacktPublishing/Hands-On-High-performance-with-QT/tree/master/Chapter%2011`), we included an example test suite with simple tests for widget and QML GUIs, if you'd like to try out Squish.

Example Squish test

When you start Squish, you will first have to create a test suite—it is sufficient only to give it a name. Second, you'll have to specify the executable for testing—you do it in the **AUT** sub-tab in the test suite's **Settings** tab, the left-most tab in the following screenshot.

Next, you will have to create a new test in the suite—you can do it by clicking on the left-most icon over the **Test Cases** panel, as can be seen in the next screenshot:

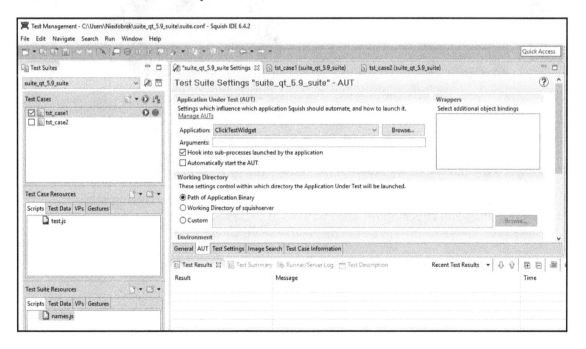

In my tests, Squish was only able to launch programs built in Release mode.

Next, we can press on the red round icon behind the test case name, as seen in the previous screenshot, to start recording for the test case. This will launch the tested application and offer an additional window for with a few action buttons, while hiding the main Squish GUI, as shown in the next screenshot:

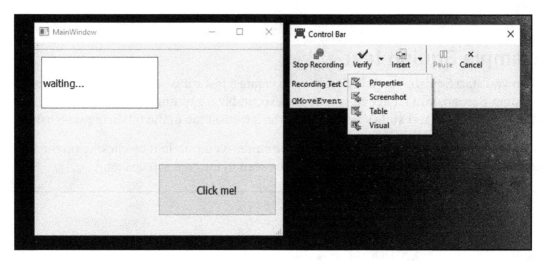

Now every action we do will be recorded in the scripting language of our choice (the default is Javascript) and can be replayed later. Additionally, if we click the **Verify** button in the Squish GUI (as shown in the previous screenshot), we will be brought back to the main Squish window, where we can select widgets and their properties and then specify their expected values to be included in the test script.

In the next screenshot, we can see an example of a recorded test case issuing mouse clicks, keyboard inputs, and checking for text contents of a `QLineEdit`:

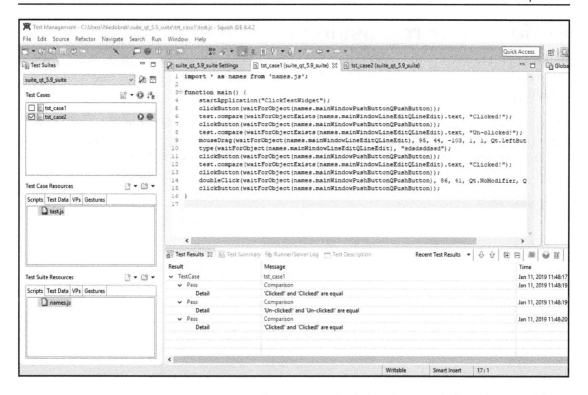

We can replay the recorded test case by clicking on the green arrow icon next to the test case's name, as can be seen from the previous screenshot. We also can see the results of a replayed test in the **Test Results** pane in the lower part of the Squish window—we see that the tests checking the text in a QLineEdit always met our expectations. Additionally, tests can be replayed from the command line, and test results will be saved to a file, using an XML format by default.

Other tools offer a similar functionality, and you have to admit that we can build up quite complex tests just with several mouse clicks. So, in summation, for GUI testing, this approach scales much better than the classic, framework-driven, unit test one.

Performance regression testing

In this book, we already mentioned the idea of performance tests, that is, tests that are set up to discover deterioration in the performance of an application. Let's now see how we could implement such a test suite.

One possibility would be to use the QTest test cases's support for benchmarks, and we showed a usage example with C++ classes earlier in this chapter. In the case of QML tests, a function whose name starts with benchmark_ will have the effect of the C++ QBENCHMARK macro, and thus we could benchmark some item's creation time as follows:

```
TestCase {
  id: root
  name: "ItemXCreationBenchmark"

  function benchmark_create_item() {
    var component = Qt.createComponent("itemX.qml")
    var obj = component.createObject(root)
    obj.destroy()
    component.destroy()
  }
}
```

Adding a qmlbench benchmark

Another possibility is to use the **qmlbench** tool (https://github.com/qt-labs/qmlbench) that we already mentioned in Chapter 10, *Qt Performance on Embedded and Mobile*. This tool only supports QML tests, but it additionally offers FPS measurements for the test cases, a metric that is also important for GUI applications.

There are two types of QML benchmarks types in qmlbench: Plain Benchmark and a CreationBenchmark. They both have a count property, which is used in FPS benchmarks and a staticCount property used in classic time measurements. An example of a plain Benchmark looks like the following:

```
import QtQuick 2.0
import QmlBench 1.0

Benchmark {
  id: root;
  property int count: 50;
  property int staticCount: 5000;

  Canvas {
```

```
   onTChanged: requestPaint();

   onPaint: {
     var ctx = getContext("2d");
     ... paint
   }
 }
}
```

A benchmark defines a time tick `t`, which can be used in an `onTChanged` handler. In the previous example, we thus benchmarked a painting on a 2D canvas. An example of a creation benchmark will look like the following:

```
CreationBenchmark {
  id: root;
  count: 50;
  staticCount: 2500;

  delegate: Item {
    x: QmlBench.getRandom() * (root.width - width)
    y: QmlBench.getRandom() * (root.height - height)
  }
}
```

We see it is rather simple, as we have to define a delegate item, and its creation times will be benchmarked. As qmlbench is open source, we can add our benchmarks and give it a try.

Using Squish

We have seen that Squish records the test cases using general-purpose programming languages such as Javascript or Python. We can, however, always edit the created script and add our time measurements. Assuming we are using Python as the scripting language, we could add a time measurement, as shown in the following code example:

```
import time

def main():
  startApplication("ClickTestWidget")

  startTime = time.time()
  clickButton(waitForObject(names.mainWindowPushButtonQPushButton))
  ... etc.
  t = time.time() - startTime
  test.log("Measured time: " + t)
```

However, because of Squish runtime instrumentation, the measured times can be higher than those of an uninstrumented application. So, we have first to establish a baseline for a Squish-instrumented application, and then we will be able to test for regressions. A disadvantage of this method is that we'll have to enhance the generated test scripts manually.

Another feature supported by Squish that can simplify automated regression tests is the ability to use virtual display software, such as **Xvnc** on Linux, to create a virtual screen for running tests on a **headless** system (for example, a server without a monitor).

 Unfortunately, this is not supported on Windows, so, in that case, we are left with a Qt Test executable started from a command line using the -platform offscreen command-line option. This will invoke a platform plugin that will create a virtual screen for the tests. This plugin is unfortunately, likewise, not compatible with Squish.

Deploying Qt applications

In this section, we will look at problems to be solved and decisions to be made when deploying a Qt application. As the platform used in our book was chosen to be Windows, we will discuss deployment in that context.

Flying parts

A typical Qt application is a single executable file, but it needs more files to be present to be able to run. The following files will be needed besides the .exe file:

- **Dynamic libraries**: By default, when we create a Qt project in Qt Creator, it will be using dynamic linking, thus our application first will need Qt's **dynamic link libraries (DLLs)**. Because we are using MinGW gcc compiler, we will also need its C++ runtime and standard library implementations, normally also as DLLs.
- **More dynamic libraries**: There are also third-party libraries we could need, such as libEGL.dll, libGLESv2.dll, and the DirectX HLSL compiler library, when we use ANGLE with OpenGL, or the OpenSSL libraries for networking.
- **QML modules**: If we are using QML, the standard modules such as QtQuick, QtQml, QtCharts, or Qt3D, will also be needed. They are distributed as DLLs and some additional files containing QML module metadata, or as pure QML files.

- **Qt plugins**: Unfortunately, the DLLs implementing Qt's C++ and QML APIs aren't enough for our `.exe` file to start. Qt also uses plugins to enable extensions, but also for fairly standard GUI functionality such as the loading and displaying of `.jpg` and `.png` files. In the same manner, there are also plugins encapsulating the platform Qt is running on. We have encountered the platform plugins when discussing Qt's usage of embedded devices, but for a desktop application, we will need the Windows platform plugin as well.
- **Language files**: If we are using Qt's built-in translation support, we will also need the `.qm` translation files and the help files, if we are also using Qt Help (or some other) framework .

We see that there are a couple of files and libraries to take care of! Additionally, we have to ensure that the Qt libraries use the correct path to find the Qt plugins, documentation, translation, and that our executable file can find the Qt libraries themselves.

Static versus dynamic builds

In `Chapter 10`, *Qt Performance on Embedded and Mobile*, we already mentioned the possibility of building our Qt application using static linking. A static build consists of a single `.exe` file, thus all DLL libraries we have to take care of in the default dynamic build just disappear. Also, the Qt plugins and QML imports can be included in a statically linked executable, further simplifying the deployment.

The previously discussed, possible usage of **link time optimization** (**LTO**) would work best with static builds as well.

Unfortunately, to be able to use static linking, Qt must be first built from source with the `-static` configuration option set. To make things worse, this qmake option is fully supported only for the commercial Qt version. Furthermore, even if we succeeded with the static build (as I did for Qt 4 back in the day), we shouldn't use it for the open source licence's sake. I'm not a lawyer, but as far as I know, open source software should be used in the form of dynamic libraries, to be easily recognized as such.

Because we are using an open source Qt version in this book, we won't further discuss static builds, and we will continue with the standard dynamic builds and deployments.

Deploying on Windows

We have seen that there is a lot to be taken into account when building a deployment of a Qt application. Fortunately, Qt provides a tool that can help us with that by scanning the created Qt `.exe` file, finding all dependencies and copying them to the deployment directory.

Windows deployment tool

The Windows deployment tool is included in the Qt 5.9 installation, can be found in `<QTDIR>/bin/`, and is named `windeployqt.exe`. We invoke it with the `.exe` file to scan, or a directory where it is placed as an argument. Additionally, if we use QML, we have to specify the directory containing the QML files, so that the QML dependencies can also be scanned.

For example, if we'd like to create a deployment of the *QmlWithModel* example from `Chapter 2`, *Profiling to Find Bottlenecks*, we have to do the following:

1. Copy the `QmlWithModel.exe` file to the deployment directory.
2. Invoke the Windows deployment tool, for example, with the following command:

```
<QTDIR>/bin/windeployqt.exe --qmldir <source_dir>
<deployment_dir>/QmlWithModel.exe
```

The tool will then copy the discovered dependencies to the deployment directory so that we will have all the needed parts in one place. It will also create the expected subdirectory structure for plugins and other Qt resources.

 The Windows deployment tool has an array of command-line options allowing the fine-tuning of the discovery and copy processes. The relevant documentation is to be found at `http://doc.qt.io/qt-5/windows-deployment.html`

Installation and paths

Now that we have found and collected all the files needed in our installation, we can use some Windows installer framework, such as the open source **NSIS** installer and **Qt Installer Framework** or the free **Inno Setup**. However, discussion of their respective features and usage patterns lies outside the scope of this book.

The chosen installer will create an executable that will, as the ultimate result, have our files copied to some directories on the target machine. What directories would they be? By default, the Qt libraries will use some hardcoded paths to look for plugins, translations, and other dependencies. However, these paths can be customized using the `qt.conf` file, a configuration file in a simple `.ini` file format, documented in http://doc.qt.io/qt-5/qt-conf.html. This file can be most conveniently placed in `:/qt/etc/qt.conf` using the Qt resource system.

With those constraints, we have following options:

- Copy the whole deployment directory as it is; the Windows deployment tool will build the expected directory structure in the deployment directory, so if we just copy it, everything will be found.
- Copy used Qt DLLs and plugins to some central place; this option is sensible if we have more than one application and we want to reuse the Qt framework's libraries. We can either keep the subdirectory structure as it is and add the Qt library path to the Window's `PATH` environment variable, or customize it as we like by using the `qt.conf` file.
- Install a complete Qt distribution in a central place; in that case, we do not need to deploy any Qt DLL with our application, only libraries and resources we have created. We can then point to the Qt libraries using Window's `PATH` environment variable. This may be an option if we are not pressed for space. In that case, the plugin subdirectory structure will be correct by default.

In that way, we can avoid issues with DLLs that cannot be loaded and plugins that cannot be found, so that our application will start without any problems.

Summary

In this chapter, we first learned how to test a Qt application, starting with the classic unit tests, their integration in Qt Creator, GUI test automation with Squish, and ending with performance regression testing. Then we had a look at the Qt application deployment problem and learned the difference between static and dynamic builds, the deployment support tools Qt has to offer, and the specific case of Windows deployment and installation.

This is the last chapter of the book, and I hope you enjoyed the ride. Maybe we didn't go deep enough into many topics, but, first, this was an intermediate-level book, and, second, you cannot go deep into everything, as some chapters could be expanded into entire books of their own. Hopefully, you can now see somehow more clearly through the mists of Qt and performance lands, and maybe you have even started to appreciate Qt more, as it spans so many fields and offers so many performance challenges.

If you thought performance optimization is only for some genius programmers working on super-cool projects, then now you hopefully know that it isn't. Admittedly, there is a lot of knowledge that has to be acquired, but all of it is the product of a human mind, and if you put a due portion of time into it, you will also be able to understand. Maybe you'll even start to enjoy learning and getting better and better at it? You've already learned a lot, and you can start your own journey if you want. Have fun, and remember—fast programs will help to save the planet; don't write slow ones because of convenience.

Questions

In the following, you will find the last set of questions to test your understanding of the topics discussed in this chapter:

1. Why would you like to test a Qt application?
2. How would you implement a performance regression test measuring the FPS rate of a QML application?
3. Do you have any ideas about deploying a Qt application to embedded Linux? Take some hints from the previous chapter.
4. You are running automated GUI tests—what problems could arise? What could be done to prevent them?
5. What does TDD mean?
6. How does Squish identify GUI elements? Can you figure it out?
7. Which deployment type is better—a static or a dynamic build?
8. Is performance optimization in Qt black magic? Be honest!

Further reading

If you'd like to deepen your knowledge about testing and deploying of applications, you might find the following books interesting:

For a standard treatment of TDD, I'd recommend *Test Driven Development: By Example,* book by *K Beck, Addison-Wesley Professional* (2002).

Mastering Qt 5, by *G. Lazar* and *R. Penea, Packt Publishing* (2018) contains an introductory chapter on the Qt Test framework and another one discussing the packaging of Qt applications on Windows, Linux, OS X, Android, and iOS.

Assessments

Chapter 1

1. What is premature optimization?
   It can be defined as blindly optimizing some parts of code without having done any runtime measurements before.

2. What did Donald Knuth really say about it?
   He said that programmers waste enormous amounts of time thinking about, or worrying about, the speed of non-critical parts of their programs, and these attempts at efficiency actually have a strong negative impact when debugging and maintenance are considered. We should forget about small efficiencies, say, about 97% of the time: premature optimization is the root of all evil. Yet we should not pass up our opportunities in that critical 3%.

3. Why do we need performance optimization techniques?
   We want to decrease power consumption and enable a smooth user experience when interacting with the program.

4. Which is the worst premature pessimization you can do?
   Choosing an inefficient algorithm, plain and simple.

5. Why is main memory slow?
   Because it needs refreshing, stores bits analogously, and lies far away from the CPU. *Far away* means outside the chip; thus, it must be read over the bus. Caches are placed directly on the chip.

6. What is ILP, and what has it to do with thread synchronization?
   ILP means instruction-level parallelism, aka out-of-order execution. The processor is allowed to re-order independent instructions (thus, also reads and writes) to achieve better performance. But when we are synchronizing two threads by reading a value of some flag, this read cannot be reordered, because all the following instructions rely on the specified ordering. Memory barrier instructions can be used to order the processor to stay away from re-ordering.

7. Is hyperthreading good or bad for performance?
Is this a paradoxical question? Not really. In hyperthreading, we don't double the processor's computing resources; we only double the instruction input. This allows the processor to pack the instructions even more tightly than with out-of-order execution only. In most of the cases, this can increase performance by about 20-30%. However, that presumes that the application is parallelizable, and that isn't already hand-tuned to use all of the core's resources efficiently. Old operating systems, which are unaware of hyperthreading (such as Windows Server 2003) are problematic too. In such corner cases, hyperthreading may not increase the performance at all, but it incurs higher power-consumption costs for nothing. The standard advice, *when in doubt, measure,* obviously applies here.

8. Why do we still use the `likely/unlikely` macros in the Linux kernel?
Some older (or simpler) CPUs won't have a sophisticated dynamic branch predictor available. If there is a static branch predictor present, the likely/unlikely macros will still be helpful.

9. Is a 64-bit program performance-wise better than a 32-bit program?
Well, you are doubling the size of your pointers and integers, so some people say that you are effectively halving your cache! And we know how important a hot cache is for performance. On the other hand, we can address much more memory, and thus go further down the memory-versus-speed lane. However, if your program doesn't need more than 2 GB of memory, then you will end up with worse performance.

Chapter 2

1. What does it really mean when Apitrace preloads an instrumented implementation of OpenGL?
This means exactly what is said here—Apitrace provides a DLL-implementing OpenGL functionality, which contains their tracing code. Preloading is a technique for loading a library manually, before the operating system has a chance to do so.

2. Isn't there a way to use `gprof` after all?
Yes, of course. Just don't use threads, and link everything statically. You just have to add the appropriate switch (`-pg`) to qmake's compiler and link options, and maybe add `gprof` as external too.
For simpler projects, this could perhaps be an option, but simpler projects normally don't have many performance problems, and if they do, a quick evaluation with **Process Explorer** would probably disclose their causes.

3. How would you look for a lock convoy or a waiting chain causing your UI to stutter or, even worse, to freeze?
   Use some tooling—either a specialized commercial tool such as Intel Inspector, or the Windows all-purpose weapon, WPF (it could be that you have to read some more of Bruce Dawson's blogs if you do).

4. What is the difference between **CPU Usage (Precise)** and **CPU Usage (Sampled)** in ETW traces?
   CPU usage (precise) is obtained from kernel events recording context switches; CPU usage (sampled) comes from sampling data and is thus less precise, as we already mentioned in the discussion of profiler types.

5. How would you find timers running amok or QML items accumulating video memory?
   You could use KDAB's GammaRay tool for that. Refer to its discussion to see how.

6. What can you do when your favorite open source performance is not supported by Qt Creator?
   Qt Creator is open source, so you either hack the support directly into your copy, or you do something for the community and write a Qt Creator plugin for that tool.

7. What is that thread and lock analysis feature some of the tools seem to have?
   Some tools can show you which thread ran when and on which processor core. Lock analysis comprises at least a visualization of currently held locks and their dependencies.

8. If you try to launch the example program directly or from some external CPU profiler, this won't work. Why? How would you fix it?
   You have to let the system know where both Qt's and MinGW's DLLs are stored so it is able to load them. This is done by setting the appropriate paths in Windows PATH environment variable.

9. If we don't use any custom ETW events in our program, will we be able see any information about the program in ETW traces?
   Yes, we will see all the kernel calls our program issues, its CPU profile, context switches, keyboard inputs, and so on.

10. Which one is better—sampling or instrumentation?
    This was a trick question! Did you fall for it? Both are good.

Chapter 3

1. What did Linus say about C++ performance?
   Well, he said nothing. He just generally trashed C++ for being too **nice**. In his own words:
   *Inefficient abstracted programming models where two years down the road you notice that some abstraction wasn't very efficient, but now all your code depends on all the nice object models around it, and you cannot fix it without rewriting your app. In other words, the only way to do good, efficient, and system-level and portable C++ ends up to limit yourself to all the things that are basically available in C. And limiting your project to C means that people don't screw that up, and it also means that you get a lot of programmers that do actually understand low-level issues and don't screw things up with any idiotic **object model** crap.*
   Think about it. Hopefully, now you understand low-level issues and don't screw up anymore.

2. What is an arena?
   An arena is a chunk of memory that is allocated for a memory manager containing allocated objects that can be efficiently de-allocated all at once. However, I've seen the word *arena* also used for any memory buffer backing a custom allocator, regardless of the de-allocation scheme.

3. What are PGO, FDO, LTO, LTCG, and WPO, and what do they have in common?
   PGO—profile-guided optimization, FDO—feedback-driven optimization, WPO—whole-program optimization, LTO—link-time optimization, LTCG—link-time code generation. They are all optimization techniques.

4. Have you looked into the compiler optimization example code from the book resources? Do you know what the **scalar replacement of aggregates** is now?
   The scalar replacement of aggregates (also known as **SROA**) is a compiler optimization technique where compiler replaces a structure, which should be stored on stack with an array of registers. In the example, the compiler is even cleverer, passing all of the structure elements in one single register.

5. What do you think? How big is the overhead of a function call?
   It was reported that cost calling a function with one to three arguments amounts to roughly 20-30 CPU clocks.

6. What is **dead-stack pinning**? Wasn't it a movie? Or was that dead-stack walking...?

   No, it wasn't a movie, and it wasn't about Luke Stackwalker either. Dead-stack pinning is a technique that can be used to avoid the dynamic allocation price when constructing a new exception object. We just instantiate the exception on the stack. However, there's a catch, as during the stack unwinding, the current stack will be released and we will lose the exception object. For that reason, this presumably dead stack is held in memory (i.e. pinned) until the matching exception handler finishes.

7. What is RTTI, and is it expensive?

   RTTI is an initialism for **Run-Time Type Information**, and, yes, it is expensive, as described in the subsection about exceptions.

8. What would change in the `mutatingFunc()` example discussed in the section on compiler optimization tricks if it were defined in the same compilation unit?

   The compiler could have a look into the function and decide whether it needed extra precaution, or if it were indeed pure.

9. What is register pressure? Hint—it has to do with one of the compiler's main tasks, that is, register allocation.

   Register pressure is a technical term describing the situation where there are more variables used than there are registers available. This will decrease performance, as some variables have to be held in memory (also known as being *spilled*). For example, function inlining will increase register pressure and spills.

Chapter 4

1. If a better algorithm uses knowledge about the structure of the data, how does that apply to sorting? Is the data to be sorted by definition devoid of any structure?

   There is one fundamental thing we know here—data can be partitioned and sorted into smaller chunks, thus decreasing the complexity from $O(n^2)$ to $O(n \log n)$. There aren't any neighborhood considerations to be taken into account. And, apart from that, sorting algorithms do use additional knowledge. Time sort (used in Python) is optimized for nearly-sorted array cases. The C++ STL's `sort` algorithm will switch from quicksort to insertion sort for small inputs or small subpartitions of the data.

2. Is using the `QStringList` class a good idea? Or should you use `QVector<QString>` instead?
   `QString` is declared with `Q_DECLARE_SHARED`, which makes it movable. `QStringList` is a typedef for `QList<QString>` and the small object optimization will be applied. So, yes, it's OK.

3. Is there any chance that Qt will start using the standard library containers in their APIs?
   They won't go away, as Qt ABI wants to stay binary compatible, as it fears that the standard changes some wording and requires changed implementation of the containers. One example of that is the C++11 standard, which effectively disallowed using COW implementations on strings. Also, as one of Qt maintainers put it, Qt still supports older platforms that do not have the C++11 standard library.

4. What is SSO? What is SVO? Where is it used?
   SSO—small string optimization, SVO—small vector optimization. They are used to optimize the performance of data-container implementations.

5. Consider the following code:

   ```
   Q_FOREACH(auto const& v, qvector) { ... }
   ```

   Is it dangerous?
   Surprisingly (or unsurprisingly) not, `Q_FOREACH()` and `foreach()` will work with Qt containers without unexpected copies.

6. Do you know now why, back in time, the COW containers were also known as **mad COW** containers?
   I think you have an idea now. Additionally, the problems are even exacerbated in a multithreaded setting.

7. Who were the Gang of Four? Are they relevant for performance?
   They were Erich Gamma, Richard Helm, Ralph Johnson, and John Vlissides. In their book, they gathered solutions to commonly encountered programming programs. And, yes, some of those solutions are relevant for performance, as we have seen in the example of the **flyweight** pattern.

8. What seems to have the greatest improvement potential when implementing data structures?
   Memory locality, of course—it beats everything else. With algorithms, it is avoiding work, though.

9. Talking about strings, what about the performance of the following code:

```
bool hasTwoDigits(const QString& numberStrg)
{
  QRegExp rx("^\\d\\d?$");
  return rx.indexIn(numberStrg) != -1;
}
```

Regular expressions must first be compiled, which will be done at runtime. Thus, to avoid a performance hit, the regexes should be defined globally. Annoying, isn't it? However, it is possible in C++17 to write a `constexpr` regex parser and move this computation to compile time. However, it is a rather advanced topic; maybe it will be in the standard library as of C++20.

Chapter 5

1. Why is a data race an **undefined behavior (UB)** in C++?
   Because changes from one thread may not yet be visible in another thread, and thus some results would be not defined! Thread visibility is a concept we haven't discussed yet, but the main concept is that different threads are allowed to work on their local cache data and only push the changes to the other thread caches when they are forced to do so. We can force such an update using a memory fence, and memory fencing is part of the implementation of mutexes and atomic variables. See also the response to question 10.

2. What is **resource acquisition is initialization (RAII)** (we have seen it already in Chapter 3, *Deep Dive into C++ and Performance*), and how is it used in `QAtomicLocker`?
   It describes an object that initializes some resource in its constructor and deinitializes it in the destructor. The `QAtomicLocker` function locks and unlocks a given mutex in that way.

3. Why cannot `volatile` variables be used to prevent race conditions?
   Volatile means *atomic* in Java and C++, and it used to mean it in pre C++11 compiler extensions, but in modern C++, it has only its original ANSI-C meaning of an externally-changed memory address. A compiler disables this caching of it in registers and forces memory access by each reference. However, it does not ensure cross-tread visibility and doesn't affect the re-ordering of reads and writes! Only use it for memory-mapped device I/O.

4. What are spurious wakes, and why aren't they banned?
Spurious wake occurs when a condition variable's `wait()` method returns without the thread being woken up. The following justification of spurious wake's existence is given in the book *Programming with POSIX Threads* (p. 80):

> *"Spurious wakeups may sound strange, but on some multiprocessor systems, making condition wakeup completely predictable might substantially slow all condition variable operations."*

- David R Butenhof

More likely, it was the inverse situation—it could be possible to exploit this requirement in some settings so as to improve the performance of the average condition wait. So, if there is the possibility for optimization, we (that is, pthreads designers) will get rid of elegance for the greater good—welcome to the dirty world of performance engineering! And Windows just followed the lead.

5. Assume you are OS (or some tool) and have just detected a deadlock. What could you do to resolve it?
We can kill one of the threads, or let one of them starve (for the greater good). Both are not very exciting alternatives, so it's better to concentrate on deadlock prevention.

6. What is cache line ping-pong?
Cache line ping-pong describes the effect when a cache line is transferred among multiple cores or CPUs in rapid succession—as in a ping-pong match. This can be caused by false sharing, but also by legitimate *true* sharing. In both cases, this is not performance-friendly.

7. If you define slots in a `QThread` subclass, what do you think will happen when they get invoked by a signal?
They will run in the thread context of the creator thread of that `QThread` class. `QThread` is a `QObject` itself, and has a default thread affinity to the thread in which it was created, which oftentimes is the main GUI thread. So, watch out!

8. What do you think the Windows system call
`InitializeCriticalSectionAndSpinCount()` does?
Citing from Windows API documentation, it *"initializes a critical section object and sets the spin count for the critical section."* Thus, we can customize the time we spend spinning before diving into kernel space.

9. What about using `QProcess` instead of `QThread`?
   A process is an kernel object that is even heavier than a thread. So, from a purely performance-oriented standpoint, it's a clear no-no. However, sometimes, there are other considerations—for example: the crash-safety feature of browser tabs.

10. What does the phrase *"flushing all the pending writes and stalling the pipeline"* from the subsection on atomic instruction costs really mean?
    In certain CPU cache architectures, such as Intel's x86 and AMD64, a write buffer is used to hold data to be written from the cache to main memory or to the next level of the cache hierarchy. Using buffering writes is a common optimization technique (batching)—we write all the data in one flush, and meanwhile the reads aren't obstructed. Local reads can also use the buffer contents.

Chapter 6

1. When would you deem a simple linear search to be a justifiable choice?
   For a couple of tens of items, it is totally OK to use a linear algorithm. But be sure that you'll never have to scale this piece of code!

2. How many items do you think can be shown without problems in a standard Qt's model-view setup?
   Model-view classes will scale up to a couple of hundred items. For very big models, you have to resort to manual optimizations.

3. What could be meant by the **Tower of Babel** performance anti-pattern?
   That colorful name describes the situation where your program burns CPU power by constantly transforming the same data among several formats. This could be a real program in bigger systems in the enterprise programming, and you'd probably never do it in a Qt program, would you? However, I liked its name.

4. Your program suffers under a performance problem. How would you try to solve it?
   Measure, profile, and try to understand the offending code location. Then, correct and measure again. Repeat until solved.

5. You have much too many items in a view—what could you do?
   We will discuss that in the section on model-view performance, but some measures you could employ are the following: setting the number of elements in advance, using a custom model that doesn't notify the view on each change, but only when all the work is done, or use `QContiguousCache` to only display a predefined **window** into the model.

6. Is it possible to avoid performance fails in your project?
   Normally, it should be possible with careful design. However, as the examples we have seen teach us, you are never totally safe from surprises!

7. What seems to be the number-one reason for performance fails?
   Probably the choice of algorithm and the data structure, and then interaction with the operating system. The other common problems, that is, memory allocations and multithreading errors, seem to be less common, probably because programmers tend to be sensitive about them.

8. What about the *do it later* performance culture and performance fails?
   We have seen the impacts of it in the discussed case of **hardware shutting down on error message** fail. If you don't think about structuring your system in a way that will ensure some basic performance, you are in for a fail! Welcome to the careless architecture and design lands, where the **Tower of Babel** and a hundred other anti-patterns bloom.

Chapter 7

1. Why will reading from `std::cin` first flush `std::cout`?
   Because they are tied by default—`std::cin.tie(&std::cout);`

2. What is the difference between a unit-buffered, a line-buffered, a fully-buffered, and an unbuffered stream?
   A unit-buffered stream will flush after each >>, a line-buffered stream after each \n, a fully-buffered stream when the internal buffers are full, and unbuffered ones after each write.

3. Why is `std::iostream` slower than `std::filebuf` and `fprintf()` slower that `puts()`?
   Because `iostream` will perform newline translation and locale-based conversions that `filebuf` doesn't have to. `fprintf()` must scan the format string in runtime; `puts()` doesn't have a format string.
   By the way, it is possible to scan a format string in compile time in C++ using template metaprogramming tricks!

4. Why does Linux kill processes simply if it feels like it?
   Because Linux overcommits the virtual memory (just like your airline does with the airplane seats) to achieve better memory usage. But if memory becomes scarce, the kernel has to make sure that it has enough memory for its internal operations, so it starts killing processes.

5. What is a page fault? Are there soft and hard page faults?
   A page fault is generated by the MMU when a program tries to access a memory page that is not currently mapped into the virtual address space. The operating system will then try to add the requested page to the mapping. If the page is unmapped but not yet swapped out to the disk, we have a soft-page fault; otherwise, it has to be fetched from the disk in the course of a hard-page fault.

6. What is thrashing?
   Thrashing is the state when the operating system is constantly running into page faults, swapping memory pages in and out, and thus inhibiting any application-level processing.

7. You are on Windows, you are starting a program, and your disk starts spinning like crazy. How would you investigate the problem?
   Just use some of the tools we discussed in Chapter 2, *Profiling to Find Bottlenecks*, such as **Process Explorer** and **Process Monitor**. For a more advanced view, start **UI for ETW** and have a look at the Disk Offset graph, which shows you a pretty accurate picture of HDD head movements.

8. You are on a 32-bit system and have to hold several big images in memory. Then, you have to read another one from the camera, but there is not enough memory left. What do you do?
   Sorry, but you will have to load off some of your memory-held images to disk to make space for the new ones! Couldn't OS do that for us? Unfortunately, it can't, as you can map only so much of a file into memory as there is free space. However, a scheme where you are mapping only the parts of the file that are currently used and unmap it afterward could be feasible. Alternatively, you could map and unmap whole files when there's no memory left, letting the OS do the whole sync-to-disk business.

Chapter 8

1. Which OpenGL version will be used if your application uses the ANGLE driver? And what is an ICD?
   It will be OpenGL ES 2.0, which is actually an embedded standard, but it will also be used on a desktop if your Windows installation doesn't have an OpenGL driver properly installed! An ICD denotes an Installable Client Driver, which will hook itself in Window's `libopengl32` library to provide an OpenGL implementation better than the supported OpenGL 1.1.

2. Which draw calls of `QPainter` are safe to use in the critical path?
   Simple compositions, simple transformations, rectangle fills, rectangular clipping, and `drawPixmap()`.
3. You can see the following OpenGL code we used in one of the examples:

```
glBegin(GL_TRIANGLES);
glColor3f(1.0, 0.0, 0.0);
glVertex3f(-0.5, -0.5, 0);
...
```

   What is your reaction?
   Come on, that's some deliberate, possibly deprecated OpenGL 1.0 stuff! Move on, at least to OpenGL 2! Look it up in this chapter's resources.
4. What is a stencil, and when will it be applied to the graphic pipeline?
   A stencil is a kind of mask you can put over an image. It will applied at the last stage of the OpenGL pipeline.
5. What optimizations are performed by the default QML scene graph?
   Batching of draw calls, texture atlases, and retention of geometry data on the GPU. And also, multithreaded rendering-on most platforms.
6. You are a platform vendor, and you'd like to take advantage of non-standard hardware features with your QML applications. What can you do?
   If needed, the standard scene graph renderer can be completely replaced using the internal scene graph backend API, as we have seen in this chapter. You have to say QML is quite flexible, don't you?
7. Why would you consider using `QGraphicView` in a new project?
   I wouldn't, because it's slower than QML and will probably be deprecated in the future.
8. What kinds of shaders are possible with OpenGL?
   The vertex shader, fragment shader, geometry shader, and the tesselation shader. Hopefully, you remember what they all are for.

Chapter 9

1. If, in the UDP protocol, there is no guarantee that the packet will arrive at the destination, why are we bothering with it at all?
   Believe it or not, in some contexts, this is an acceptable trade-off. For example, in the **VoIP** (**Voice-over IP**) context, dropping one or two packets of the conversation is usually OK, and a price we are glad to pay for improved latency!

2. How can we enable a network cache in Qt? What will get cached there?
   We can use `QNetworkAccessManager::setCache()` to enable it. This will cache HTTP contents (such as the HTML page, JSON data, and so on) that we get from the network.

3. What is an IP protocol?
   An IP protocol sends data from IP address X to an I/O address Y, and thus has to find a way to reach Y starting from X. A UDP does not do much more than this, but additionally multiplexes data for several ports on X and Y.

4. Is there a Qt cache for DNS? How can we use it?
   Qt uses a DNS cache internally. However, it is non-persistent and will be populated only after the application has started. It relies, in turn, on the caching mechanisms of the underlying OS to avoid the network round-trips.

5. Why would you consider using HTTP/2?
   Probably to use stream multiplexing over a single connection—we can have up to 100 streams instead of the allowed six parallel connections! Then, there is the server push and graceful connection shutdown using the **GOAWAY** frame.

6. What HTTP-like protocols are supported by Qt? Is REST supported?
   HTTP(S)/1.1, SPDY, HTTP/2, and WebSocket are all supported. REST is not a protocol, but an architectural style for defining HTTP endpoint APIs. So, as long as HTTP is supported, REST will be too. HTTP/3 and QUIC are not supported at the moment.

7. What are some examples of well-known ports? And what are they anyway?
   They are fixed ports for application-level protocols running over TCP and UDP, officially assigned by the IANA agency. Here are some examples: 80 and 443 for HTTP and HTTPS, 20 for FTP, 22 for SSH, 23 for Telnet, 53 for DNS, 25 for SMPT (email transfer), 143 for IMAP (email reading), or 7 for simple Echo.

8. Have you ever heard of OSI's 7-layers protocol stack model?
   These days, you won't hear about it very often, but back in the day, it was the grand schema for the taxonomy of communication protocols. It is much more fine-grained than the crude transport/application divide we introduced; for example, SSL and TLS would be classified as presentation-layer protocols.

9. What are the performance gains from reusing a TCP connection?
   First, we spare the connection setup overhead, and, second, we skip the slow-start phase of TCP congestion control.

10. What is the TLS protocol? Isn't it the same as SSL?
    This is a kind-of trick question—**Transport Layer Security** (**TLS**) is the successor of the original **Secure Socket Layer** (**SSL**) protocol, which shouldn't be used anymore. However, in everyday usage, we are somehow still speaking of SSL as a kind of generic term for that kind of protocol.

Chapter 10

1. On what embedded hardware could we use Qt 5.9 and higher?
   Preferably, 256 MB or more of dynamic RAM, CPU running at 1 GHz and some graphic hardware acceleration: OpenGL ES 2.0 or OpenVG. We can go down with CPU clocking and dispense with graphic acceleration if we are not afraid of simplifying our UI.

2. You could ask, what's the fuss about fast startup on embedded? My car's digital console starts in no time! Are there any explanations?
   Take it from me, they are cheating. An automotive-embedded system will begin to boot as soon as the driver unlocks the door! Sometimes, this can give you entire seconds for the system to boot.

3. What is a SoC? What is an MCU?
   System on a Chip (SoC) is a chip containing a CPU, graphics card, WiFi, and other periphery controllers. **MCU** is an abbreviation of **microcontroller unit** and is basically a much more poorly equipped SoC used in lower-end embedded systems.

4. Should I be bothered by floating-point operations on embedded?
   Well, it depends. If our processor doesn't have an FPU co-processor, then they will be emulated in software and induce a big performance hit! However, the hardware we normally are using Qt on is not very likely to lack an FPU.

5. What does the Wayland plugin for embedded Linux do?
   The Wayland plugin interfaces with Linux Wayland driver, which provides a lightweight windowing system that replaces an older and rather heavyweight X11 system. Thus, instead of a single, full-screen window, we can show several (decorated) windows in parallel.

6. What is the worst possible polling interval for 3G mobile radio access?
   For our example, a 3G radio state machine; if an application polls the server every five seconds, it will stay in the full power mode forever; if it's polling every 17 seconds, it will stay forever in high and low power states, never reaching the power-saving standby state.

7. What would a mobile device be most likely to do?
   It'd like to go to sleep. Waking it up will incur battery life costs, as well as keeping it awake. Waking up its sub-components such as a network radio unit or a GPS unit will do the same.

8. What is a tile-based architecture, and why is it widespread on mobile? Why aren't we using it on desktop?

Tile-based rendering splits the frame into several so-called tiles and renders them separately, which is less memory- (and thus power-) intensive than rasterizing the entire frame at once. We want to save power on mobile, don't we? Less memory also means lower space requirements.

On desktop, the power conservation was traditionally less important than the rendering performance, but lately even some desktop GPUs are beginning to make use of tile-based rendering.

9. The GPU performance of Raspberry Pi 3 is often (incorrectly) quoted to be 24 GFLOP. What could be the reason for that?

Raspberry Pi 3 has the same GPU chip as its predecessors; however, it is clocked at a higher frequency. In that way, the same hardware is able to achieve a higher performance.

Chapter 11

1. Why would you like to test a Qt application?

First of all, for correctness, and then for regression, and also for regressions in performance—remember Qt performance-regression tests and `https://testresults.qt.io/grafana/`?

2. How would you implement a performance-regression test measuring the FPS rate of a QML application?

We already developed a graphical FPS display in `Chapter 8`, *Optimizing Graphical Performance*. We could use the same technique of hooking into signals emitted by the QML scene graph and computing the needed statistics.

3. Any ideas about deploying Qt application to embedded Linux? Take some hints from the previous chapter.

As we discussed in the previous chapter, Qt Creator supports the copying of a cross-compiled binary to a target device. When the development is finished, the executable will be included as a separate packet in the Linux build tool such as Buildroot or Yocto.

4. You are running automated GUI tests—what could the problems be? What could be done to prevent them?

   Screen savers, dialogs of virus scanners, or other tools popping up unexpectedly, or generally, other users and programs using the keyboard and the screen. In Qt 5, on Windows, the alternative is to use the **offscreen** plugin—a plugin that will provide a virtual screen only to be used by our tests. When starting the `QTests` executable from the command line, we can use the `-platform offscreen` command-line option to enable it.

5. What does TDD mean?

   This stands for test-driven development. The idea is that writing the tests is driving your development, instead of tests being retroactively applied to an existent code base.

6. How does Squish identify GUI elements? Can you figure this out?

   It uses Qt object names, that is, the `QObject::objectName` property.

7. Which deployment type is better—a static or a dynamic build?

   Static deployment has a smaller binary and consists of only one file. The downside is that it is monolithic, and must be updated as a whole. When using dynamic build, we have the option to update a single DLL without touching other parts of the system. However, we have to keep the DLLs backward-compatible so as to avoid the so-called **DLL hell**.

8. Is performance optimization in Qt black magic? Be honest!

   Hopefully, you responded with *no*. For performance optimization, we first have to know the basic principles of performance, and then the design and implementation of a specific Qt feature. Both parts were explained in that book (hopefully, they were explained well).

Other Books You May Enjoy

If you enjoyed this book, you may be interested in these other books by Packt:

Qt5 Python GUI Programming Cookbook
B.M. Harwani

ISBN: 9781788831000

- Use basic Qt components, such as a radio button, combo box, and sliders
- Use QSpinBox and sliders to handle different signals generated on mouse clicks
- Work with different Qt layouts to meet user interface requirements
- Create custom widgets and set up customizations in your GUI
- Perform asynchronous I/O operations and thread handling in the Python GUI
- Employ network concepts, internet browsing, and Google Maps in UI
- Use graphics rendering and implement animation in your GUI
- Make your GUI application compatible with Android and iOS devices

Mastering Qt 5 - Second Edition
Guillaume Lazar

ISBN: 9781788995399

- Create stunning UIs with Qt Widgets and Qt Quick 2
- Develop powerful, cross-platform applications with the Qt framework
- Design GUIs with the Qt Designer and build a library in it for UI previews
- Handle user interaction with the Qt signal or slot mechanism in C++
- Prepare a cross-platform project to host a third-party library
- Use the Qt Animation framework to display stunning effects
- Deploy mobile apps with Qt and embedded platforms
- Interact with a gamepad using Qt Gamepad

Leave a review - let other readers know what you think

Please share your thoughts on this book with others by leaving a review on the site that you bought it from. If you purchased the book from Amazon, please leave us an honest review on this book's Amazon page. This is vital so that other potential readers can see and use your unbiased opinion to make purchasing decisions, we can understand what our customers think about our products, and our authors can see your feedback on the title that they have worked with Packt to create. It will only take a few minutes of your time, but is valuable to other potential customers, our authors, and Packt. Thank you!

Index

www.ingramcontent.com/pod-product-compliance
Lightning Source LLC
Chambersburg PA
CBHW080611060326
40690CB00021B/4650